Consultation in
Early Childhood Settings

Consultation in
Early Childhood Settings

by

Virginia Buysse, Ph.D., and **Patricia W. Wesley, M.Ed.**

FPG Child Development Institute
The University of North Carolina at Chapel Hill

·P A U L·H·
BROOKES
PUBLISHING C⁰.®

Baltimore • London • Sydney

Paul H. Brookes Publishing Co.
Post Office Box 10624
Baltimore, Maryland 21285-0624

www.brookespublishing.com

Typeset by Auburn Associates, Inc., Baltimore, Maryland.
Manufactured in the United States of America by
Victor Graphics, Baltimore, Maryland.

The authors are grateful to Gina Harrison for her design inspirations.

The stories in this book are based on the authors' experiences. These vignettes are composite or fictional accounts that do not represent the lives or experiences of specific individuals, and no implications should be inferred.

Library of Congress Cataloging-in-Publication Data

Buysse, Virginia.
　　Consultation in early childhood settings / by Virginia Buysse and Patricia W. Wesley.
　　　　p.　　cm.
　　Includes bibliographical references and index.
　　ISBN 1-55766-774-8 (pbk.)
　　　1. Psychological consultation.　　2. School psychology.　　3. Early childhood education—Psychological aspects.　　I. Wesley, Patricia W.　　II. Title.

BF637.C56B89 2005
362.7—dc22
　　　2004017224

British Library Cataloguing in Publication data are available from the British Library.

Contents

About the Authors

Virginia Buysse, Ph.D., earned her doctoral degree in early intervention and early childhood special education from The University of North Carolina at Chapel Hill. She is Senior Scientist at the FPG Child Development Institute and Research Associate Professor in the School of Education at The University of North Carolina at Chapel Hill.

Dr. Buysse began her career as a preschool teacher. She has since directed or conducted a number of research projects on a variety of topics, including practices related to serving Latino children and families; consultation in early childhood settings; parent leadership development; friendship and peer acceptance among young children with disabilities; and the cost, quality, and outcomes of preschool inclusion.

Dr. Buysse is on the editorial boards of *Exceptional Children, Journal of Early Intervention, Infants and Young Children, Topics in Early Childhood Special Education,* and *Young Exceptional Children.* She also serves as co-editor of *Early Developments,* a newsletter that is jointly published by the FPG Child Development Institute and the National Center for Early Development & Learning.

Patricia W. Wesley, M.Ed., is Senior Scientist at the FPG Child Development Institute at The University of North Carolina at Chapel Hill, where she is also Clinical Instructor in the School of Education. Following a decade as the director of an inclusive preschool, in 1990 she became the director of Partnerships for Inclusion, a statewide training and consultation project supporting the inclusion of children with disabilities and their families in all aspects of community life. In this role, she has developed, implemented, evaluated, and published an on-site model of consultation to enhance quality in early childhood programs. She also has developed several community approaches for building broad-based acceptance of people with disabilities.

In addition to early childhood inclusion and consultation, Ms. Wesley's interests include parent leadership and communities of practice in early childhood education. She is a frequent guest reviewer for several professional journals and a popular keynote speaker on the state and national lecture circuit.

Foreword

When I was a preschool special education teacher, my time during the school day was spent teaching, reading stories to, managing, and playing with 4- to 5-year-old children who had a range of developmental delays. There were interactions with other adults (e.g., assistant teachers, assorted therapists, administrators) and very important work with parents, but work with adults was not part of my main job. Although this traditional, self-contained model of early childhood special education still exists in many school districts, times have indeed changed.

Since the mid-1970s, early childhood special education has evolved. A strong initiative has emerged to provide special education services to children with disabilities in inclusive settings. From a classroom perspective, inclusive settings may be conceptualized as classes containing typically developing children who are of a similar age to the child with disabilities (Odom et al., 2004). The *Twenty-Fourth Annual Report to Congress on the Implementation of the Individuals with Disabilities Education Act* (U.S. Department of Education, 2002) indicated that 326,466 preschool children with disabilities (approximately 54% of the children served by IDEA) received special education services in some form of inclusive early childhood setting or in their homes during the 1999–2000 school year (the last year for which figures were available).

Providing inclusive services for preschool children with disabilities is problematic for some school systems. Because general education most often begins with kindergarten (i.e., at age 5), there may not be classroom options for preschool-age (3- to 5-year-old) children with disabilities. School systems have responded in innovative ways, and different models of inclusion have emerged (Odom et al., 1999). In some cases, school systems start their own preschool classes for children from the community and include children with disabilities in other classes. Many states have begun funding prekindergarten programs for children who are at risk for school failure (i.e., mainly children from low-income communities). These programs are often placed in public schools and could be an option for inclusion. Similarly, public schools sometimes work with Head Start programs to create options for inclusive placement. A primary model for inclusion has been placement in community-based programs—that is, private or publicly funded preschool or child care programs.

For preschool inclusion to be viable and effective for preschool children, more than physical placement is necessary—a planned, individualized, and systematic provision of instructional services has to occur. In most of the inclusive options described previously, the lead early childhood education teacher will not have training in special education and may have limited experiences in working with children with disabilities and their families. Yet, this person sees the children on a daily basis and is the professional in the classroom who is likely to have the greatest developmental impact on the child. To provide support for this key individual (or set of individuals), a new professional role emerged in early childhood special education—the itinerant service provider.

The role expectations for the itinerant service provider are different from those for a classroom teacher. In most cases, the itinerant service provider is a consultant to the classroom teacher (or family in a home-based intervention) rather than a teacher who works directly with children, although these roles are sometimes mixed. This shift in role expectations and responsibilities has created a need in the field for professionals who can effectively work with other teachers, professionals, and families. For early childhood special education teachers who have been working in the field for a while, their preservice training probably did not include consultation skills. Plus, there have been very few sources for training materials about consultation that are explicitly designed for early childhood special education.

Precisely when we need it, *Consultation in Early Childhood Settings* has filled the gap in knowledge and training. Drawing from their many years of work on inclusion, consultation, and community partnership as well as from the research and scholarly literature, Virginia Buysse and Pat Wesley have crafted the most authoritative and practical model for consultation with early childhood care providers. Their book adds needed definition and clarity to the consultation process and documents the evidence of effectiveness existing in the research literature. The step-by-step model of consultation is precisely articulated and serves as a powerful guide for new and experienced teachers, as well as other professionals (e.g., speech-language pathologists, occupational therapists, physical therapists) who deliver their services through consultation. The authors wisely begin the process with the consultant's self-reflection and evaluation of his or her own skills. Next, they describe the best ways of entering the consultation setting and establishing a positive relationship with service partners; the importance of this step in the consultation process cannot be understated. The process continues from assessment through goal setting and implementation and ends with evaluation. Having the full scope and sequence of the consultation process makes this book an extremely valuable resource for early childhood consultants. Also of value are the forms provided for documenting features of the process and a hypothetical case study that follows one family and child through the consultation process. Virginia Buysse and Pat Wesley have crafted a resource that early childhood consultants will want to have on their bookshelves—and in their cars as they drive out to work with teachers in early childhood settings or families in their homes.

Samuel L. Odom, Ph.D.
Otting Professor of Special Education
School of Education
Indiana University, Bloomington

REFERENCES

Odom, S.L., Horn, E.M., Marquart, J., Hanson, M.J., Wolfberg, P., Beckman, P.J., Lieber, J., Li, S., Schwartz, I., Janko, S., & Sandall, S. (1999). On the forms of inclusion: Organizational context and individualized service delivery models. *Journal of Early Intervention, 22,* 185–199.

Odom, S.L., Vitztum, J., Wolery, R., Lieber, J., Sandall, S., Hanson, M.J., Beckman, P., Schwartz, I., & Horn, E. (2004). Preschool inclusion in the United States: A review of research from an ecological systems perspective. *Journal of Research in Special Educational Needs, 4,* 17–49.

U.S. Department of Education (2002). *Twenty-fourth annual report to Congress on the implementation of the Individuals with Disabilities Education Act.* Retrieved August 7, 2004, from http://www.ed.gov/about/reports/annual/osep/2002/index.html

Preface

The idea for *Consultation in Early Childhood Settings* grew out of a desire to share empirically based knowledge with professionals who find themselves thrust into the role of early childhood consultant. Because both of us have experienced this challenge as practitioners, we know firsthand what it is like to make the difficult transformation from working directly with children and families to working collaboratively with other adults in many different settings. Learning how to apply a systematic process for sharing content expertise to reach mutually determined goals for children and families is not an easy task. The fact that most early childhood professionals graduate from colleges and universities without any preparation in consultation makes this task more difficult. Those who are fortunate enough to somehow acquire expertise in consultation soon discover that there is little infrastructure to support effective consultation practice in early childhood settings. Nor are there sufficient opportunities to reflect and grow within the broader community of consultants. We hope that this book begins to address some of these needs in the early childhood field, which we view as encompassing child care, early education, and early intervention.

This book also should be useful to classroom teachers, parents, specialists, and others who find themselves cast in the role of consultees, the recipients of consultation services, often without requesting these services or even recognizing that these services exist. Like many consultants, we have witnessed the bewilderment of a classroom teacher who is encountering consultation for the first time and wondering why "an expert" has selected her classroom for special attention. We hope that this book unveils any misconceptions about the consultation process for consultees and assists them in recognizing the expertise that they bring to the consultation process as well as the critical importance of their contribution in achieving desired consultation outcomes.

We hope that *Consultation in Early Childhood Settings* addresses some of the confusion that exists in the early childhood field about the terminology describing our work with other adults. Although terms such as *consultation* and *collaboration* are often used interchangeably, we have used precise language throughout to promote the shared meaning and understanding of consultation for the field. We view consultation as a unique service delivery model, distinct from other help-giving or collaborative models such as teaming, coaching, co-teaching, training, technical assistance, family-centered practices, mentorship, and supervision. We define *consultation* as an indirect, triadic service delivery model in which a consultant and a consultee work together to address an area of concern or common goal for change. Although seemingly straightforward, this definition does not reveal completely the complexity of consultation practice across many dimensions that include the theoretical model of consultation, the goal of consultation, the specific role of the consultant and consultee, and the focus and nature of the interactions between the consultant and consultee. Our aim has been to uncover each of these layers to help readers develop a fuller understanding of how consultation works and how it might be applied to their own practices. We describe, for example, how consulting roles must shift across the consultation process depending on the expectations of the consultee and whether the consultation task involves responding to an immediate crisis or a long-term goal. Our decision to weave together goals related to program quality and child-specific interventions reflects the belief that these issues are inextricably linked and should not be treated in isolation.

In identifying the content for this book, we had to look beyond the early childhood field to draw from the larger body of knowledge from other disciplines and theoretical traditions, most notably the mental health professions and school-based consultation in special education and school psychology. We believe that the eight-stage process of consultation outlined in this book holds great promise for the early childhood field; nonetheless, many questions about consultation in early childhood settings remain unanswered. At a time when policy makers advocate for evidence-based practices established largely through scientific research, there is little empirical evidence to support specific consultation practices in early childhood settings. Established guidelines for involving family members in the consultation process with other professionals do not exist. Valid concerns about the efficacy of consultation as compared with direct services for children and families must be recognized, even though there is no direct evidence to either support or refute these concerns. Yet, early childhood practitioners cannot be expected to simply suspend their practices until the necessary evidence is acquired. Until these foundations can be established in the early childhood field, we believe that it is necessary to support professionals who are already engaged in consultation practice by providing them with a consultation framework and a systematic process based on the empirical and theoretical foundations from other disciplines.

PURPOSE

We have envisioned a number of purposes for *Consultation in Early Childhood Settings*. First and foremost, the book is designed for practitioners of consultation (both consultants and consultees) from various human service systems (e.g., child care, early education, early intervention, mental health, public health) to help them navigate the consultation process together. Regardless of whether the goal of consultation is to assist an individual child or to improve an entire program, we view the process as essentially the same and, therefore, applicable to a variety of consultation contexts. University faculty and others involved in professional development may find the book helpful in developing academic training programs and continuing education activities to promote effective consultation practice in early childhood settings. Administrators may find the book useful to support the professional growth and development of consultants and consultees and to engage them in reflective practice as a means of improving consultation. Policy makers may use the book to examine how current educational policies support or hinder consultation practice and to consider ways to address obstacles to consultation in early childhood settings.

ORGANIZATION

The book is divided into three sections. Section I presents the conceptual and philosophical framework for our model of consultation. Chapter 1 discusses the rationale for consultation, describes the history and origins of consultation, elaborates a *definition* of consultation, and describes the limited research on consultation in the early childhood field. A review of the existing research reveals the absence of a conceptual framework for consultation as well as the lack of guidelines for evaluating its effectiveness. Chapter 2 describes the knowledge, skills, and dispositions of an effective early childhood consultant. Five domains in which mastery is considered essential for effective consultation include 1) child development theory and early childhood practices, 2) developmental disabilities and early intervention and early childhood special education practices, 3) communication, 4) knowledge of consultation stages and strategies, and 5) ethics and professionalism.

Section II outlines the actual model. Chapters 3–10 describe the consultation stages by using a consistent format that covers Key Consultation Tasks, Critical Considerations for the consultant and consultee, Communication and Interpersonal Strategies, and What If? questions (describing aspects of consultation that can go wrong and presenting possible solutions to address these issues). The process chapters introduce checklists and forms that can be used to support consultation practice, monitor the process, and evaluate its effectiveness. A special feature of this book is a case illustration that runs throughout the eight-stage process in Chapters 3–10, beginning with entry into the consultation setting and concluding with the summary conference as part of the last step in the process. The case illustration is designed give the reader a window into a realistic practice setting, complete with excerpts of consultation dialogue and examples of completed forms.

Section III addresses outcomes, applications, and recommendations. Chapter 11 offers additional considerations (beyond those described in Chapter 9, which covers Stage Seven: Evaluation) regarding the evaluation of consultation processes and outcomes. A logic model is proposed to guide the planning of an evaluation of consultation. In addition to methods for monitoring the evaluation process, Chapter 11 presents consultation outcomes at the level of the child, the consultee, and the program.

Chapter 12 discusses the contexts and settings associated with consultation in early education and intervention. The chapter identifies aspects of the sociopolitical context that contribute to recent changes in the field and examines how contexts and settings coincide with systems of care to influence consultation practice, as well as the specific challenges to consultation within each of these contexts.

Finally, Chapter 13 offers recommendations for moving the field toward a consensus on what constitutes effective consultation practice in early childhood settings. These include 1) develop a conceptual framework for consultation practice, 2) create professional standards, and 3) evaluate consultation through scientific research.

To my husband, Bob, and my children, Kate and Nick,
who have always encouraged and supported me in my work
—VB

To my colleagues at Partnerships for Inclusion, whose experiences
and insights have enriched my understanding of consultation
—PW

Section I

Conceptual and Philosophical Framework

Chapter 1

Why Consultation?

New Roles for Early Childhood Professionals

In a relatively short amount of time, the professional roles and responsibilities of early interventionists and special educators have changed dramatically. This transformation has come about largely in response to policies and practices that support embedding interventions for young children with disabilities in natural environments. As a result, professional roles have expanded from primarily providing *direct* therapy and instruction to also providing *indirect* services in the form of collaborative partnerships with parents and teachers. Although the need for professionals to work directly with children with disabilities continues, there is an urgent need for viable methods of working collaboratively with other adults to address their priorities and concerns regarding children's learning and development.

Before delving into ways of collaborating with others, it is helpful to review all of the professional roles and goals that constitute one's professional practice, as well as how these specific roles relate to one another (Buysse, Wesley, & Able-Boone, 2001). Figure 1 represents three broad professional goals that provide a framework for considering the multiple roles of the early interventionist: 1) designing, implementing, and evaluating intervention with children and families; 2) promoting high-quality care and education; and 3) promoting professional development and the advancement of the field. By defining professional roles and identifying their

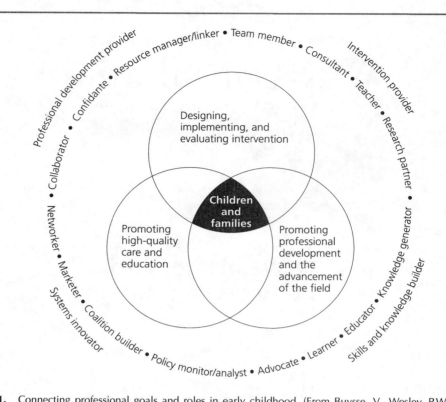

Figure 1. Connecting professional goals and roles in early childhood. (From Buysse, V., Wesley, P.W., & Able-Boone, H. [2001]. Innovations in professional development: Creating communities of practice to support inclusion. In M.J. Guralnick [Ed.], *Early childhood inclusion: Focus on change* [p. 185]. Baltimore: Paul H. Brookes Publishing Co.; adapted by permission.)

interrelatedness, one can form a more cohesive picture of interventionists' work than by considering professional competencies, education, and training alone. At the core of intervention is the desire to enhance the quality of life for children and families. The goal most closely associated with this mission is the design, delivery, and evaluation of intervention in the form of direct services to children and families. The other two goals are familiar to professionals but require greater attention now than ever before. As more interventionists deliver services in community early childhood settings, a greater emphasis on collaboration with other adults is needed to address their priorities and concerns for specific children as well as to improve the overall quality of the early childhood program for all children.

Interventionists still require a foundation of knowledge and skills related to working directly with young children and their families. Indeed, this foundation of knowledge about child development and evidence-based early intervention practices constitutes the *content* of our professional practices in both direct and indirect service delivery. It is not a sufficient foundation, however, for understanding the systematic *process* of transferring this content expertise to reach shared goals in collaboration with others.

Consultation is one approach that has been advocated to achieve such collaboration in the early childhood field (Buysse, Schulte, Pierce, & Terry, 1994; Buysse & Wesley, 2001; File & Kontos, 1992; Hanson & Widerstrom, 1993; Palsha

& Wesley, 1998; Wesley, 1994). Consultation is not a profession per se. Rather, it is a role that can be assumed by professionals from many different disciplines and is a powerful tool for collaborative problem solving and change (Brown, Pryzwansky, & Schulte, 1998). One of the primary justifications for adopting a consultation model stems from the efficiency of providing assistance to a larger number of clients in a more timely fashion than could be accomplished through individual treatment approaches alone. In addition, consultation holds the promise of producing positive change, not only in the client (e.g., the child) but also in the consultee (e.g., the teacher), the program (e.g., the curriculum or learning environment), and, potentially, the entire system.

Empirical evidence that documents the effectiveness of consultation practice in schools is accumulating (Busse, Kratochwill, & Elliott, 1995; Medway & Updyke, 1985; Sheridan, Welch, & Orme, 1996), although little research has examined consultation processes and none has evaluated consultation's outcomes in early education and intervention. Erchul and Martens (2002) noted the difficulty of conducting research on consultation outcomes, particularly with regard to demonstrating benefits to a third party (i.e., the client) through interventions targeting a second party (i.e., the consultee). Despite these methodological challenges, the authors concluded that there is ample evidence that consultation is effective, citing meta-analyses and reviews across more than 100 controlled studies that yielded modest to high effect sizes (from .55 to .95).

Hundreds of books and several journals (e.g., *Journal of Educational and Psychological Consultation, Consulting Psychology Journal*) suggest that consultation is a unique form of service delivery with its own theoretical and empirical foundations distinguishing it from other forms of collaboration and help-giving relationships (Zins, Kratochwill, & Elliott, 1993). In formulating recommended consultation practices and evaluating their effectiveness in early childhood settings, it is critical to look beyond the field's limited literature and draw from the larger body of knowledge and theoretical traditions from other disciplines, most notably mental health and school-based consultation in education.

The sections that follow examine the history, origins, and definitions of consultation from other disciplines. Then, the chapter reviews the limited research on consultation in early education and intervention and offers a consultation approach that holds promise for application in early childhood settings. We say that this approach "holds promise" because it remains to be validated through scientific research. In the meantime, the proposed approach offers professionals already engaged in the practice of consultation a systematic process and other key elements of consultation that have been found effective outside of early education and intervention.

THE HISTORY AND ORIGINS OF CONSULTATION

The roots of contemporary consultation practices can be found in a wide range of disciplines that include the clinical or expert model in medicine, mental health consultation in psychiatry, and organizational development and behavioral consultation in psychology, as well as other forms of consultation adapted for specific purposes in education and community psychology (Brown et al., 1998). Each model has contributed important dimensions to the practice of consultation, some of which are controversial and continue to spark debate, such as the expert versus collegial nature of consultation and the extent to which the consultant should exert control over the consultation process. Two approaches, the mental health model and the behavioral model, have made significant contributions to current consultation theory and practice and are relevant for developing a consultation approach in early childhood settings.

Mental Health Model

It is impossible to discuss the history and origins of consultation without mentioning the mental health model. Virtually every reliable source on consultation mentions the contributions of Gerald Caplan's mental health model to the development of contemporary consultation practice (e.g., see Brown et al., 1998; Erchul & Martens, 2002; Wallace & Hall, 1996).

The origins of the mental health model stem from Caplan's work with adolescent immigrants in post–World War II Israel. As the director of a mental health clinic in Jerusalem, Caplan and his staff found it impossible to provide individual psychotherapy and other treatment to the more than 16,000 youth throughout Israel who needed mental health services. Instead of serving individual clients in their Jerusalem clinic, Caplan and his staff traveled to approximately 100 institutions throughout Israel and concentrated their efforts on working with the professionals in these institutions to address the priorities and concerns related to the people they served. These efforts resulted in a new model of delivering mental health services in the form of collegial discussions with providers; in turn, this approach led to providers returning to work with different perspectives and more effective strategies for addressing concerns. (For a comprehensive description of the mental health model and the historical context in which this particular approach to consultation was developed, the reader is referred to original works by Caplan [1970] and Caplan and Caplan [1999], as well as to the many other reviews and critiques this work has inspired.)

Caplan's definitions and ideas about consultation have made a significant contribution to contemporary consultation practice, although some of these ideas are more relevant for mental health than for educational contexts. Features of the mental health model of consultation that have been widely adopted or incorporated into other consultation approaches include the following (Brown et al., 1998; Erchul & Martens, 2002):

• The triadic nature of consultation (i.e., the consultant, the consultee, and the client)

- A nonhierarchical and voluntary relationship between the consultant and consultee

- A taxonomy of approaches to consultation (e.g., consultee-centered, client-centered, program-centered)

- A focus on work-related problems rather than on personal problems of the consultee

- The recognition that the ultimate responsibility for the client's welfare rests with the consultee

- A focus on helping the consultee address similar problems independently in the future

Behavioral Model

The behavioral model also has contributed to the development of consultation and influenced its theory and practice. Bergan's (1977, 1995; Bergan & Kratochwill, 1990) problem-solving approach to consultation was based on principles of behaviorism and operant learning that consider behavior a function of environmental factors that can be controlled by people in the environment to produce desired changes. Because the behavioral model is based on sound theoretical foundations and a systematic problem-solving paradigm with clear action steps, it remains the most widely used model by practitioners in U.S. schools and has been validated empirically more than any other approach (Brown et al., 1998; Erchul & Martens, 2002).

The behavioral model shares several key features with the mental health model (e.g., the triadic nature of consultation, a systematic process for addressing shared goals) but also differs in several important ways. Henning-Stout (1993) identified the problem-solving orientation as one of the most generalizable and empowering skills that a consultee can gain from the behavioral approach to consultation. In consultation, *problem* is defined as the discrepancy between the actual situation and an ideal state. In behavioral consultation, it is this discrepancy between what actually exists (e.g., a child who has severe physical disabilities and no means of verbal communication) and what the consultee desires (e.g., a way for the child to communicate her choice of foods during snack time) that brings the consultant and consultee together in the first place. Dougherty (2000) noted that the goal of all consultation is to solve problems. He further suggested that the term *problem* does not necessarily imply that something is wrong with the client or the consultee but, rather, refers more broadly to an undesirable situation requiring change.

The consultee and consultant work together to identify and define the problem and jointly create an intervention that is acceptable to the consultee (e.g., teaching the child to use a picture communication system). The immediate goal in most situations is to remediate an area of concern identified by the consultee; however, assisting the consultee to reframe a problem (i.e., view it from different perspectives) and helping him or her to prevent similar problems from occurring in the future often constitute less explicit but equally important goals of behavioral consultation. As a result, behavioral consultation can be viewed as a powerful tool for producing positive changes in the client as well as enhancing the knowledge and skills of the consultee.

In comparison to the mental health model of consultation, the behavioral model focuses less on the interpersonal aspects of the consulting relationship and concentrates more on the technical aspects of facilitating the consultation process. This process consists of a series of specific activities within four problem-solving stages: problem identification, problem analysis, plan implementation, and problem evaluation. One of the most controversial aspects of this approach concerns the extent to which the consultant should exercise control over the consultee through various communication strategies to facilitate the process and ensure the effectiveness of the intervention (Brown et al., 1998; Erchul & Martens, 2002). Chapters 3–10, which describe a collaborative framework for the early childhood field, address this issue of how the consultant should provide professional support and attempt to influence the process. Other notable contributions of the behavioral model to contemporary consultation practice include protocols for conducting initial and subsequent interviews with consultees, specific steps in the intervention process, and a framework for evaluating consultation effectiveness.

Each approach to consultation—the mental health model and the behavioral model—has contributed to the development of contemporary consultation, and aspects of each can be applied to consultation practice in early childhood settings. The mental health model notes the importance of preventing future problems and of addressing the consultee's immediate concerns. The behavioral model reminds interventionists to focus on the client as well as on the consultee and offers a clearly specified process for identifying the goals of consultation, developing and implementing a plan to address those goals, and determining ways to evaluate the outcomes of consultation. The following section presents definitions of consultation from the literature and provides a definition for the early childhood field.

DEFINING CONSULTATION

Unfortunately, a consensus on the definition of consultation does not exist. The term *consultant* is used so frequently that there is some danger that people will embrace the title without fully comprehending its implications for theory and practice (Hansen, Himes, & Meier, 1990). Common usage of the term *consultation* generally implies the giving and receiving of technical advice, but this definition does not capture the complexity of consultation and is far removed from those offered by various scholars of consultation theory and practice. In the early childhood field, the term *consultation* has been used to mean various things, from having structured and goal-directed interactions within a consulting relationship to simply checking in from time to time with a classroom teacher (Dinnebeil, McInerney, Roth, & Ramaswamy, 2001). This section provides the reader with several definitions from reliable sources on consultation, identifies common elements or threads across these various definitions, and, finally, offers a specific definition of consultation for the early education and intervention field.

Definitions from the Literature

Consultation has been defined many ways in the literature. Dougherty defined consultation in schools and human service settings as "a type of helping relationship in which a human service professional (consultant) delivers assistance to another person (consultee) so as to solve a work-related or caretaking-related problem the consultee has with a client system" (2000, p. 18).

Wallace and Hall offered a broad-based definition of psychological consultation for use in a variety of settings and contexts. In their view, consultation is

> A broad helping approach in which qualified psychological consultants help consultees (1) resolve work-related issues pertaining to individuals, clients, or programs that they are responsible for, (2) become active agents in achieving solutions to problems, or (3) strengthen consultees' work-related competencies to address similar issues in the future. (1996, p. 10)

Erchul and Martens provided a definition of school-based consultation:

> School consultation is a process for providing psychological and educational services in which a specialist (consultant) works cooperatively with a staff member (consultee) to improve the learning and adjustment of a student (client) or groups of students. During face-to-face interactions, the consultant helps the consultee through systematic problem solving, social influence, and professional support. In turn, the consultee helps the client(s) through selecting and implementing effective school-based interventions. In all cases, school consultation serves a remedial function and has the potential to serve a preventive function. (2002, pp. 13–14)

Other scholars identified the essential elements of consultation in general rather than offering a specific definition (Brown et al., 1998; Zins et al., 1993). The major elements of consultation identified by these authors include the following:

- It is an indirect method of service delivery in that the consultant generally does not work directly with the client.

- It is initiated by either consultee or consultant.

- It is triadic in that it provides indirect services to a third party (client or clients).

- It is a joint, systematic problem-solving process.

- Roles and goals of consultation vary with the consultee's needs and stages in the process.

- The consultant may be internal or external to the organization.

- Consultees may accept or reject suggestions.

- The consulting relationship is characterized as voluntary, temporary, collegial or cooperative, confidential, and focused on work-related issues.

- The goals focus on remediation and prevention.

- It is influenced by the organizational context and requires a systems or ecological perspective.

A Definition for Early Education and Intervention

A review of the various definitions of consultation that exist in the literature reveals essential features common across all definitions, such as the triadic nature of consultation, the collegial nature of the consulting relationship, and shared responsibilities across all stages of the consultation process. The definition that we propose for consultation for the early childhood field embraces many of these key elements and is closely adapted from the definition put forth by Erchul and Martens (2002). It can be differentiated from other definitions in several important ways. Perhaps most important, it specifies that parents and other caregivers be viewed as legitimate consultees and specialists from various disciplines outside of education be viewed as legitimate consultants. Furthermore, in our definition of *consultation,* the client can be an individual child, more than one child, or an entire early childhood program. Finally, our definition differentiates consultation from other forms of collaboration by including a description of the respective roles of the consultant and consultee as delineated by Erchul and Martens (2002). Our proposed definition is as follows: In early education and intervention, *consultation* is defined as an indirect, triadic service delivery model in which a consultant (e.g., early childhood special educator, therapist) and a consultee (e.g., early childhood professional, parent) work together to address an area of concern or a common goal for change. (Figure 2 displays the triadic nature of the consultation process.) Through a series of meetings and conversations, the consultant helps the consultee through systematic problem solving, social influence, and professional support. In turn, the consultee helps the client(s) with full support and assistance from the consultant. The purpose of consultation is to address the immediate concern or goal as well as to prevent similar problems from occurring in the future.

Distinguishing Consultation from Collaboration

Consultation shares several elements with other help-giving relationships and models of collaboration. It can be distinguished by its focus on a nonhierarchical

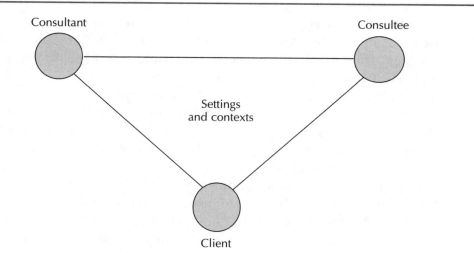

Figure 2. Triadic nature of consultation.

relationship between the consultant and the consultee and the process itself, which is described in more detail later. It is important but somewhat difficult to grasp the distinction between consultation and collaboration. Brown et al. (1998) suggested that the term *collaborative consultation* may be an oxymoron, a view not shared by Idol and colleagues, among others (Idol, 1989; Idol, Paolucci-Whitcomb, & Nevin, 1986; Parsons, 1996). Brown and colleagues suggested that this is the case primarily because collaboration in the schools can and usually does involve two professionals providing direct service to the client, whereas direct service is not a defining component in any of the various models of consultation. Erchul and Martens (2002) stated that the issue of whether to collaborate or consult is not as straightforward as one might expect. For example, they noted that organizational contexts or other factors often force the consultant to adopt a hands-on approach with the client rather than relying on time-honored consultation methods of supporting and encouraging the consultee. This is particularly true when the consultant is internal—that is, employed by the same organization as the consultee. In the field of early intervention, a further complicating issue stems from the fact that itinerant teachers in early childhood settings often play both an indirect and a direct service delivery role, depending on the needs of the consultee and the client. It is important for the reader to be aware of this debate in the literature and to consider the meaning of consultation and collaboration throughout the remaining sections. We consider collaboration a valuable goal in consultation that has potential to optimize resources, consultee commitment, and each party's satisfaction with the process.

Distinguishing Consultation from Coaching

Consultation can be distinguished from coaching in several important ways. Consultation and coaching have very different histories, origins, and theoretical foundations. Although it is beyond the scope of this book to provide a comprehensive comparative analysis, it should be noted that the foundations of coaching stem from athletics, business, and, more recently, from teacher education and adult learning theory; whereas consultation is rooted in mental health, applied behavior analysis, and the special education field, as noted previously. In terms of the application of these models in early childhood settings, it appears that coaching has been used most often with both early intervention professionals and families of young children with disabilities in home settings and other natural environments, although there is a growing interest in the use of coaching to support teaching practices in early education classrooms. By contrast, consultation has been used more frequently with educators in early childhood classrooms but also could be applied to collaborative work with families and other adults who work with very young children in a variety of community settings.

According to the definition offered by Hanft, Rush, and Shelden, "coaching in early childhood is an interactive process of observation, reflection, and action in which a coach promotes, directly and/or indirectly, a learner's ability to support a child's participation in family and community contexts" (2004, p. 4). This definition points to several other differences between consultation and coaching. First, coaching refers to the recipient of coaching as a "learner" and stresses the importance of the learner selecting what he or she wants to learn. In consultation, the "consultee" is considered a full partner in a relationship characterized by mutual decision-making as well as self-determination. Second, consultation is defined more narrowly as an indirect service delivery model, whereas coaching can refer to either a direct or indirect service model. Although consultants often move back and forth between their consulting roles and other roles (i.e., providing instruction or therapy services to children), direct service is not a defining component of consultation. Third, consultation commonly is used to address goals related to an individual child, a group of children, a consultee, an early childhood program, or even an entire system; whereas the goal of coaching focuses more narrowly on the adult learner's ability to address child-specific interventions.

Finally, although there are some similarities in the stages of the process employed by each of these models (e.g., observing, gathering information, evaluating the model's effectiveness), there are important differences as well. For example, developing a plan in conjunction with the consultee to address shared goals is a key component of consultation, but, in the coaching model, this element is addressed more informally and more spontaneously through reflective questioning.

DETERMINING THE PURPOSE AND GOALS OF CONSULTATION

The early childhood field has not reached consensus regarding the purpose and goals of consultation. Professionals who are thrust into a consultant role because of inclusive policies and practices often express confusion about consultation and wonder about its effectiveness (Dinnebeil et al., 2001; Sadler, 2002). Our research confirms these conclusions, suggesting that professionals in consultation roles in natural environments are not always sure who their client is and wonder whether to focus their intervention efforts on the child, family, teacher, or program (Wesley, Buysse, & Skinner, 2001). Similarly, they do not know which consultation methods are best suited to address various consultation goals or if these methods even exist. The confusion stems, in part, from the fact that most states have not articulated how indirect services in early education and intervention should be provided, nor have they defined the specific roles and responsibilities of professionals who provide these services (Dinnebeil et al., 2001). With little to guide them, consultants in early education and intervention often borrow strategies from more familiar models of collaboration and help giving, such as family-centered practices, but they may not have a clear understanding of the purpose and goals of consultation. It is our contention that the purpose of consultation can encompass any number of goals that generally fall under the following areas: addressing a child's individual needs, changing or improving the consultee's practices and beliefs, and improving global program quality.

Research on Consultation in Early Education and Intervention

As mentioned previously, research examining consultation practice in early education and intervention is limited. Extant research has examined early education professionals' beliefs and perceptions about the processes of consultation but has not investigated the effectiveness of consultation by using randomized, controlled studies. Much of the existing research has served to underscore professionals' lack of comfort with the consulting role. Dinnebeil and colleagues, for example, found that 91% of special educators who served as itinerant teachers reported using consultation, but most also reported being uncomfortable with specific strategies that primarily involved direct contact with the early childhood classroom teacher; most of the strategies that they used frequently involved providing direct services to children (Dinnebeil et al., 2001).

In related research, we conducted several studies that employed focus groups and structured interviews to examine the ways in which consultants viewed their work, particularly with respect to factors that contribute to or reduce their professional comfort and whether there exists a shared understanding of the meaning of consultation practice (Wesley, Buysse, & Keyes, 2000; Wesley et al., 2001). The major conclusion from this line of research was that consultants' comfort with consultation was affected by multiple factors, including the characteristics of the child, the consultee, and the program, as well as their own knowledge and skills and the availability of resources. The following subsections summarize the findings across each of these dimensions.

Professional Comfort with Consultation

Child Characteristics

Consultants described greater discomfort when the child had a severe disability or multiple disabilities, especially when sensory deficits or behavioral problems were involved. More severe disabilities caused greater discomfort because consultants did not believe that they had the expertise they needed to provide all of the answers. These results are somewhat troubling because they echo the findings from an earlier study in which the comfort level of child care providers was found to decrease as the severity of the child's disability increased (Buysse, Wesley, Keyes, & Bailey, 1996). These findings also raise questions about how consultation can be an effective method of service delivery in situations in which both the consultee (the recipient of consultation) and the consultant (the provider of consultation) experience discomfort with the severity of a child's disability.

Consultee Characteristics

Paradoxically, although consultants stated that one of the purposes of their consultation was to help consultees acquire new educational beliefs and practices, they expressed frustration when these differed from their own. Some consultants mentioned that it was necessary to convince consultees that the consultant was not there to monitor the quality of the teaching in the classroom. Another concern was that consultees did not have the same expectations as the consultant for the consultant's role and responsibilities in the classroom. One of these differences concerned the expectation of consultees that consultants would pull children out of the classroom for special instruction or therapy. Consultants viewed this approach as exemplifying a belief among consultees that it was possible to apply quick fixes or magic tricks to address complex problems and that the primary responsibility for the child's welfare rested with the consultant. Where families were concerned, comfort with consultation had to do with consultants' perceptions of how stable or resourceful families were. Their comfort increased when families were perceived as having the ability and resources to carry out activities suggested for the child and decreased when families denied the existence of their child's disability.

Program Characteristics

Another major source of comfort or discomfort originated from characteristics of the programs that served as consultation sites. An inadequate staff–child ratio, a large group size, a curriculum that was not developmentally appropriate, high staff turnover, and low staff qualifications were all factors that created challenges and professional discomfort for consultants. Consultants described the challenges of providing consultation in a wide range of early childhood environments, from low-quality programs with few material resources and inadequate teacher preparation to academically focused programs in which children were required to sit and complete worksheets for long periods. Some consultants expressed uncertainty about whether the purpose and goals of consultation could encompass improving the global quality of the early childhood program as well as addressing the individual priorities and needs of a particular child. Others viewed inadequate program quality as an obstacle to effective consultation but did not view action in this area as part of their responsibility as a consultant. Still others expressed a belief that consultation related to a specific child could be used as a stepping stone to address issues related to the broader program in that child-specific recommendations would improve the consultee's knowledge and skills and eventually benefit other children.

Consultant Characteristics

The majority of consultants did not elaborate on the possibility that there were characteristics about themselves that affected their professional comfort with consultation. Many identified a tension between being a generalist and a specialist or an expert. Although the consultants (whose backgrounds were primarily in early childhood education or early childhood special education) viewed expert status as conveying power, many sought to avoid this designation and made efforts to distinguish themselves in attitude and actions from other specialists such as speech-language pathologists and physical therapists. This was largely due to consultants and consultees in the studies perceiving these other specialists as not willing to "get their hands dirty" and participate in the day-to-day routines of the classroom. Yet, consultants also expressed the need to establish credibility in the eyes of their consultees, and this required specialized content knowledge about all conditions they encountered. Although consultants suggested that better communication skills would take them beyond merely providing information to increasing the likelihood of achieving consultation goals, they also described limited time for meaningful communication and dialogue with classroom staff.

Resources

Consultants also indicated that their professional comfort increased with the availability of resources such as additional information and training about the process and outcomes of consultation practice. They also identified the following as needed resources: team collaboration, flexible funding, and access to content experts and print materials on a wide range of topics. Many expressed an interest in obtaining information about research on consultation effectiveness in early education and intervention, particularly regarding whether children who received direct versus indirect services through consultation made more or less progress.

The Absence of a Conceptual Framework for Consultation

Further analysis of interviews with consultants revealed the absence of a clearly defined conceptual framework for implementing consultation as well as the lack of guidelines for evaluating its effectiveness in early childhood settings. On the basis of previous research with early childhood consultants (Buysse et al., 1994), we suspected that consultants' beliefs and practices about consultation would be premised on a collaborative model, but this proved not to be the case. Consultants spoke of "collaboration" and "being a diplomat," but then described telling consultees what to do and being frustrated by their lack of follow-through. As consultants, they operated without an understanding of a systematic process for moving through consultation stages such as establishing a consulting relationship, jointly assessing needs, collaboratively identifying priorities and strategies for change, implementing those strategies, and evaluating outcomes. Few referred to past experiences and training as a source for current practices, and none identified principles for implementing change. Many consultants expressed the belief that consultation with child care providers would not be effective until somebody described the consultant's role and how the consultation process would unfold, although consultants did not view engaging consultees in a dialogue about consultation roles and goals as part of their responsibility. In short, consultants lacked an understanding of the consultation process.

An obvious implication of these findings is the need for a clearly defined conceptual framework for implementing consultation and evaluating its effectiveness for the early childhood field. The next section provides an overview of such an approach. Then, subsequent chapters offer additional details about each stage of the consulting process from entry into the consultation setting until the summary conference.

A PROPOSED FRAMEWORK FOR CONSULTATION IN EARLY EDUCATION AND INTERVENTION

We propose a framework for consultation in early childhood settings that builds on research-based knowledge from other disciplines and theoretical traditions, most notably the mental health professions and school-based consultation. Although the proposed framework is based on sound theoretical and empirical foundations, the effectiveness of this or any consultation approach for early education and intervention must be validated through scientific research. In the absence of such evidence, we view the proposed model as a promising approach that invites additional research to document its processes and outcomes for young children, their caregivers, and systems of care.

The proposed framework integrates strengths from both the mental health and behavioral models of consultation, along with principles of social influence and support, and is called an integrated model of consultation (Erchul & Martens, 2002). The integrated model incorporates the emphasis on prevention and the consulting relationship from the mental health model with a focus on the client and a clearly specified problem-solving approach from the behavioral model (Erchul & Martens, 2002). In this model of consultation, the process is viewed as three interrelated tasks—problem solving, social influence, and professional support—that are accomplished within a collegial consultative relationship. Through a series of consultative meetings and interviews, the consultant both influences and supports the consultee throughout the problem-solving process. The help that a consultant offers the consultee is based on the three interrelated tasks and may take the form of suggesting a new strategy such as embedding interventions into daily routines (problem solving), encouraging the consultee to implement the strategy during center time (social influence), or providing training or coaching the consultee to help him or her learn specific techniques related to using the strategy (professional support). The consultee acquires new knowledge and skills, which are applied to interventions that directly benefit the client and can be used to prevent similar problems from occurring in the future.

The stages of consultation reflect a process that is not unfamiliar to professionals who must plan and evaluate interventions for young children and their families. Although consultants often rely on checklists, observations, and data to support consultation practice, the process essentially involves a series of conversations between the consultant and the consultee. The conversations focus on building rapport and establishing a productive working relationship; identifying the consultation focus and defining a common goal for change; and identifying, implementing, and evaluating strategies to address this goal.

Before presenting the stages of the process, it is important to note several issues that contribute to the complexity of consultation. First, the process of consulting with another adult requires the consultant to operate on two planes simultaneously: He or she must implement a set of activities or tasks that unfold sequentially over time to address the area of concern while concentrating on the interpersonal aspects of the consulting relationship (Brown et al., 1998). Later in this book, the description of the process touches on both of these dimensions, as well as on the specific communication strategies that are essential to be effective in both domains at every stage.

Another issue concerns the need for early interventionists and itinerant teachers to understand the delicate balance between their direct and indirect service delivery roles: shifting as needed from providing direct therapy and instruction to children to offering indirect services in the form of collaborative consultation to children's parents and teachers (Dinnebeil et al., 2001; Sadler, 2002). Consultation involves a mix of factors that affect the consultant's focus and methods. These include, for example, whether the consultee is experiencing a crisis requiring immediate intervention and the degree to which resources are available to support a mutual process of diagnostic observation and intervention planning. Although the balance between direct and indirect services is important, we agree with Parsons that it is more functional to view the nature and form of consultation as a "multidimensional, integrated activity that takes shape and distinctiveness by moving along continuums reflecting consultee-felt need, consultant expertise, and degrees of collaborative involvement" (1996, p. 36).

Finally, it is important to keep in mind that the consultation process can vary across consultees, even when a single model of consultation is employed. De-

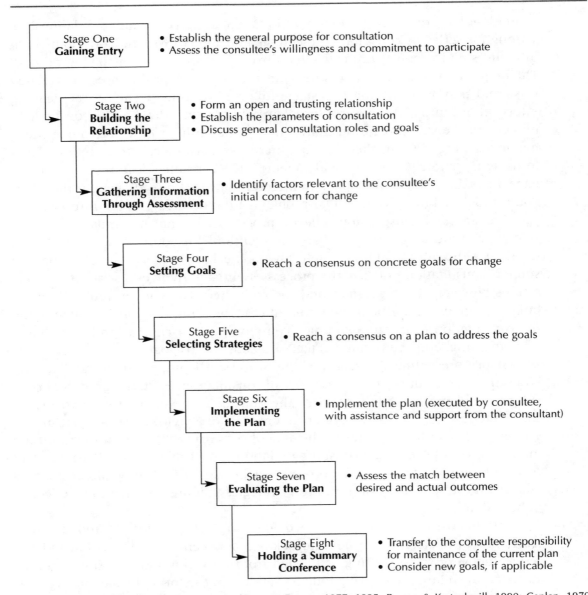

Stage One
Gaining Entry
- Establish the general purpose for consultation
- Assess the consultee's willingness and commitment to participate

Stage Two
Building the Relationship
- Form an open and trusting relationship
- Establish the parameters of consultation
- Discuss general consultation roles and goals

Stage Three
Gathering Information Through Assessment
- Identify factors relevant to the consultee's initial concern for change

Stage Four
Setting Goals
- Reach a consensus on concrete goals for change

Stage Five
Selecting Strategies
- Reach a consensus on a plan to address the goals

Stage Six
Implementing the Plan
- Implement the plan (executed by consultee, with assistance and support from the consultant)

Stage Seven
Evaluating the Plan
- Assess the match between desired and actual outcomes

Stage Eight
Holding a Summary Conference
- Transfer to the consultee responsibility for maintenance of the current plan
- Consider new goals, if applicable

Figure 3. Stages of the consultation process. (*Sources:* Bergan, 1977, 1995; Bergan & Kratochwill, 1990; Caplan, 1970; Caplan & Caplan, 1999.)

pending on the situation, a step in the process may be skipped, combined with another step, or revisited at a later time.

The stages of consultation outlined in Figure 3 and elaborated in subsequent chapters were drawn from reliable sources on school-based consultation and include our own applications for consultation practice in early childhood (Bergan, 1977, 1995; Bergan & Kratochwill, 1990; Buysse & Wesley, 2004; Caplan, 1970; Caplan & Caplan, 1999; Wesley & Buysse, 2004). We believe that the consultation steps can be adapted to a wide variety of purposes, such as improving global program quality, addressing individual educational goals, and enhancing the knowledge and skills of the consultee. We believe that the steps also can be adapted to a wide variety of contexts, including community-based child care and prekindergarten programs, neighborhood play and recreation groups, Head Start programs, public school prekindergarten classrooms, clinical settings, home-based early intervention services, and family child care homes.

CONCLUSION

This chapter presented a conceptual framework for consultation in early childhood settings that integrates the mental health and behavioral approaches found to be effective in other professions. Equipped with the stages of the consultation process—together with the consultant's knowledge, skills, and dispositions outlined in Chapter 2—early childhood consultants and consultees will have a firm foundation to achieve shared goals and positive change.

Chapter 2

Consultant Knowledge, Skills, and Dispositions

It is not surprising that early interventionists who provide itinerant services to 13–20 children with various developmental delays and disabilities and their families each week express frustration and concern about their roles (Wesley et al., 2001). Although they continue to serve children and families directly, they do so in many different early childhood settings and in collaboration with general early childhood personnel, various disability specialists, and other professionals from community agencies, some of whom may be serving a child with a disability for the first time. Early interventionists continue to rely on knowledge and skills related to disability and intervention in working directly with children, but their consultation with other adults stretches them beyond the knowledge base and practices that have guided them in the past. Early intervention consultants must have more than mastery of disability-related content; they also must understand the process of consultation to serve as catalysts for change and to share accountability with their consultees for the client's progress. This chapter considers the knowledge, skills, and dispositions needed by the effective consultant.

To begin thinking about what makes a successful consultant, it may be helpful to envision a typical consultation scenario. Consider an early childhood special educator who is visiting a $3\frac{1}{2}$-year-old-girl with cerebral palsy who is enrolled in a community child care program. The special educator first met the child's teacher and saw the classroom when she visited the program prior to the child's individualized education program (IEP) meeting. At that time, the teacher and the special educator briefly discussed the hope that the special educator (consultant) and teacher (consultee) would work together to promote the child's (client's) adjustment and progress in the new setting.

Now the consultant goes to the classroom twice per week and spends up to an hour or more working directly with the child, as well as with the consultee to address specific goals that are included on the IEP. Although the consultant is present in the program to focus on issues related to one particular child, the consultee and her teaching assistant are responsible for 17 other children who are also present full time in the classroom. The consultant recognizes that to maximize opportunities for the child with cerebral palsy, the consultee will need to implement interventions when the consultant is not present in the classroom. With this awareness comes the reality that the consultee has never worked with a child who has a disability, lacks training in intervention strategies, may have assumed the consultant would be responsible for all the child's special education goals, and has expressed concerns about meeting the needs of the child while also meeting the needs of the other children she serves. It is also apparent to the consultant that modifications of some classroom materials and activity centers are needed to enhance the child's participation and increase natural opportunities for functional goal work. In addition, the consultant is concerned about the curriculum and the teacher's ability to adapt it to ensure the child's full participation.

The consultant and the consultee acknowledge that meeting each other before the child started attending the classroom was beneficial, as is the family's involvement and support. They are realizing quickly, however, that more is needed in their collaboration than the brief, twice-weekly discussions about how to encourage the child to pull to stand and where to store her leg braces when she is not using them. From the consultant's perspective, the need initially appeared to be coaching the teacher through the acquisition of some new skills and techniques while the consultant continued direct services; however, this has grown into a need to address more general program elements such as room arrangement and the teacher's philosophy of early childhood education. From the consultee's perspective, services promising an extra set of hands in the classroom and some suggestions for serving the child with a disability have expanded to affect various aspects of the entire program, possibly including the schedule, the curriculum, and the teacher's own approach to instruction—something the teacher had not bargained for when the child joined her class. (This consultation scenario is presented in detail as an extended case illustration that appears at the ends of Chapters 3–10. Table 1 serves as a guide for reading the case illustration.)

MORE THAN TECHNICAL EXPERTISE

As illustrated by the preceding scenario, an effective consultant simultaneously must understand many worlds. One is the world of early intervention, in which

Table 1.   What to look for in the case illustration

Stage number and name (location of case study)	Description
Stage One Gaining Entry (Chapter 3)	The consultant presents him- or herself as approachable and creates a climate that invites questions and comments from the consultee. He or she shares information about his or her role and the consultation process.
Stage Two Building the Relationship (Chapter 4)	The consultant comments about his or her observations of the classroom and asks questions to gain additional information. The consultant avoids offering a quick fix when the consultee asks in their second meeting, "What should I do?"
Stage Three Gathering Information Through Assessment (Chapter 5)	The consultant uses open-ended and closed questions to achieve a thorough understanding of the consultee's concerns and clarify the focus of the assessment process. The consultant expands the assessment to include an examination of the classroom and program environments. The consultant recognizes that the assessment results have indicated a need in an area the consultee has described as a strength. The consultant frames the discussion of the findings positively and sets the stage by sharing his or her own related professional experience.
Stage Four Setting Goals (Chapter 6)	The consultant uses a combination of facilitation and interpretation skills to make sense of the assessment results and to help the consultee set goals.
Stage Five Selecting Strategies (Chapter 7)	The consultant asks the consultee which strategies have been tried before and found to be effective. He or she incorporates relevant approaches into the development of new strategies.
Stage Six Implementing the Plan (Chapter 8)	The consultant acts as a sounding board for the consultee and tries to reflect the consultee's feelings while demonstrating patience, understanding, and willingness to continue to problem solve.
Stage Seven Evaluating the Plan (Chapter 9)	The consultant and consultee identify new areas of need and schedule time to explore those areas in the near future.
Stage Eight Holding a Summary Conference (Chapter 10)	The consultant solicits feedback from the consultee about his or her satisfaction with the overall consultation experience. Together, the consultant and consultee make plans to modify the process to address the consultee's concerns.

therapy, instruction, and intervention techniques are tailored for an individual child in partnership with the child's family and are often introduced to the child on a one-to-one basis. Another is the world of the early childhood classroom and curriculum, through which many children, most of whom are developing typically, are served in groups by one or two adults. Finally, there is the world of consultation, in which a combination of interpersonal and communication skills, content expertise, and ongoing support achieve the changes necessary to create an inclusive environment in which children with and without disabilities thrive. The consultant must meet the needs of the client and consultee through multiple activities that play out over many months while managing the interpersonal dimensions of the consulting relationship. This dual focus on the activities and the relationship is illustrated in the remarks of one veteran consultant who has been working in child care programs for 10 years:

> You have to float up and look down at the consultation situation and see your-
> self and the consultee working together. It's not enough to show that teacher
> how to position the child in the block center or use the communication board.
> You need to know how to inspire the teacher to create many varied opportu-
> nities for the child to interact with others. You need a sense of when the
> teacher's ready to try new things and a way of introducing changes that she
> buys into! (B. Dennis, personal communication, February 3, 2003)

Much discussion in the field of early intervention and special education focuses on core competencies needed to serve young children with disabilities and their families. Lists of required courses for university graduate degrees and published descriptions of recommended or best practices provide easily accessible summaries of these professional competencies (e.g., see Sandall, McLean, & Smith, 2000). Often absent from these lists and descriptions, which enumerate various direct service practices, is any reference to the process of consultation—for example, the competencies related to developing and monitoring the consultation relationship, guiding the consultation process through predictable stages that have been validated through research, or selecting communication strategies to maximize implementation and empowerment. Because the expansion of professional roles to include indirect service delivery has occurred so rapidly, early intervention research and preservice education have not kept pace with the practice field's needs for knowledge and skills related to consultation. To fill this gap, this book draws on the literature on psychological consultation and organizational development and from our own experience and limited research in early intervention consultation to identify five domains in which mastery is essential to effective consultation in the early education and intervention field. The following section considers key tasks of consultation and offers a brief review of the literature about consultation skills and characteristics.

KEY TASKS, SKILLS, AND CHARACTERISTICS

The need to identify consultation tasks is prerequisite to the identification of essential consultation skills. Chapter 1 described our definition of consultation in early intervention, including the people, activities, and overall purpose of consultation. Chapter 1 also described Erchul and Martens's (2002) integrated model of school consultation, which draws on the strengths of both the behavioral and mental health consultation models. This model reflects findings from relational communication research and the social psychology literature's principles of social power and influence. It incorporates three interrelated tasks involved in school consultation: problem solving, social influence, and support or development. We believe that the model is applicable to early childhood consultation, especially in the way that the tasks interrelate. In the field of school psychology, the consultant may be called in by the teacher to solve classroom problems, especially to reduce the discrepancy between observed and desired student behavior; conversely, in early intervention, the consultant's involvement may be a support routinely provided through the child's individualized family service plan (IFSP) or IEP. Although the consultant and the teacher work together to solve problems, the consultant's orientation is asset based, emphasizing strategies that build on the child's abilities and strengths. The consultant may use his or her social influence to encourage the teacher to change behaviors, attitudes, or even beliefs to benefit the child and family. The extent to which the teacher is able to implement agreed-on plans also depends on the consultant's ability to support his or her development as the teacher expands his or her professional knowledge and experience related to the child.

To accomplish the three tasks of solving problems, using social influence, and providing support for professional development, a consultant must possess a range of skills and characteristics. Consultant knowledge and skills have been discussed at some length in the literature, with various sets of competencies being set forth based on scientific research and, to a larger degree, on the opinions of experts in the field (e.g., Brown, 1993; Brown et al., 1998; Dougherty, 2000; Horton & Brown, 1990; Idol & West, 1987; Kratochwill, VanSomeren, & Sheridan, 1990; Lippett & Lippett, 1986; Parsons & Meyers, 1984). Although different models of consultation emphasize different areas, most authors stress the importance of competence in the specific discipline related to the consultation (e.g., early childhood special education); knowledge about consultation and group processes; and effective interpersonal, communication, and problem-solving skills. Dougherty (2000) provided a good summary of essential consultation skills in his description of the following areas:

- Interpersonal: putting the consultee at ease through the use of small talk and humor; demonstrating respect and authenticity in interactions; creating a base of social influence by building the consultee's belief in the consultant's trustworthiness, competence, and similarities to the consultee

- Communication: using nonverbal behaviors, active listening, questioning, clarifying, summarizing, providing information and feedback

- Problem solving: using objectivity in gathering, analyzing, and interpreting information; designing responsive interventions; predicting ramifications

- Skills in working with organizations: determining the communication channels in the work place, identifying the organization's standards and values, assessing the types of available internal resources and determining how to use them

- Group facilitation: focusing and maintaining attention on relevant issues, managing meeting agendas, facilitating discussion and the development of the group process, providing feedback

- Responsiveness to cultural diversity: neither under- nor overemphasizing cultural variables, refraining from value judgments, building on the life experiences of the consultee

- Ethics: respecting confidentiality, adhering to accepted guidelines for professional behavior

It also is widely recognized that consultants need certain personal characteristics in addition to knowledge and skills to be effective. These characteristics include

- The drive and desire to make a difference (Bianco-Mathis & Veazey, 1996)

- A high level of awareness of his or her values (Caplan, 1970)—for example, regarding child rearing and early childhood education—and an awareness of the potential differences in values among consultees (Brown et al., 1998)

- The ability to see things through different perspectives, including culturally differing frames of references (Hunsaker, 1985; Soo-Hoo, 1998; Varney, 1985; Zins et al., 1993)

- Genuineness or the ability to be sincere without presenting a false front (Zins et al., 1993)

- Determination, energy, and persistence (Maher, 1993)

- A personal and professional growth orientation (Dougherty, 2000)

Other characteristics mentioned in the literature are confidence characterized by a positive outlook about oneself, others, and the consultation process; trustworthiness; humor; helpfulness; a commitment to creativity; and a willingness to take risks (Dougherty, 2000; Lippett & Lippett, 1986). More than likely, one's own personal and professional experiences provide ample examples of how such characteristics and attitudes affect relationships; however, research on the *characteristics* of effective consultants is slim compared with the abundance of information about consultation *skills* (Brown et al., 1998; Knoff, McKenna, & Riser, 1991). It is noteworthy that research has found the strength and outcome of the consultation relationship to be related directly to the consultee's positive attitude toward the consultation process and commitment to change (Villa & Thousand, 1996; West & Idol, 1990). This finding underscores the importance of the consultant's ability to understand and monitor the intricacies of interpersonal interactions. The Knowledge and Skills Inventory for Consultants summarizes recommended competencies related to basic knowledge, systems change, personal characteristics, communication, problem-solving, and professional development (see Form 1 for a sample; also see the appendix at the end of the book for a full-size, blank version of this form).

CRITICAL DOMAINS

Building in part on Dougherty's (2000) key areas of consultation skills and the limited literature reporting consultation characteristics, we propose five domains in which mastery is essential for effective consultants in early intervention:

Knowledge and Skills Inventory for Consultants

Please check the appropriate box to rate the extent to which you agree or disagree with the statement regarding your knowledge and skill as a consultant.

	1 Strongly disagree	2 Disagree	3 Agree somewhat	4 Agree	5 Strongly agree
With regard to basic knowledge, I					
1. Understand the stages/phases of the consultation process					
2. Understand the need to match possible consultation approaches and specific consultant situations, settings, and needs					
3. Am able to discuss the purpose of consultation in the early childhood setting and the roles of the consultant and consultee					
4. Am familiar with the major areas of child development: a. cognitive b. language and literacy c. motor d. socioemotional					
5. Am familiar with disabilities and their impact on development					
6. Can identify quality indicators in the child care center or home					
7. Understand the early childhood and early intervention service system					
With regard to systems change, I					
8. Strive to understand the philosophical/theoretical perspective of the early childhood program in which I am consulting					
9. Am able to identify positive and negative effects that might result from efforts to change part of the program					
10. Can implement strategies to empower individuals and systems to change when necessary					
11. Am able to modify myths and attitudes that impede successful inclusion of children with disabilities					
12. Am able to identify and link resources between early childhood teachers and other agencies					
With regard to personal characteristics and skills, I					
13. Am respectful, open, and caring in consultation interactions					
14. Can establish and maintain a sense of rapport and mutual trust with all persons involved in the consultation process					
15. Maintain an enthusiastic attitude and positive self-concept throughout the consultation process					
16. Demonstrate a willingness to learn from others throughout the consultation process					
17. Am creative in examining problems and options					
18. Facilitate the consultation process by demonstrating flexibility					
19. Respect divergent points of view, acknowledging the right to hold different views and to act in accordance with convictions					

(continued)

From Klein, S., & Kontos, S. (1993). *Best practices in integration in-service training model: Instructional modules* (pp. 35–39). Bloomington: Indiana University; adapted by permission.

	1 Strongly disagree	2 Disagree	3 Agree somewhat	4 Agree	5 Strongly agree
With regard to communication skills, I					
20. Communicate clearly and effectively in oral and written form					
21. Use active listening and responding skills such as paraphrasing, clarifying, and summarizing to facilitate the consultation process					
22. Am perceptive in grasping and validating stated and unstated meanings and affect in communication					
23. Am able to elicit information from persons involved in the consultation process					
24. Enable others to examine their viewpoints of a situation or stated problem and to consider other possible views or explanations					
25. Manage conflict skillfully throughout the consultation process to maintain collaborative relationships					
26. Am reinforcing of others involved in the consultation process					
With regard to collaborative problem solving, I					
27. Identify and clarify problems and needs using a variety of data					
28. Pursue collaborative "brainstorming," withholding premature evaluation of ideas, to generate possible solutions to problems and means to objectives					
29. Integrate feasible goals and objectives into a plan of action that includes consultees as equal partners					
30. Elicit information to evaluate the effectiveness of the planned activities and interventions					
31. Provide information from my own area of expertise when needed by others without overwhelming or failing to acknowledge others' expertise					
32. Recognize and respond appropriately to the belief systems of others involved in the consultation process					
With regard to my own development, I					
33. Maintain a high standard of ethics related to such issues as confidentiality, personal and professional boundaries, and consultation efficacy					
34. Am able to assess my own effectiveness by using children's progress, parent and staff feedback, and self-rating					
35. Request and accept constructive feedback and suggestions for improvement					
36. Am able to make changes based on this feedback					
37. Seek professional development through conferences, workshops, meetings, individual study, and reading					

From Klein, S., & Kontos, S. (1993). *Best practices in integration in-service training model: Instructional modules* (pp. 35–39). Bloomington: Indiana University; adapted by permission.

Form 1. (From Klein, S., & Kontos, S. [1993]. *Best practices in integration in-service training model: Instructional modules* [pp. 35–39]. Bloomington: Indiana University; adapted by permission.)

1) child development theory and early childhood practices, 2) developmental disabilities and early intervention/special education practices, 3) communication, 4) consultation stages and strategies, and 5) ethics and professionalism (Wesley & Buysse, 2004). Although these domains encompass roles and skills that the literature has identified as critical to consultation effectiveness, the domains have not been validated through scientific research (see Figure 4).

The five domains and their related skills support the three tasks of Erchul and Martens's (2002) integrated model and the development of the consultative relationship. Although the first two child-related domains are related to the technical content needed by the consultant and the remaining three adult-oriented

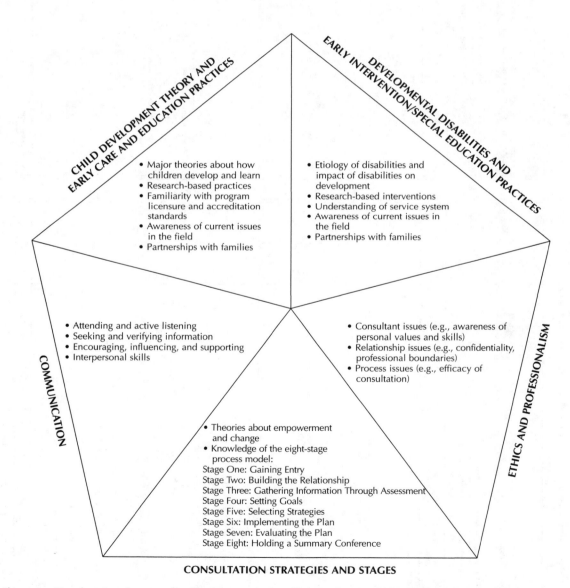

CHILD DEVELOPMENT THEORY AND EARLY CARE AND EDUCATION PRACTICES

- Major theories about how children develop and learn
- Research-based practices
- Familiarity with program licensure and accreditation standards
- Awareness of current issues in the field
- Partnerships with families

DEVELOPMENTAL DISABILITIES AND EARLY INTERVENTION/SPECIAL EDUCATION PRACTICES

- Etiology of disabilities and impact of disabilities on development
- Research-based interventions
- Understanding of service system
- Awareness of current issues in the field
- Partnerships with families

COMMUNICATION

- Attending and active listening
- Seeking and verifying information
- Encouraging, influencing, and supporting
- Interpersonal skills

ETHICS AND PROFESSIONALISM

- Consultant issues (e.g., awareness of personal values and skills)
- Relationship issues (e.g., confidentiality, professional boundaries)
- Process issues (e.g., efficacy of consultation)

CONSULTATION STRATEGIES AND STAGES

- Theories about empowerment and change
- Knowledge of the eight-stage process model:
  Stage One: Gaining Entry
  Stage Two: Building the Relationship
  Stage Three: Gathering Information Through Assessment
  Stage Four: Setting Goals
  Stage Five: Selecting Strategies
  Stage Six: Implementing the Plan
  Stage Seven: Evaluating the Plan
  Stage Eight: Holding a Summary Conference

Figure 4.   Five domains of mastery for effective consultation. (*Sources:* Parsons, 1996; Wesley & Buysse, 2004.)

domains are related to the processes required to share that content, the reader is cautioned against applying such a simple dichotomy. Both technical and process expertise are critical throughout consultation and within each domain.

Child Development Theory and Effective Practices

Any consultant working with young children must have an understanding of basic major developmental theories that serve as the foundation for professional beliefs and practices. In addition to theory, thorough knowledge of evidence-based practices for promoting children's development and learning during the early years should inform the selection of interventions during the consultation process. Familiarity with various early childhood program licensure and accreditation standards is a plus, as the consultant strives to understand the factors affecting the classrooms in which he or she may be working. Moreover, consultants should maintain an awareness of fundamental issues or tensions in child care and early education—for example, the tensions between developmentally appropriate practice and the increasing academic focus of kindergarten and prekindergarten programs (Wesley & Buysse, 2003) and between parent and professional concerns about early childhood transitions (Pianta & Cox, 1999). Consultants can refer to publications of the National Association for the Education of Young Children (NAEYC; http://www.naeyc.org) and to their states' departments of education for descriptions of minimal professional competencies, program standards, and positions statements on current issues. Professional journals such as *Child Development* and *Early Childhood Research Quarterly* include articles describing practices that have been demonstrated through research to promote children's development and learning.

Developmental Disabilities and Early Intervention/Special Education Practices

Although knowledge of typical child development and evidence-based early childhood practices is a necessary foundation, it is not sufficient for effective consultation involving children with disabilities. Early intervention consultants' primary expertise lies in their knowledge of developmental disabilities including etiology, an understanding of the impact of disability on all areas of development, and related interventions. Thorough understanding of and firsthand experience with the service system are crucial, from child referral and diagnosis to development and evaluation of an education plan. A minimum requirement is mastery of fundamental concepts and skills in areas such as family-centered philosophy and practice; service delivery in natural environments; interagency collaboration; and individualized, activity-based interventions. Consultants can refer to publications of the Council for Exceptional Children (http://www.cec.sped.org), particularly those of its Division for Early Childhood (http://www.dec-sped.org), for information about professional standards and evidence-based practices. Professional journals such as the *Journal of Early Intervention, Exceptional Children, Zero to Three,* and *Topics in Early Childhood Special Education* are rich sources of research findings related to the education and care of young children with disabilities.

Communication

Because consultation is basically an interpersonal exchange, the consultant's success depends largely on his or her skills in communication and relationship building (Gutkin & Curtis, 1982). Communication is the process of exchanging messages to create meaning between two or more people (Tubbs & Moss, 1977, as cited in Parsons & Meyers, 1984). Effective communication creates a condition in which the message perceived and responded to by the receiver corresponds to the one intended by the sender (Parsons & Meyers, 1984). An effective consultant is aware of the personal, interpersonal, and environmental factors that affect this correspondence (e.g., body language, warmth, objectivity, meeting space free of excessive distractions) and is proficient in communication skills that promote mutual engagement and collaboration in a helping process. These skills include the ability to communicate ideas in a helpful, nonthreatening manner that is consistent with the purpose of the communication (e.g., to elicit or provide information, to influence, to confront); responsive listening; reflecting content and feelings; questioning; probing; clarifying; and summarizing (Cormier & Cormier, 1985; Parsons, 1996). For example, the consultant may use many open-ended questions during the first visit with the consultee to learn about his or her experiences in the classroom and style of teaching. The consultant may make a special effort to be aware of his or her own posture and eye contact with others as he or she expresses pleasure in meeting new adults and children. At the same time, the consultant must understand the nonverbal messages of the consultee, who is in turn sizing up the consultant's values and behaviors (Zins et al., 1993). Table 2 summarizes three skills areas that equip the consultant with effective tools for communication.

Zins and colleagues (1993) summarized the literature on two theories in which competent interpersonal communication in consultation can be grounded: personal construct theory and causal attribution theory. A *personal construct* refers to the beliefs that serve as a paradigm or cognitive framework for understanding the consultation situation. Personal construct theory is supported by the findings that one can communicate and solve problems more effectively by conceptualizing the situation and the consultee from multiple perspectives rather than from a single viewpoint (Delia, O'Keefe, & O'Keefe, 1982; Hunt, 1983, as cited in Zins et al., 1993). Consultants who adopt a flexible approach that is open to suspending or reframing their perceptions along the way may help consultees rethink their own beliefs and constructs related to their understanding of a problem's definition or solution. For example, consider the following situation: A consultant visits

Table 2.   Tools for effective communication in consultation

	Function	Example
Attending and active listening		
Body language	Physical posture characterized by a relaxed, open manner and good eye contact demonstrate interest and concern.	Leaning slightly toward the speaker while sitting, hands relaxed in the lap
Reflecting content	Paraphrasing the content of a message is one way to let the speaker know you understand what has been said.	"You've tried limiting the number of toys and materials in each center."
Reflecting feelings	Using your own words to identify the feelings expressed in a message is one way to let the speaker know you understand his or her sentiments and sense the world as he or she perceives it.	"You're pretty excited about Jon coming to your classroom!"
Encouraging words	Acknowledging the speaker through simple verbalizations encourages the speaker to continue.	"Yes." "Uh-huh." "Please go on."
Seeking and verifying information		
Questioning	Probing through the use of different types of questions yields information that helps to define an issue or concern.	"How many teachers are assigned to this room?" (closed question) "In what ways do you acknowledge cultural differences in your program?" (open-ended question)
Silence	Waiting patiently and quietly while another person thinks or prepares to answer a question lets the speaker know you want to hear from him or her.	N/A
Clarifying	After encouraging the speaker to elaborate or expand on a topic, reflect the message and ask if you understand what has been said.	"Tell me more about departure time . . . Do I understand what happens correctly?"
Building	Adding to the speaker's ideas or statement lets the other person know you value his or her input.	"Yes, and . . ." "That's a great starting point for . . ."
Summarizing	Integrating the relevant facts into a succinct statement is one way of obtaining closure when speakers appear to have said everything they have to say.	"Let's see. We've identified two goals today . . ."
Seeking consensus	Verifying information and agreement throughout the process prevents misunderstandings.	"Would you say that increasing literacy opportunities in the classroom is our biggest priority now?"
Encouraging, influencing, and supporting		
Self-disclosing	Sharing one's personal or professional experiences or perspectives helps establish rapport and minimize perceptions of power.	"I struggled with the same issue when I taught preschool."

(continued)

Table 2.   *(continued)*

	Function	Example
Demonstrating	Showing or modeling a desired behavior can boost success during implementation.	"Watch how I hold his hand over the spoon."
Coaching	Making periodic suggestions can support or improve skill development.	"Try pointing to the picture and then showing Ennis the sign."
Informing	Sharing information and knowledge enhances understanding.	"Her behaviors are characteristic of children with Asperger syndrome."
Drawing inferences	Forming and sharing hypotheses is an important part of solving problems and uncovering possible meanings of behaviors.	"Chih Ing may need a little more encouragement and assistance to use the new communication cards."
Evaluating	Forming and sharing conclusions helps practitioners determine when they have been successful in implementing their strategies.	"The strategy you used in the transition to nap time worked well today."

a child care provider who is preparing to enroll a child with physical disabilities for the first time. Jenna, the child care provider, proudly shows Ann, the consultant, a corner of the classroom where she has arranged some toys, a mat, and pillows for the new child. Jenna explains that she has created this area for the child with disabilities so that he can be apart from the other children. Rather than assuming that Jenna's motive for creating a separate area is based on a belief that children with disabilities should be kept separate, Ann acknowledges the work that went into creating the special area and asks Jenna to describe what she has in mind. Through this discussion, Ann learns that Jenna hoped to make a space where the child would be safe from the active play of his classmates and where he could have easy access to his favorite toys. By looking at the situation through Jenna's eyes, Ann recognizes that much thought about the child's needs went into the arrangement of the area. Rather than approaching the consultation process with the idea that Jenna has a negative attitude about inclusion, Ann now is able to build on the strength of Jenna's willingness to address the individual needs of children. Ann can affirm the importance of safety and access to toys while introducing the value of having easy access to social interactions and cooperative play. As the relationship with Jenna develops and trust is built, Ann may consider letting Jenna know how her explanation helped the consultant change what could have been an inaccurate first impression.

Attribution theory and research enriches understanding of the problem-solving task of consultation. *Attribution theory* refers to how people make casual explanations and describes the behavioral and emotional consequences of those explanations (Ross & Fletcher, 1985). A consistent finding in the literature on attribution research is that in describing the problems of another person, people view that individual's personal traits or characteristics as the primary causal factor but view the situation or environment as the primary cause of their own problems (Graham & Folkes, 1990; Martin, 1983; Zuckerman, 1979, as cited in Zins et al., 1993). This realization may help the consultant and consultee avoid errors in attribution, which would increase the effectiveness of their communication and collaborative relationship.

Consultation Stages and Strategies

A defining characteristics of consultation that distinguishes it from other forms of helping relationships is the process. The process may vary somewhat, depending on the particular model of consultation employed (e.g., mental health, behavioral, organizational), but the stages across these models are generally the same and reflect a process that is familiar to professionals who must plan and evaluate interventions for young children and families. The stages presented here are drawn from reliable sources on school-based consultation (Bergan, 1977, 1995; Bergan & Kratochwill, 1990; Buysse & Wesley, 2004; Caplan, 1970; Caplan & Caplan, 1999; Wesley & Buysse, 2004) and are developed in detail in Chapters 3–10. They include 1) Gaining Entry, 2) Building the Relationship, 3) Gathering Information Through Assessment, 4) Setting Goals, 5) Selecting Strategies, 6) Implementing the Plan, 7) Evaluating the Plan, and 8) Holding a Summary Conference. In addition to understanding the purpose and essential tasks of these stages, consultants need knowledge and specific sets of skills in the following areas (to name a few) to boost the effectiveness of consultation across the stages: the change process and the importance of consultee motivation, problem solving, managing resistance, conflict resolution, planning and record keeping, data collection and analysis, group facilitation, interagency collaboration, and gaining access to community resources. The consultant's (and consultee's) understanding of the eight-stage framework guides the consultation process and ensures the voluntary and collaborative nature of the relationship.

Once they are familiar with the stages of consultation and their related strategies, consultants should be able to adapt them to a variety of consultation settings and concerns. Effective consultants are flexible and responsive to the unique demands and opportunities of each situation and are able to shift the focus and content of consultation services to address different levels of concern. For example, they are aware when the focus of concern changes from client or consultee skills to program- or systems-level components, and they know when to use different strategies or resources to address these changes. Consider the following situation: Elsie, a consultant, and Maria, a teacher who has a boy with autism enrolled in her class, discuss strategies for preparing the child for transitions between activities. Elsie suggests showing the child a photograph of materials used in the next activity before starting the transition and showing him a photograph of his juice cup prior to snack time. When Elsie shares that she has seen some teachers use photographs of field trip destinations as a way to prepare all of the children for an upcoming trip, Maria states that her program makes arrangements for children with disabilities to stay at the center on field trip days. She says that the staff have discussed this policy because they realize it may not seem fair to the children or families. Maria thinks the staff need guidance about how to ensure safety on inclusive field trips. Elsie recognizes that to address this program-level challenge, she will need different skills and resources than those that have worked in the classroom. Chapter 5 provides more information about shifts in consultation focus.

Ethics and Professionalism

As a set of principles that govern the conduct of a profession, ethics provide important parameters for viewing consultants' responsibilities. Many aspects of consultation practice pose unique ethical challenges for professionals. These include the triadic nature of consultation; the possibility of multiple clients; potential value conflicts between consultant, consultee, and system; the limits of confidentiality; and accountability for client welfare, safety, and progress (Brown et al., 1998; Dougherty, 1990; Parsons, 1996). Yet, such rules or guidelines in the early childhood field do not address all of the issues about which consultants must make decisions on a regular basis. For example, what action should a consultant take if he or she is aware that a program's staff–child ratio is periodically out of compliance with state regulations? How candid should the consultant be when asked by families about the quality of a program with which he or she is engaged in consultation to improve global quality? In his book *The Skilled Consultant: A Systematic Approach to the Theory and Practice of Consultation*, Parsons (1996) identified three categories of ethical concern in consultation: consultant issues, relationship issues, and process issues. The following subsections use this organization to introduce key principles for the ethical consultant.

Consultant Issues

Consultant issues include the consultant's competence and values and the need to recognize the boundaries of each. The concern over the absence of ethical guidelines that address consultation in the early childhood field is made more urgent by the fact that competencies deemed essential to early intervention consultation are not scientifically tested or even universally defined, a point made by Parsons (1996) about consultation practiced by school psychologists. Although the early childhood field increasingly values professional reliance on scientifically derived knowledge, there can be pressure on the consultant in daily practice to respond to problems in areas for which he or she may lack adequate preparation. This is due, in part, to the unpredictable nature of child care and the relative isolation of consultants from mentors or colleagues.

Ethical guidelines for early intervention consultation should address knowing when to say no, when to seek support, and when to refer a consultee to another resource that could best serve the client. Similarly, it is imperative that the consultant "clarify, and where possible articulate, his or her personal and professional values and the role they may play in the consultative process" (Parsons, 1996, p. 230). Such values include, for example, those related to the consultant's desire to engage in consultation and the consultant's feelings about collaboration, diversity, and child rearing, among many others. A related practice not specified by the early intervention profession is the need for the consultant to help consultees (individuals and/or systems) to identify their own values and the relationship of those values to their actual practice. Although few people would dispute the benefit of having the consultant and consultee clarify their values during the early stages of consultation, from a practical standpoint it is more likely that such conversations will evolve around situations that highlight the compatibility or incompatibility of values. Values that may help or hinder the consultation process include, for example, those about gender equality, competition versus cooperation, children's rights, and cultural sensitivity (Parsons, 1996).

Relationship Issues

One dimension of professionalism in consultation is the consultant's ability to make the rights and needs of the client and consultee his or her primary concern (Parsons, 1996). Parsons suggested that the consultation relationship be characterized by informed consent, confidentiality, professional boundaries, and the ethical use of power. *Informed consent* means that consultees must be provided with information that will help them make decisions concerning participation in the consultation process. This includes information about the role of the consultee and that of the consultant, the nature of the relationship, and the consultation stages and process. *Confidentiality* is the foundation on which a trusting consultation relationship is built. Consultants must delineate the confidentiality policy clearly with the consultee and the conditions under which confidentiality can be broken—for example, in the case of child abuse or neglect. *Establishing clear professional boundaries* requires the consultant to know the difference between his or her own personal feelings and needs and the professional needs, concerns, and feelings of the consultee. An ethical consultant monitors the consulting relationship and identifies strategies that help maintain these boundaries. *The use of power* to influence the attitudes and behaviors of others is fundamental to consultation practice (Newman, 1993). An ethical consultant is aware of his or her role in influencing the consultee and of the distribution of power within the consulting relationship and promotes the consultee's right to accept or reject suggestions and the relationship itself at any time.

Process Issues

The dynamics of the consultation process itself create a number of ethical considerations including questions about who the client is and the efficacy of the consultation services (both in terms of the consultant's competence and the support in scientific research). For example, consultants in early intervention have expressed confusion about whether they will be held accountable for outcomes related to the early childhood programs in which they are consulting as well as the children and families on their caseload (Wesley et al., 2001). Although the program director ultimately is accountable for the program, the ethical consultant is careful not to make recommendations that conflict with a program's regulatory standards, and he or she should maintain an awareness of the potential impact of changes on internal program policies or initiatives. The consultant conscientiously facilitates communication among him- or herself, the child's teacher (the consultee), and the child's family. To the greatest extent possible, the consultant must use techniques in managing the consultation process that have been shown to be effective through research. Increasingly, professionalism in early intervention is characterized by the commitment to increase one's own knowledge and skills and to incorporate new research findings that support specific interventions into practice.

A WORD ABOUT BELIEFS AND DISPOSITIONS

In his description of the five disciplines for learning organizations, Senge (1990) suggested that more than competence and skills are needed for personal mastery, although those are certainly important. He described the need for professionals to learn continually, to have insight and knowledge of self and clarity about what is happening in the present. Such clarity involves an energetic attempt to understand all aspects of a situation, including tensions and negative reactions in interpersonal relationships and the discrepancy between one's vision for change and reality. This description of personal mastery illustrates the importance of values and attitudes to the effective leader and can also be applied to the effective consultant. An effective consultant should take stock of the knowledge, skills, and attitudes that he or she brings to each interaction with the consultee and reflect during the interaction and afterward on areas in which the consultant's own personal and professional growth is needed.

Because consultation is in its most basic essence a series of interpersonal interactions, consideration of assets that contribute to lasting, positive relationships is warranted. The following list presents examples of beliefs and dispositions that may enrich the consultation process and contribute to positive outcomes and that are based on a collaborative approach. For the purpose of this discussion, the word *disposition* is used to refer to intrinsic habits that characterize a professional's approach to practice.

1. Consultees are professionals who have dignity and deserve respect.

2. Both the consultant and consultee bring valuable expertise, perspectives, and experience to the consultation process.

3. It is exciting to share techniques and skills that equip consultees to solve problems in the future.

4. Conflicts are opportunities for personal and professional growth.

5. The consultee's active participation in problem solving and plan development makes follow-up during implementation more likely.

6. The consultant and consultee are responsible for monitoring and discussing their roles and the dynamics of their relationship.

7. Consultation practice is improved when consultants engage in continuous learning through their work and collective reflection with others about their practice.

8. Because the consultant's own values, world view, and culture will affect the consultation process, consultants benefit from knowing themselves. Being sensitive to and valuing the unique cultural experiences of others and the role cultural differences play in the identification and resolution of problems are equally important.

9. It is not necessary for the consultant to have all of the answers.

In addition to a foundation in child development theory and the common emphasis on building trusting professional relationships, early childhood consultants share a core set of values that although difficult to quantify are critical to their practice. Ethical consultation supports the value of children's emotional and social development as a foundation for later school success, of play and exploration as a vital way of learning, of practices that are culturally sensitive and respectful, of reciprocal relationships with families, and of experiential and research-based knowledge as a foundation for practice.

CONCLUSION

Possessing all of the knowledge, skills, characteristics, and dispositions described in this chapter is a daunting proposition, especially given the fact that many practicing consultants have received no formal training in consultation other than that provided through on-the-job experience (Dougherty, 2000). Consultants who wish to increase the likelihood of successful consultation outcomes may wonder where to begin to improve their effectiveness. No single book teaches the knowledge, skills, and attitudes necessary for professional mastery in consultation, and as Dougherty (2000) suggested, developing the skills to become more effective is a process that continues throughout every consultant's career. It is helpful to keep in mind that most consultants are not experts in all areas, nor is it likely that they have none of the abilities necessary for competence. By becoming familiar with the literature on effective consultation and engaging regularly in deep discussions with colleagues about consultation practice, early childhood professionals can begin to assess their strengths and needs as consultants. Although considering conceptually the characteristics and skills of effective consultants is a good starting place, attempts also should be made to develop mentorships and other trusting professional relationships, including those with consultees, through which candid feedback about performance can be obtained.

Model for the Consultation Process

Chapter 3

Gaining Entry

STAGE ONE

Stage One of the consultation process involves the consultant's initial contact and first meetings with the consultee. The goal of the entry stage is for the consultant to become familiar with the consultation site and the early childhood staff with whom he or she will be working. As the consultant and consultee begin to get to know each other, they begin a conversation about the general purpose and process of consultation.

When the consultant is an early childhood special educator or a therapist visiting a classroom in which a child with an IFSP or IEP is enrolled, the consultant and the early childhood teacher probably understand that the consultant's role will be to help that child succeed in the classroom. As illustrated in the following chapters that describe the eight-stage consultation process, however, this understanding may be limited to knowing which child is on the consultant's caseload and the child's general goals. The consultant and consultee may not share the same expectations about their respective roles. For example, the consultee may not anticipate spending much time with the special educator and may in fact be counting on the special educator to remove the child with a disability from the classroom each time he or she visits. The consultant may expect to spend time meeting with the consultee and observing the child in group activities and may have no plans to work directly with the child in or out of the classroom during early visits. Chances are that neither consultant nor consultee has the privilege of choosing to work with each other the way consultants and their clients in the business world often do but, rather, find themselves in a professional relationship because of the way in which early intervention and education services are delivered to children with disabilities in inclusive settings. In part, the entry stage serves as a springboard for discussion about the stages and desired outcomes of consultation.

When the consultant is an early childhood educator working in a classroom to promote global quality as part of a community- or statewide quality enhancement initiative, there may be an opportunity during the entry stage for consultant and consultee to determine whether they want to work with each other. For example, early discussions may explore the match between the consultant's services and availability and the program's needs. If the match is confirmed, then the consultant and program staff continue to share information as a way of getting to know each other and preparing for the consultation process.

KEY TASKS

Initial contact between consultants supporting IFSP or IEP implementation and classroom teachers too often involves the consultant simply arriving at the classroom on the first opportunity after itinerant services are recommended. Ideally, the consultant would initiate contact with the classroom teacher or program administrator to discuss and schedule a first visit. Sometimes a program representative, teacher, parent, or other potential consultee calls the agency or consultant providing specialized services and describes the concern or need that has prompted the call, and the consultant schedules a visit to learn more. This is often the way that a school psychologist, for example, may begin work with a teacher who has asked for help managing a student's challenging behavior. Consultation focusing on quality enhancement also sometimes is initiated in this way when community child care programs signal their interest in participating in a rated license or accreditation process by requesting that a consultant contact them.

During entry, the consultant goes to the program and meets the people with whom he or she will be working—ideally the classroom teacher and assistant if the focus is a child with a disability and also the program administrator, especially if the focus is program quality. They jointly discuss the presenting concern and overall purpose of consultation (e.g., to support a particular child's IEP, to address a challenging behavior, to improve playground safety, to increase the level of a rated license). In either case, if other program staff do not know the consultant already, the consultant may want to find an opportunity during the initial visits to describe briefly his or her work history and current professional activities. By sharing information about recent experiences and current interests, the consultant not only builds his or her own credibility in an easygoing way but also presents possible areas in which the consultant and consultee may find they have things in common.

During these first contacts, an effective consultant also builds an understanding of the program's history and current mission. This is particularly helpful if the consultant has no previous experience with the program. The consultant may want to determine whether he or she knows anyone who has consulted with or provided training to the program before and could serve as a resource. The consultant should also ask the program staff about previous experiences related to the general consultation focus. For example, has the program served a child with disabilities before? Has it ever served a child with a disability whose needs were similar to those of the child whom the consultant is visiting? What steps has the program taken in the past to improve quality? In general, what needs remain in this area? The purpose of this line of inquiry is to build knowledge about the program staff's general resources and interests.

The consultant and consultee need to begin a conversation about the process of consultation, continuing to clarify its general purpose and their respective roles, expectations, and activities. Consultees who have a sense of control are more likely to participate fully in the consultation process (Gutkin & Conoley, 1990). Therefore, the consultant should strive to demystify consultation by describing it as a systematic process in which interventions are developed, implemented, and evaluated to address the consultee's concerns and solve problems (Hughes, 1997). The consultant should then introduce the stages of consultation, pointing out that they are not necessarily linear and that the consultant and the consultee may move back and forth among them (see Figure 3 in Chapter 1). In his or her description of the process, the consultant needs to explain the rationale for each stage, a process that will be repeated as the consultant and the consultee approach each stage in the months ahead. The consultant should note that the consultee will play an active role throughout the process and that his or her participation is especially important during the stages of goal setting and implementation. The consultant's attitude should reflect confidence and excitement about collaborating with the program, especially about the opportunity to learn from the consultee. Based on his or her experience, the consultant may make suggestions about which resources will be needed to support the consultation process. For example, the consultee will need relief from direct responsibility for children to meet with the consultant during every stage of consultation. It also will be helpful to know if there is a source of funds, material donations, or volunteer labor to draw upon in the event that additional toys or furnishings are needed.

Based on this description of the process and on clarification of the consultation's purpose, the consultee and consultant will begin to develop a mutual understanding of how the consultant's services could address the program's needs. When the consultant is visiting the program to serve a child with a disability, this match may not be so much a question of whether the consultant is the right person for the job as it is a discussion of how the consultant's approach and expectations compare with those of the program. For example, how do the consultant and the classroom teacher envision working together? In what ways will the family be involved in the consultation process? How will the consultant integrate his or her services into the classroom? If the program has asked for assistance to raise its global quality or obtain a higher licensure or accreditation, the discussion of the fit between consultant and program may involve a greater examination of the consultant's qualifications and experiences and the program's expressed goals.

Toward the end of the entry stage, a key task for the consultant and consultee is to discuss the logistics of future communication. Which communication methods are preferred? Which times are convenient for scheduling visits? Do both agree that the visits should be confirmed in advance? The consultant and the consultee also should establish the boundaries of confidentiality for information about the children and program, including the consultant's firm commitment not to share sensitive information among the programs in which he or she is working. During this discussion, the consultant must clearly express the circumstances under which sensitive information would be shared with others, such as observed child neglect or abuse.

The consultant may find it helpful to use a Contact Summary form to describe briefly all contacts with the program, including telephone calls and visits (see Form 2 for a sample; also see the appendix for a full-size, blank version of this form). This form provides an opportunity to summarize discussions, actions taken, and plans for the next contact, and it can be used throughout the consultation process. The consultant may want to complete this form independently after each consultation contact has concluded, especially after early visits, when the consultant focuses attention on the consultee and does not want to be absorbed in paperwork. As consultation progresses, the consultant and the consultee could work together in summarizing information on page one of this form, which then can be photocopied for the consultee's records. The consultant records his or her own reflections about the consultation contact on page two of the form and keeps this page in his or her own file. These notes may include the consultant's perceptions about a range of complex issues, including interactions with the consultee, the consultee's expectations for consultation services, previous strategies that have addressed goals effectively, observations about the classroom or program, and thoughts concerning implementation.

CRITICAL CONSIDERATIONS

Because the consultant is interested in learning as much as possible about the program, he or she may want to consider doing a bit of homework between initial visits. Information about the program's history of services and mission can be obtained through discussions with colleagues or families in the community. The consultant can learn much about a program's operational policies by reading parent and staff handbooks and documents describing relevant minimum standards and licensing requirements. It is desirable to rely on visits to the program and interviews with consultees, as well as printed and web-based materials, as methods of gathering information.

An effective consultant is aware that the consulting relationship develops within a cultural context that is characterized by the unique experiences and

Contact Summary

Consultant _____

Consultee _____

Classroom _____

Date _____ Program _____

Contact initiated by

Type of contact

☐ On-site consultation ☐ Consultant

☐ Telephone call ☐ Consultee

☐ Observation

☐ Other (specify): _____

Duration
(in hours and in minutes)

Prep _____

Travel _____

Contact _____

Purpose of contact _____

Focus of concern _____

Summary of activities and discussion _____

Decisions reached _____

Action steps for consultant _____

Action steps for consultee _____

Date of next consultation _____

(continued)

From Wesley, P.W. (2000). *Improving the quality of early childhood programs: The PFI model of consultation* (p. 42). Chapel Hill: The University of North Carolina, FPG Child Development Institute; adapted by permission.

Consultant reflections, Stage number _____ :

These questions are designed to help you think about the consultation strategies you have used as well as consultee reactions and perspectives related to these approaches. Depending on which stage you are in, address the targeted issues (below) in your reflections.

Stage One: What specific strategies did you use to learn about the program and the consultee? How well do you think the consultee understands the purpose and process of consultation?

Stage Two: What strategies did you use to build trust? What have you learned about the consultee, the program, and the focus of concern?

Stage Three: What ideas and activities did the consultee contribute during the information gathering/assessment stage? What is the consultee's understanding of the priorities for focus?

Stage Four: What specific strategies did you use to ensure collaboration during goal setting? How do you know if the consultee feels ownership of the goals?

Stage Five: How did you determine the potential success of each strategy? How confident does the consultee feel about implementing the strategies?

Stage Six: In what ways did you model flexibility, encouragement, and problem-solving skills with the consultee during implementation? What adjustments were needed in the Intervention Plan? How does the consultee feel about his or her ability to implement the plan in your absence?

Stage Seven: How do you and the consultee know you have accomplished the desired outcomes? Describe any unanticipated outcomes or the impact of the consultation process. How do you and the consultee feel about the outcomes and your relationship?

Stage Eight: What specific strategies did you use to encourage the consultee to disclose his or her view of the consultation relationship and his or her overall satisfaction with the outcomes? What are the consultee's overall perceptions of the consultation process? What work, if any, remains to be done, and what are the plans for the next steps? What new goals should be addressed through future consultation?

From Wesley, P.W. (2000). *Improving the quality of early childhood programs: The PFI model of consultation* (p. 42). Chapel Hill: The University of North Carolina, FPG Child Development Institute; adapted by permission.

Form 2. (From Wesley, P.W. (2000). *Improving the quality of early childhood programs: The PFI model of consultation* [p. 42]. Chapel Hill: The University of North Carolina, FPG Child Development Institute; adapted by permission.)

understandings of the people in the work setting. Their ethnicity, age, gender, religious beliefs, professional training and experience, and possibly even their sexual identification all influence how they present and process information (Soo-Hoo, 1998). The consultant should consider when and how to acknowledge the influence of these factors with the consultee, realizing that denying professionals' social and cultural differences may result in a relationship that seems cordial but is limited in depth (Donahue, Falk, & Provet, 2000). For example, a young consultant who is in her first year of work after graduate school and is consulting with a 65-year-old woman who has cared for children in her family child care home for more than two decades may want to express her belief that the differences in their ages and experiences will prove to be an asset to the consultation process. She may state her hope that the provider will be open to new ideas and that she herself will learn from what the provider has found worked in the past. In Stage One, the consultant begins the process of gathering information as a way to become acquainted with the consultee and his or her program but in a manner that seeks to understand the consultee's frame of reference—that is, the way that the early childhood teacher sees the world. To understand the concerns of the consultee and the issues affecting the consultation process, the consultant must achieve sufficient understanding to be able to view the world as the consultee views it (Soo-Hoo, 1998; for more details about using a frame of reference approach, see Chapter 12).

Beginning with the first contact, the *consultant* is interested in learning answers to the following questions:

- What is the program's mission and reputation in the community? Is a scrapbook or other written material about the program available for review?

- How is the program organized overall—general funding, licenses and accreditation, number of classrooms and children, ages of children served, and so forth?

- How long has the program served children with disabilities? If so, what disabilities have these children had?

- How are staff members organized (in terms of horizontal and vertical relationships)?

- How do staff members relate to the children and families? That is, what attitude do staff express? What is their communication like? How are families involved?

- What are staff assumptions about early childhood education?

- Do staff members seem to adhere to the same professional practices?

- What resources are available to the early childhood program in general? What resources are available to the classroom and the teacher?

- What are the program's cultural norms (e.g., relationships, values, rituals, ceremonies, stories, jokes)?

- Which program accomplishments are the staff most proud of? What is the program's current goals or needs?

- Are there organizational needs that are not being met (e.g., strained community relationships, inadequate supervision, lack of professional development opportunities)?

- Are there other current or planned initiatives that would have an impact on the consultation process (e.g., staff getting ready for accreditation through the NAEYC, director planning an increase in enrollment, another consultant working in the classroom)?

- Has the program received consultation in the past? What type? What did program staff think of it?

During entry, the *consultee* may be wondering

- About the consultant's experience and qualifications

- How the consultant was selected to work with the early childhood program

- How frequently the consultant will visit and what the consultee's role will be in the consultation process

- Whether the consultant has his or her own goals for the child or classroom (or for the consultee)

- Whether he or she will have to follow the consultant's recommendations

- Whether the consultant will be working directly with the child, in or out of the classroom

- About other services available to support children with disabilities in the early childhood program

- Whether the consultant can address classroom issues that are not directly related to the child with a disability

- To whom the consultant will report

- Whether and how the consultant will communicate with the child's therapists

- Whether information shared with the consultant will be treated confidentially

- What colleagues in the early childhood program think about the consultant being in the consultee's classroom

- How long the consultant will work with the program

- Whether the consultant has funding or other resources to share with the program

- How information about the consultant's visits and ideas will be shared with families and how families will be involved

- Whether the same consultant will come each time

COMMUNICATION STRATEGIES AND INTERPERSONAL APPROACH

The entry stage offers the first opportunity for the consultant to begin to understand the early childhood program and to demonstrate openness to learning about the consultee, classroom, and clients (children and families). The consultant should show enthusiasm about being in the program, listen carefully, pay attention to written materials provided about the program, and ask questions in an interested but easygoing and conversational way. Although the purpose of initial contacts is to get to know the program, the first meeting should not seem like a drill or formal interview. The consultant listens first and then determines how to garner additional information. For example, although gathering information about the size and operating hours of the program will be easy, understanding the program's work culture and organizational needs will require keen observation during many visits.

At the same time, the consultant is beginning to establish a positive working relationship with the consultee that includes trust, respect, genuineness, competence, and objectivity (Caplan, 1970). She must consciously take responsibility for developing this optimal working relationship and use a variety of attending behaviors (e.g., showing empathy and positive regard), verbal behaviors (e.g., acknowledging what the consultee says, sharing information), and nonverbal behaviors (e.g., sitting with the consultee in a relaxed but professional posture; Caplan & Caplan, 1999). The consultant should share information about him- or herself in a sensitive way that is mindful of any differences between the consultant's and the consultee's educational, professional, and cultural backgrounds. The consultant also needs to respect the line between professional and personal information and be careful not to appear too friendly or to divulge inappropriate details about his or her life. For example, during first visits, if the consultant learns that the consultee is in the middle of a divorce, the consultant's sharing her own divorce experience at this time could risk setting the stage for personal conversations of this intimacy level at every contact.

The consultant must put him- or herself in the shoes of the consultee, considering how the relationship is starting and anticipating the consultee's questions and concerns. The consultant should present him- or herself as approachable and create a climate that invites questions and comments from the consultee. For example, the consultant may ask from time to time, "Can you think of anything that it would be helpful to discuss that we haven't touched on?" (see the case illustration at the end of this chapter for more information).

WHAT IF?

What if the consultant is asked to provide immediate action—for example, to address an urgent need created by a child who is harming property or others or to conduct staff training on an issue of pressing concern? How can the consultant respond to the crisis and, at the same time, lay the groundwork for a collaborative problem-solving process in the future?

A key task of the consultant in the early stages of the consultation process is to establish a collaborative relationship with the consultee by fostering a shared and mutually beneficial approach to better understanding the presenting concerns. If the consultant is successful, then his or her skills and help are viewed as supplemental to the situation; they serve to strengthen the consultee's ability and self-confidence in handling the situation and similar ones in the future (Zins et al., 1993). Sometimes, as in the example of a consultee's urgent need, the consultant finds that he or she must shift from this collaborative approach to a more directive one.

Effective consultants understand that programs occasionally experience problems that create significant stress and, with the help of the consultee, are able to discern which "crises" do not merit emergency attention. These consultants recognize that to jump into a role of taking charge will change the consulting relationship, at least temporarily, and they weigh this situation with the consequences of taking no action (Parsons, 1996). Solving problems too soon or too often may build dependency rather than empowerment in the consultee. Requesting a consultant's immediate help at a time when he or she is trying to build trust may tempt the consultant to try a rescue, perhaps even in an area in which he or she lacks expertise. When faced with a dilemma such as a consultee's need for immediate help with an aggressive child or the need for all staff to be trained in a critical area by a certain time, the consultant should ask the following:

- Can another person provide the emergency intervention?

- Do I have enough information, experience, and expertise to address the crisis?

- Is the urgent situation related to the presenting concerns about which it is clearly my role to consult?

- What are the consequences of no action (e.g., will other people or property be harmed or put at risk)?

Following these guidelines, a special education consultant's role is not likely to encompass providing staff training to meet professional development requirements soon to be monitored through a licensing inspector. Conversely, assisting to decrease a child's aggressive behavior possibly would be a part of the consultant's job.

If the consultant decides to provide intervention addressing the urgent need, he or she should elicit the consultee's ideas and participation to the extent that is feasible in selecting, implementing, and evaluating any action. It is also important for the consultant to reflect on how emergency action might affect the consulting relationship. For example, the consultee may believe that he or she has failed professionally by not solving the crisis or may defer to the consultant in similar future situations.

Occasionally there are times when a classroom teacher experiences disequilibrium within the larger program or service system. For instance, there may be tension between this teacher and other teachers concerning the curriculum used in his or her classroom, or perhaps the philosophy of the program as a whole differs from that espoused by the administrative agency. Consultees may feel that such situations deserve urgent attention and that the consultant, by virtue of being an outsider, has the power to make an immediate difference. Yet, the very nature of these systemic conflicts requires thorough, multilayered, and collaborative assessment and planning. When the consultee reports stresses at the program or system level during the entry stage, the effective consultant is careful to document and consider these concerns as he or she continues visits to learn more about the program. The consultant should explore with the consultee the complexity of assessing needs at the systems level during Stage Three and consider whether he or she is the right person to provide systems-level consultation. Although a number of techniques have been suggested as useful diagnostic tools for systems-focused consultation (Parsons, 1996; Whitt & Kuh, 1991), a consultant in the early childhood classroom probably would not include such a broad focus in consultation. Rather than planning an intervention, he or she would use information about the internal and external forces shaping the practices and expectations of the program as a way to better understand the consultee's world.

CONCLUSION

It may be helpful for the consultant to keep in mind that sometimes during the entry stage, while he or she is interested in learning as much as possible about the consultation setting, the consultee is focused on learning more about the consultant—his or her credentials, work experience, and reason for being there. As the consultant and consultee move into Stage Two, when building the relationship is the focus, the consultant typically concentrates on fine-tuning understanding of and rapport with the consultee; yet by this time, the consultee may be thinking more about the classroom and all of the ways that the consultant potentially could help. Taking this into consideration, along with the fact that getting to know the program and consultee is a process that develops throughout the consultation stages, it is easy to see how the first two stages of consultation can blur together. Key points during Stage One are to begin a conversation about the purpose and process of consultation and to set the stage for a positive, collaborative relationship that will be explored and defined more clearly in Stage Two.

Gaining Entry: Stage One
Case Illustration

Consultant: Karen

Consultees: Lakesha, Molly

Parents: Juan and Patricia

Child: Benita

Karen works as an itinerant teacher for a large metropolitan school district. Much of her previous preparation and training focused on working directly with young children with disabilities and their families, but in recent years, she has acquired considerable experience and expertise as a consultant in inclusive early childhood settings. Although she still works directly with children and families sometimes, her primary role now consists of providing indirect services through consultation to early childhood teachers and other professionals. Her current caseload consists of 14 3- and 4-year-old children, each with an identified disability and an IEP. The children are enrolled in nine different early childhood settings that range from Head Start programs, to community-based child care centers, to public school classrooms that include some blended programs.

Lakesha is the lead teacher in a classroom with 18 children enrolled. She has one teaching assistant, Molly. Lakesha has an associate's degree in child development from a community college and is working on her early childhood teaching certification through a local university program. The center where Lakesha works, Wee Care Child Care, is a licensed program with moderately good quality, based on the Early Childhood Environment Rating Scale–Revised Edition (ECERS-R) and the state's rated license.

Juan and Patricia Alvarez and their 3½-year-old daughter Benita are new to the area. Benita has cerebral palsy but has never received special services or attended a center-based early childhood program. Benita's parents enrolled her in Wee Care Child Care when Patricia took a job at the plant where Juan works. The child care program's director referred Benita to the public school system for evaluation. The school system's preschool coordinator worked with Juan and Patricia to have Benita assessed and to schedule an IEP conference for her. Prior to the conference, Karen visited Wee Care and observed Benita in Lakesha's classroom to get a better idea of Benita's developmental delays and physical challenges. Depending on the recommendation of the IEP team, Karen might provide itinerant services to Benita at Wee Care. During the visit with Karen, Lakesha mentioned that she had never previously worked with a child who has cerebral palsy, but she was looking forward to having an extra set of hands in the classroom and getting new ideas from Karen.

The IEP conference was held to discuss goals and objectives for Benita and to consider the recommendation to provide services to Benita in Lakesha's class. Benita's parents wanted Benita to continue at Wee Care because the center's hours of operation accommodated their work schedules. It was decided that

Benita's therapy and instructional goals would be addressed through itinerant special education services. Karen explained that itinerant services would involve twice-weekly visits to the classroom and spending up to an hour there to work with Benita as well as with Lakesha, to support and assist her as Benita's teacher. Karen also offered to stay in contact with Benita's parents to get their input and help them address similar goals at home. After the meeting, Karen called Lakesha to schedule an appointment during naptime on the following Tuesday.

During their next meeting on Tuesday, Karen learned more about Wee Care and its philosophy of inclusion. She reintroduced herself to the director and met a couple of the other teachers. She learned that a speech-language therapist she knew from the local early intervention program for infants and toddlers was working with a boy in a classroom down the hall. Karen also learned that the program staff had very little experience working with children who were English language learners. As the visit continued, Karen and Lakesha focused on Benita, as shown in the following conversation.

Karen: I thought we should discuss how we might work together to address Benita's goals in the classroom. I'm really excited about working with you and your staff. You said that this was the first time you had worked with a child with disabilities. Is this also your first time working with a consultant?

Lakesha: No, the state child care licensing consultant comes once or maybe twice a year, so I wouldn't say it was my first time.

Karen: That's right. The state licensing consultant. We're both called consultants, but we actually have very different goals and ways of carrying them out.

Lakesha: Yeah, she doesn't really pay much attention to individual children. She's mainly interested in our records and our staff–child ratio—things like that.

Karen: Well, why don't I tell you a little bit about how the consulting process usually works in my experience. Then, you can be thinking about whether this approach is right for you and whether you have other ideas or suggestions for how we might work together. How does that sound?

Lakesha: Okay.

Karen: Well, first off, I just want to say that I'm going to need your insights about Benita and your classroom. Each of us brings a different area of expertise to the consulting process. You know your program and the children and families you serve better than anyone. You also bring to the table many years of experience and training in working with young children. What I bring are ideas for working with children with disabilities and suggestions for helping your program meet the needs of all children and families. So, together we could make a great team.

Lakesha: Sounds good to me, but I'm still not sure how we would work together. Aren't you here mainly to work with Benita, to do those things on that IEP?

Karen: Yes, I am, but I hope you and I can work together, too. Benita is the main reason I'm here, but I'll only be here twice a week. You are the person she will get to know best. She will be with you 5 days a week! I think she will have the best opportunity to learn and progress if you and I work as partners to implement the IEP. Together we'll figure out how you can support Benita's development when I'm not here. Is that something you are willing to do?

Lakesha: Yes, I see what you mean, but I really don't know anything about children like Benita.

Karen: And I've got a lot to learn about your classroom. Here's how the process usually works. I've found it's good to spend some time getting to know a teacher before we delve into working together to address a child's goals in the classroom. You and I may want to decide together how we will gather information about Benita's adjustment and needs and then share it with each other and Benita's parents. We also need to decide on our roles in developing a plan to implement Benita's IEP. I won't always be around, so it is important when I am not here that you are confident about implementing the IEP and any other goals we develop together.

Lakesha: So we'll figure out together just what Benita needs?

Karen: Right. Part of the process involves gathering some additional information. My role will be to learn as much as I can from you about what happens in your class and any concerns you might have about supporting Benita's development. Often, teachers request that I spend time in the classroom as part of this process. That way you and I can share ideas about any needed changes to accommodate Benita. Once we have a better idea of what we want to do, we'll work together to select a strategy or several strategies to address the goals we've identified. Here's where your experience will be really helpful. We'll want to consider strategies you've already tried or used with other children, as well as some new ideas. We'll choose strategies that you are comfortable with.

Lakesha: Let me see if I'm getting this. We are going to come up with ideas together for the best way to work on Benita's IEP goals, and we'll also see what else we may want to do to help her fit in.

Karen: Yes, that's the idea. It will be helpful to write our ideas down as a sort of plan that we can refer to. Then, the next phase of the process involves actually implementing the plan we've developed. Sometimes it's necessary to make a few changes to the strategies we've selected or try a different approach. Then, we'll stand back to evaluate the plan to determine if it accomplished what we wanted. The process occurs over a series of weeks or months and then often starts over again to address a new goal. That's it in a nutshell. How does this fit with the way you were envisioning us working together?

Lakesha: It sounds great. I must admit that I originally thought that you would be spending more time working with Benita in the classroom, but I like the idea of us working together to come up with a plan, and I hope you can help with implementing it. I'm glad we'll be writing down our ideas.

Karen: Yes, it will be important for us to write down what we hope to accomplish and how we'll go about it. I'm looking forward to this. I always learn so much from this type of collaboration! Now we need to talk about setting times when it will be possible for us to sit down and talk. Can you think of anything else that we haven't gone over that we should discuss?

Lakesha: Well, no, it's a lot to grasp! And it sounds like the process takes a while. When could we get started?

Contact Summary

Consultant _Karen_

Consultee _Lakesha_

Classroom _Threes_

Date _9/10/04_

Program _Wee Care Child Care_

Type of contact

☑ On-site consultation

☐ Telephone call

☐ Observation

☐ Other (specify): _____

Duration (in hours and in minutes)

Prep _20 minutes_

Travel _45 minutes_

Contact _30 minutes_

Contact initiated by

☑ Consultant

☐ Consultee

Purpose of contact _Discuss Benita's goals in the classroom, get to know Lakesha and the program better, and discuss the consultation process._

Focus of concern _Lakesha expressed a need for support in addressing Benita's mobility and communication goals in the classroom._

Summary of activities and discussion _Much of the time was spent discussing the consultation process and clarifying the goals and our respective roles in this process._

Decisions reached _We agreed to meet weekly to address Benita's goals and Lakesha's concerns about how to work with her. Lakesha invited me to observe Benita before our next meeting._

Action steps for consultant _Gather additional information about the program (e.g., mission statement, daily schedule, class list), observe Lakesha's classroom before our next meeting, and talk to the speech therapist about her experiences with this program._

Action steps for consultee _Consider additional priorities or concerns that we can address through consultation._

Date of next consultation _9/16/04_

(continued)

From Wesley, P.W. (2000). *Improving the quality of early childhood programs: The PFI model of consultation* (p. 42). Chapel Hill: The University of North Carolina, FPG Child Development Institute; adapted by permission.

Consultant reflections, Stage number _One_ :

These questions are designed to help you think about the consultation strategies you have used as well as consultee reactions and perspectives related to these approaches. Depending on which stage you are in, address the targeted issues (below) in your reflections.

Stage One: What specific strategies did you use to learn about the program and the consultee? How well do you think the consultee understands the purpose and process of consultation?

Stage Two: What strategies did you use to build trust? What have you learned about the consultee, the program, and the focus of concern?

Stage Three: What ideas and activities did the consultee contribute during the information gathering/assessment stage? What is the consultee's understanding of the priorities for focus?

Stage Four: What specific strategies did you use to ensure collaboration during goal setting? How do you know if the consultee feels ownership of the goals?

Stage Five: How did you determine the potential success of each strategy? How confident does the consultee feel about implementing the strategies?

Stage Six: In what ways did you model flexibility, encouragement, and problem-solving skills with the consultee during implementation? What adjustments were needed in the Intervention Plan? How does the consultee feel about his or her ability to implement the plan in your absence?

Stage Seven: How do you and the consultee know you have accomplished the desired outcomes? Describe any unanticipated outcomes or the impact of the consultation process. How do you and the consultee feel about the outcomes and your relationship?

Stage Eight: What specific strategies did you use to encourage the consultee to disclose his or her view of the consultation relationship and his or her overall satisfaction with the outcomes? What are the consultee's overall perceptions of the consultation process? What work, if any, remains to be done, and what are the plans for the next steps? What new goals should be addressed through future consultation?

I tried hard to put Lakesha at ease about working with a consultant. This is Lakesha's first experience with consultation, so I made sure I took the time to explain the process. I also created opportunities for Lakesha to ask questions and comment on whether the process matched her expectations and priorities. It will be important to reinforce basic concepts about consultation over the next several sessions. Lakesha may need a little more encouragement to assume an active role in planning and implementing intervention strategies. I'm very excited about the opportunity to work with Lakesha, and I think Benita and the entire class will really benefit from this experience.

From Wesley, P.W. (2000). *Improving the quality of early childhood programs: The PFI model of consultation* (p. 42). Chapel Hill: The University of North Carolina, FPG Child Development Institute; adapted by permission.

Form 2. Completed Contact Summary form. (From Wesley, P.W. [2000]. *Improving the quality of early childhood programs: The PFI model of consultation* [p. 42]. Chapel Hill: The University of North Carolina, FPG Child Development Institute; adapted by permission.)

Chapter 4

Building the Relationship

STAGE TWO

The relationship between the consultant and consultee begins with first contacts and continues throughout the consultation process, but much of the foundation for a lasting and trusting consulting relationship is laid in Stage Two. The goal of this stage is to build rapport while gathering more details about the consultee and the classroom. Because the classroom is a part of a bigger program that may contribute to the success or limitations of consultation, the consultant must build relationships not only with the consultee but also within the program and system in which the consultee works (Parsons, 1996). The consultant may find it beneficial to get to know the program director and other teachers he or she is likely to encounter while moving about the center. The consultant may want to look for naturally occurring opportunities to meet board members or other community members who are involved in the program.

KEY TASKS

Key to establishing a positive relationship is the consultant's effort to spend time visiting in the program, participating in the daily routine (with the permission of and guidance from the consultee), and observing the classroom operation and interactions. These first visits set the stage for shared partnership and responsibility throughout the consultation process, and they go a long way to providing the consultant with an understanding of the workplace culture.

Stage Two will likely overlap with Stage Three (Gathering Information Through Assessment). Although the consultant will be learning more about the program and therefore about the program's needs and concerns with each visit, the difference between Stages Two and Three relates to the primary focus of the consultant and consultee. During Stage Two, the consultant's questions and comments serve to create a full picture of the child and classroom from which the assessment process will grow. For example, the consultant may use his or her observations of the classroom's day-to-day operation to inform his or her suggestions about methods for data collection. The consultant also may want to make a point of meeting the children and some of the families served by the consultee as a way of rounding out the picture. During Stage Three, the consultant and consultee will devote time to planning and conducting specific strategies for gathering more information, specifically about the presenting concerns, whether they are a particular child's, the program's, the consultee's, or, more likely, a combination of these.

The success of these early visits is influenced by the personality and style of the consultant. An effective consultant shows respect for the consultee and his or her situation from the very first contact. This means demonstrating a nonjudgmental attitude, empathy, and sincerity, without presenting a false front (Caplan, 1970). By approaching the consultation process with enthusiasm and giving the consultee full attention, the consultant can help the consultee feel relaxed and make a lasting positive impression. The consultant may want to visit the classroom at different times of the day to better understand what a typical day is like. He or she may want to make written information about his or her agency available to classroom staff to share with their colleagues. If the consultant's main focus is not a specific child but the quality of the overall program, then he or she should get to know other adults working in the program as well as the classroom teacher. The consultant may offer to meet with teachers and assistants in classrooms not participating directly in the consultation process as a way to inform them about his or her presence in the program and to answer any questions.

At this stage, the consultant should continue to discuss the consultation process, including stages and roles, with the consultee. They may discuss initial ideas for how decisions will be made along the way and how to resolve differences when they arise. For example, they may agree that consensus is required between consultant and consultee before any new goals are added to the intervention plan and that differences will be resolved whenever possible by considering the evidence base supporting the selection of classroom strategies.

CRITICAL CONSIDERATIONS

Much of what a consultant does to get to know a consultee may come naturally—presenting a friendly disposition and showing pleasure in becoming acquainted with an early childhood program. Effective consultants are able to incorporate information gathering strategies as a part of this early relationship building in a way that reflects a genuine interest in the consultee and his or her work environment. These strategies may include interviews, document review, and keen observation.

The *consultant* wants to learn answers to the following questions:

- What is the consultee's general background and history with the program?

- What decision-making authority does the consultee have?

- What are the consultee's general perceptions of the program strengths and needs?

- What supports does the consultee have in the program (e.g., training, library, mentor, caring and knowledgeable supervisor, active families)?

- Has the consultee participated in consultation in the past? What was the focus? What were the outcomes? What did the consultee think of it?

- What are the consultee's assumptions and expectations of the consultation process (e.g., roles, stages, focus)?

- How does the consultee see him- or herself and the consultant working together?

- Does the consultee have fears or concerns about the consultation process?

- What are the consultee's past experiences with implementing change? What sorts of changes has he or she made, and what motivated them?

The *consultant* is forming ideas about

- The consultee's relationship with children, families, and co-workers

- The consultee's willingness to engage in self-reflection

- What aspects of his or her own consulting style and approach fit with the consultee's style and approach toward change

- What he or she has in common with the consultee

- How stable, predictable, and consistent the classroom and overall program are

- Whether the information the consultant was provided upon initial contact about the program's philosophy, policies, and practices hold true as he or she learns more about the classroom

- Whether the information the consultant was provided upon initial contact about the program's needs match his or her observations now that he or she has spent time in the program

The *consultee* may be wondering

- What, if anything, the consultant has been told about the classroom and the consultee

- About the specifics of how he or she and the consultant are going to work together

- What he or she and the consultant may have in common

- The extent to which the consultant really understands the day-to-day business of the program and what life in the classroom is like

- Whether the consultant is willing to "get his or her hands dirty"

- How to fix a current and pressing problem in the classroom

- What the families and other teachers will think about the consultant's presence in the room

- How the children will react to the consultant

- Whether the consultation process will mean extra work for the consultee

- In what other programs the consultant is working

- Whether the consultant has ever worked with a child similar to the one in the consultee's classroom

- About the consultant's relationship and communication with the child's family

A special consideration during the entry stage and during the stage of building the consulting relationship is the possibility that the consultee will ask for the consultant's expert advice related to teaching practices or situations in the classroom. Early childhood teachers' experience with consultants may be limited to professionals who monitor the program for compliance with state standards, such as child care licensing regulations. It is the job of such regulators to provide directions for "fixing" what is not working. An effective consultant is cautious not to fall into the trap of providing a quick fix. He or she is aware that offering expert advice too early may threaten the collaborative relationship and prepares in advance possible responses to the consultee's early requests to "tell me what I should be doing" (see the case illustration at the end of this chapter).

COMMUNICATION STRATEGIES AND INTERPERSONAL APPROACH

The consultant must rely on strong interpersonal skills to create a collaborative basis for the relationship. He or she should be aware of his or her personal demeanor, including nonverbal communication such as facial expressions, mannerisms, eye contact, and posture, while presenting a professional demeanor characterized by organizational skills, calm communication, and comfort with the process (Hughes, 1997). Asking predominantly open-ended questions is important, as "yes/no" or other closed questions narrow information about the consultant's perspectives and feelings and "why" questions may make the consultee feel defensive this early in the relationship. The consultant may ask questions about his or her own observations to determine whether what he or she has observed is typical, or the consultant may interpret situations aloud as a way to clarify his or her understanding (see the case illustration at the end of this chapter).

Consultants often find it advantageous to talk and dress in a style similar to that of the consultee as a way of being attuned to the setting's culture (Wesley et al., 2001). For example, if most teachers dress informally (e.g., the female teachers wear slacks to work), the consultant may want to consider doing likewise. The consultant should make sure that his or her actions are consistent with his or her stated values (e.g., she respects children and thus gets on their level to speak with them, she understands the daily demands of the consultee's job and thus does not try to carry on a conversation while the consultee is directly involved with children). Manner in the classroom is a powerful way to communicate respect (Donahue et al., 2000). The consultant should be aware of the ongoing demands on the consultee and jump in to help when appropriate, showing that he or she is not afraid to offer assistance. He or she also should be sensitive not to overstep his or her role in the program—for example, by repeatedly initiating activities with the children that conflict with the planned schedule or by advocating for the needs of one or two children at the expense of others. At the same time, the consultant should consider the cultural differences between him- or herself and the consultee. For example, the consultant is aware of how his or her perspectives about child rearing or schooling reflect his or her own experiences and culture, and the consultant recognizes how another person's differing views are influenced by that person's experiences and culture. Consider, for example, a consultee's expressed concern about a child's home life. Leah, the consultee, describes the state of the child's clothing and hair and even the snacks she brings to preschool as red flags indicating trouble at home. Leah remarks on the child's facial expressions and general body language as signs of fatigue and probable loss of sleep. The preschool in which Leah has worked for 12 years serves an upper-middle class neighborhood; historically, there has been little diversity among the children or staff. Conversely, Tonya, the consultant, has visited and provided consultation in dozens of early childhood programs in diverse communities. Tonya listens carefully to Leah's descriptions of the child, but her own observations of the child during several visits do not raise concerns about the child's home or family. Tonya believes that more information is needed but is aware that the differences in her experiences with young children and those of the consultee will influence the way that they define problems and concerns.

The consultant observes on many different levels during this stage of building rapport. He or she observes the relationships within the classroom and across the program, among children, between children and adults, and among adults. With these observations comes a better understanding of the dynamics of the classroom and the power structure among the staff—that is, who makes what sorts of decisions. This is important whether the focus of consultation is a child with a disability or the global quality of the program. The consultant also tries to discern the types of traditions or social rituals that staff enjoy. For example, how do they recognize staff birthdays or holidays? Do they share coffee in the morning? Do they ever have potluck lunches? The consultant may begin to find out a little about the consultee's personal life as a way to share common experiences and interests, including such areas as hobbies, parenting, or family pastimes. Although none of this information alone can guarantee a collaborative relationship, each piece of information helps to inform the consultant's and consultee's understanding and appreciation of each other.

WHAT IF?

What if the consultant discovers that the consultee is resistant to consultation? Perhaps it was not the consultee's idea to invite the consultant to work in the classroom in the first place, or perhaps the consultee has a very different idea about what the consultant's role should be—namely, that the consultant should focus on fixing problems without involving the consultee. Although it is rarely the case that itinerant special educators working in inclusive classrooms are called in by the program's administrator to help with a "deficient" classroom, this scenario is often reported by consultants in quality enhancement programs and is worth exploring (Munn, 2003).

Tensions are sure to be created when a program representative other than the prospective consultee requests the consultant's assistance without speaking first with the classroom teacher. As described in Chapter 3, special education consultants frequently are assigned to work in classrooms with children who have disabilities as a part of the IFSP or IEP process. Classroom teachers may be unwitting consultees. So that consultation can start off without either party feeling put upon, it is good practice for the consultant to clarify during the first contact who is making the referral and why. Often this is as simple as explaining a bit about the IFSP or IEP process and how services are coordinated and delivered for children requiring special help. If a program administrator has called to request help in a particularly challenging classroom or to initiate a quality enhancement project, the consultant will want to know whether the teacher has been involved in making the decision to request consultation. If not, then the consultant should state clearly that he or she would like to clarify with the teacher the background for the referral and ascertain the teacher's willingness to participate in the consultation process.

In other words, when the consultant meets the teacher, it is best to be up front about the way that he or she has entered the program. If classroom quality is the referring concern, the consultant may say, "The program director shared some concerns with me about the challenges of this classroom. I am not sure I can help, but I would like the opportunity to work with you to tackle some of those challenges." The consultant, understandably, may experience initial resistance and defensiveness from the prospective consultee. It may take several visits and extra effort by the consultant to get beyond this and establish a collaborative relationship with the teacher. An effective consultant is sensitive to the consultee's feelings and, as a result, may want to share an experience of being asked to consider making changes about something over which he or she felt little control at first. The consultant may want to spend more time in the early visits getting to know the teacher and helping out in the classroom, thereby demonstrating an eagerness to learn. The consultant also may find it helpful to stress the fact that few classroom challenges are caused by any one factor and that typically a combination of influences contributes to day-to-day problems. By pointing out that two heads are often better than one, the consultant can begin to lay a foundation for trust and win a positive reception from the consultee.

It is helpful for the consultant to keep in mind that some resistance to the prospect of change is natural. No one wants to undo the status quo, which is predictable and preferable to the unknown experience of doing things a different way. Although there is a lack of empirical research about resistance to consultation, descriptive accounts in the consultation literature alert consultants to various other reasons for and expressions of resistance (Wallace & Hall, 1996). Such reasons include holding unrealistic expectations about outcomes (e.g., the consultee believes the consultant can fix all problems without involving the consultee), hidden agendas (e.g., the program director believes having a consultant in the program will make her look good at the time of license renewal), and poor communication (e.g., the consultant has not clearly presented a reason for her presence in the classroom). Through experience, consultants learn to recognize defensive postures as possible signs of resistance—for example, a teaching assistant's asking the consultant at each visit, "When was the last time you changed 30 diapers in one day or tried to soothe four children at once as they went to sleep?" Rather than reacting defensively, the effective consultant acknowledges how stressed the consultee must be feeling and restates his or her own commitment to collaboration in a joint effort to make things better.

CONCLUSION

As noted in Chapter 2, the process and outcome of consultation are affected by the relationship between the consultant and the consultee, especially the consultee's positive approach to the consultation process (Villa & Thousand, 1996; West & Idol, 1990). The effective consultant works hard to promote open communication, collaboration, and an atmosphere of trust and acceptance. Because building the relationship does not occur at any one point in the consultation process, the consultant uses his or her interpersonal skills to ensure that all interactions with the consultee are rewarding. The consultee who believes the consultant is interested in him or her and the situation (e.g., child, classroom, program) is more likely to accept help and ideas (Brown et al., 1998).

Building the Relationship: Stage Two
Case Illustration

Consultant: Karen   Parents: Juan and Patricia
Consultees: Lakesha, Molly   Child: Benita

Lakesha and Karen agreed that over the next few weeks, Karen would try to spend time in Lakesha's classroom during breakfast, circle time, activity time at interest centers, and outdoor play. Karen wanted to see how Benita was adjusting and to gain a better understanding of Lakesha's classroom schedule and daily routine. Earlier, when Karen and Lakesha discussed the classroom curriculum, Lakesha said that she didn't rely on a single curriculum but liked to pull activities and materials from various sources—another reason why Karen thought it would be useful to observe Lakesha's classroom in action. She wanted to get a better sense of whether the learning activities were teacher directed or child centered or if a balanced approach was used. Karen especially wanted to observe how Benita used her language and motor skills in the classroom. She also was interested in how classroom activities promoted early literacy and social-emotional development for all children.

Although Lakesha liked Karen and was excited about working with her, she was a little nervous about having Karen in her classroom. She could not help wondering whether she and Karen held similar or different views on a range of issues such as classroom management, the role of academic learning, and dealing with children's challenging behaviors. She knew that unlike herself, Karen had seen many other classrooms, and Lakesha wondered how hers would measure up. She also worried that collaborating with a consultant could mean a lot more work for her.

Following Lakesha's suggestion, Karen arranged her schedule to be able to arrive for her visit in time to introduce herself to several parents who were dropping off their children. Karen explained that she was collaborating with Lakesha and Molly to develop new ideas for the classroom related to serving children with disabilities. She also had an opportunity to greet Benita and her father when they arrived. When Lakesha welcomed Karen, she offered to reorient the consultant to the classroom. Karen made a mental note of the classroom schedule, room arrangement, and organization of each interest center. She noticed that the classroom was very busy with visual displays and seemed cluttered and difficult to navigate without stepping over or going around furniture and equipment. Throughout the morning, Karen participated as she observed the classroom, assisting children and adults as needed. She encouraged Benita to play in the dramatic play center and helped her participate in "cooking dinner" with several other children.

On the next visit, Karen arrived during outdoor play and noted that Benita spent most of her time in the sandbox, watching the other children play on the equipment or ride the tricycles. She watched to see how Lakesha and Molly would handle this. Eventually, Molly approached Benita, picked her up, and began talking to her in a soothing voice. Karen was impressed with how sensitive and nurturing Lakesha and Molly were in their interactions with all of the children, and they were both very attentive to Benita.

When Karen and Lakesha met later on, they worked on getting to know each other a little better, as shown in the following conversation.

Lakesha: It was great having you here this week. We could use an extra set of hands here every day. I didn't realize that you were willing to jump in like that when you said that you were coming to visit. It was so helpful. Have you ever worked as a teacher in a child care program?

Karen: Thanks, Lakesha. I really enjoyed it. I taught a preschool classroom for 10 years before I started this job, so I really appreciate how important your job is. I also know how hard it can be and how much you must mean to the children and their families. It was really helpful for me to see your classroom in action and get a sense of your daily schedule and routines.

Lakesha: Well, we try to stick to our general routine, but you know that's hard sometimes.

Karen: Oh, I remember very well! Would you say that the days I observed were fairly typical days?

Lakesha: I'd say they were typical days. We pretty much stuck to the usual schedule and were able to do what we had planned. Over the past couple of weeks, we rearranged the block center, and I think the children like it better now. Oh, and there were two children sick today, so I guess in that way it wasn't a normal day. I'm curious about what you saw today. Anything in particular you'd like to point out?

Karen: I was impressed with how warm and responsive you and Molly were to all of the children. You both took time to greet each child and parent as they arrived, and you attended to each of their individual needs throughout the day. The classroom really has a nice, positive tone. It's pretty obvious that all of the children are attached to you and Molly, and they also play and interact well with each other. Am I reading that right?

Lakesha: It's nice of you to notice. Yes, I think the children really get along pretty well. We've really worked hard on that here at Wee Care, and we're trying to get all the certifications we can for our program. Right now we are gearing up for the NAEYC accreditation.

Karen: How is preparation for the accreditation going?

Lakesha: It's a lot of work, but we all know how important it is. And we think it will be a good way to let the families know we care about the children and about our program.

Karen: I agree! I noticed that there are lots of opportunities for children to make choices and follow their interests throughout the day. It looks like you and Molly make an effort to build on the children's lead throughout the morning. Can you tell me more about your approach to teaching?

Lakesha: Yes, I think what you saw is pretty much the way we teach. It's a lot easier to start with where the children's attention already is when you are trying to show them something new.

Karen: This will make it easy to address Benita's goal of interacting during play with another child. The children appear busy and engaged with activities most of the time. It's clear they enjoy themselves, and Benita seemed interested in what they were doing. What did you notice about Benita's activities today, about what she did in the classroom?

Lakesha: She is sweet and quiet. I think she is still settling into the classroom. I think she will participate more when things are a little more familiar and she gets to know the children better.

Karen: Yes, I had that observation too, and you may be right about her settling in. It will be important to keep an eye on that. I noticed she spent a good deal of time today watching the other children play. Because Spanish is Benita's home language, it may take her awhile to adjust to a new place where everyone speaks English. We might be able to come up with some ways to help her become more involved in classroom activities.

Lakesha: Do you think there is something we should be doing now? I mean, do you know how I could involve Benita a little more in class activities? What should I do?

Karen: We could work on that together. I agree it's time to start drawing Benita out! And it seems from her evaluation that she may understand more English than she speaks. But first, we'll need to gather some more information about times when Benita is interested and actively engaged with activities and times when she is watching others or tuning out. If you like, we can talk more about that when we meet next time.

Lakesha: Great. I'd like any ideas you might have for how I can improve the classroom.

Karen: Alright. And I'm hoping that you will help me figure out how I can best assist you as Benita's teacher. I really see us working together every step of the way.

Chapter 5

Gathering Information Through Assessment

During the assessment stage, the goal of the consultant and consultee is to gather and interpret information, making it possible to define more clearly the consultee's presenting concerns or needs. It is important during assessment to clearly formulate a shared understanding of the problems that will serve as the basis for goal setting in the next stage. The consultant should make several visits to the classroom that may involve data collection and meetings with other people in addition to the classroom teacher. A consultant supporting children with IFSPs or IEPs may need information and perspectives from the child's family or physical therapist, for example, as she learns more about how to target her consultation. Although IFSPs and IEPs specify long-term goals and short-term objectives, they provide little guidance about factors affecting implementation. A consultant focusing on program quality enhancement should include not only classroom teachers but also teacher assistants and possibly the program director in the assessment phase.

In Stage Three, it is helpful to keep in mind that although the initial focus of concern may concentrate on the child with disabilities, the process of gathering additional information may indicate needs in other areas as well. Consultation ultimately may address consultee-related needs such as a teacher's desire to learn new instruction techniques to meet the varying needs in an inclusive classroom or program-related needs such as the need to link a program with community resources and professional organizations. Although the program itself initiates consultation to support an early childhood center's acquisition of a higher rated license or accreditation, the assessment process may reveal concerns related to a specific child or teacher.

KEY TASKS

By Stage Three, the consultant and consultee should have a clear understanding of how the consultant became involved with the program and the general purpose of consultation. Now they want to gather enough information to be able to agree on the definition of the problem or concern that they hope to address through the consultation process. They can discuss strategies for maximizing their mutual participation in the assessment process and the methods that they will use to gather information during this stage. This discussion may involve sharing information about instruments and taking a look at existing data about the child, the classroom, or the overall program. They should discuss who else may need to be involved in the assessment process and make arrangements for these people to participate, realizing that individuals may be more positive about change if they have been involved in the early identification of the targets of change (Alpert, 1995). Although the consultant and consultee develop and strive to adhere to an agreed-on time frame for assessment, they also must acknowledge the possible need to extend the assessment phase or to add new strategies once the assessment process gets underway.

To prepare for and inform the assessment process, the consultant should invite the consultee to identify classroom strengths, needs, and resources and to document these on the Classroom Strengths, Needs, and Resources form, which becomes a part of the consultation file (see Form 3 for a sample; also see the appendix for a full-size, blank version of this form). This process can be a natural extension of a conversation begun during Stage Two as the consultant began to learn about the program. The form can provide helpful information during the goal-setting stage (Stage Four).

The consultant can introduce assessment as a continuous process with many layers that benefits from multiple perspectives, perhaps using the following process to do so. First, he or she discusses the need for both hard data about the focus area (e.g., child's participation and progress, classroom environment) and soft data related to the teacher's or family's perspectives, frustrations, and wishes. Then, the consultant offers multiple methods of assessment that may include individual interviews using both open-ended and closed questions, group meetings, questionnaires or consultee self-assessments, checklists, rating scales, observation and data collection in the classroom, and document review (e.g., existing data) and is open to learning about assessment methods suggested by the consultee.

Prior to assessment, the consultant takes time to arrange any needed training or resources to enable the full participation of the consultee or other program staff

---

Classroom Strengths, Needs, and Resources

Consultee _____

Classroom _____

Date _____

Program

Strengths (e.g., all staff participate in professional development activities, written philosophy of inclusion, accredited by the NAEYC, spacious classrooms)

1. _____
2. _____
3. _____
4. _____
5. _____

Needs (e.g., lack age-appropriate playground equipment, director position vacant)

1. _____
2. _____
3. _____
4. _____
5. _____

Resources (e.g., dependable substitute teachers, program "adopted" by church club, volunteer parent carpenter)

1. _____
2. _____
3. _____
4. _____
5. _____

From Wesley, P.W. (2000). *Improving the quality of early childhood programs: The PFI model of consultation.* Chapel Hill: The University of North Carolina, FPG Child Development Institute; adapted by permission.

Form 3.   (From Wesley, P.W. [2000]. *Improving the quality of early childhood programs: The PFI model of consultation.* Chapel Hill: The University of North Carolina, FPG Child Development Institute; adapted by permission.)

during the assessment process (e.g., introduces the consultee to data collection strategies or new instruments). He or she observes the situation with the big picture of the program in mind to know and make sense of the current classroom situation and to begin formulating ideas about why it is that way and what it will take to change it. The consultant facilitates a discussion about the consultee's view of the ideal situation and hoped-for outcomes to help the consultee begin to recognize the creative tension between the ideal and current situation (Scott, 2000).

The consultant ensures that assessment is joint and that he or she and the consultee complete their parts according to an agreed-on time frame. This guarantees that any data provided by observation instruments such as checklists or rating scales reflect the same current period. The consultant also considers the value of having the consultee complete the same instruments as the consultant to provide at least two perspectives about the same items. For example, if the general focus of consultation is to enhance program quality, the consultant and the consultee (e.g., classroom teacher, assistant, director) each could complete an environment rating scale (e.g., Infant/Toddler Environment Rating Scale–Revised Edition [ITERS-R]; Harms, Cryer, & Clifford, 2003).

After assessment, the consultant arranges for and facilitates a meeting (or possibly several meetings) to discuss the results, ensuring that sufficient time is available for all participants (which may include the child's family and others who participated in the assessment process) to feel that this meeting is complete. The consultant assesses the consultee's confidence at this point and invites him or her to help facilitate this meeting, as this is an important formal opportunity for the consultee to begin taking charge of the consultation process. The consultant ensures that notes are taken during the meeting (using a flipchart can be helpful when more than two people are meeting) and, with the consultee, determines the meeting rules, which may include the following (Scott, 2000):

- Everyone participates.

- Listen without interrupting.

- Share different perspectives.

- Back up ideas with specific examples.

- No blaming or judging allowed.

Data are presented in a format and in terms that can be understood easily and that assist consultees in interpreting and analyzing the data. The consultant models synthesizing and summarizing information shared during the meeting, focusing on data most relevant to the concerns and needs expressed by the consultee. He or she seeks agreement about key points concerning the data before moving on.

Regarding data interpretation, the consultant helps the consultee to identify and write down themes that may emerge in assessment results (e.g., the need to monitor and facilitate the child's engagement in play with peers, the need to align classroom practices with the program's health policy). He or she ensures that the notes taken during the meeting are shared among participants, with ideas summarized as goals on the Intervention Plan form during the next stage (see Form 4 in Chapter 6). Then, the consultant elicits a "concise, accurate, and complete formulation of the problem" that includes factors contributing to the problem and makes the relationship between the data collected and the definition of the problem explicit (Hughes, 1997, p. 14). After the meeting, the consultant engages in ongoing reflection about who is involved in the assessment process and considers who should be involved in a future meeting to develop goals for change based on the assessment results (Stage Four). For example, time sampling and observational checklists completed during a 2-week period indicate that 3-year-old Allie is not interacting with her classmates during the periods of the day when children enjoy activity centers and outdoor play. These data, the teacher's (consultee's) daily log, and parent description of Allie's behavior during social gatherings with the family's friends suggest that Allie approaches other children but does not try to communicate with them or engage in their activities. The consultant and consultee agree that on her own, Allie has demonstrated an interest in many of the toys and materials that she observes the other children playing with but that she may lack the verbal skills needed to gain entry into their activities. They decide to concentrate their focus on this problem and to invite Allie's mother to their next meeting to develop related goals.

CRITICAL CONSIDERATIONS

Early in Stage Three, the consultant begins to develop hypotheses about what may be influencing the presenting problem and the consultee's perspectives about that problem. In formulating these hypotheses, the consultant must consider variables such as the consultee's skills, attitudes, beliefs, culture, and physical and emotional well-being, as well as child and classroom characteristics. The consultant should weigh these hypotheses, along with other factors, including the consultee's ideas and suggestions in determining what recommendations to make about assessment methods. The consultant and consultee may or may not realize the full scope of consultation at this time—that is, whether it will affect primarily the child, the teacher, or the program—but they recognize the potential of the assessment process to reveal needs at all levels.

For example, if the consultant is working with the consultee to implement a child's IEP, then the IEP certainly provides initial guidance for a consultation focus on the child. The consultant and consultee should discuss the IEP goals and how easy or challenging these goals are to address in the classroom. They also should examine the child's adjustment to the classroom routine and his or her relationships with other children. It may be constructive for the consultant and the consultee to share their views about the ideal situation vis-à-vis the child's participation in daily activities and accomplishment of each IEP goal and begin to compare that ideal with data indicating what is actually going on in the classroom. When the classroom teacher, as a consultee, has a method for organizing the information that he or she has about the child, collaboration with the consultant may be more fruitful (Wolery, Brashers, & Neitzel, 2002). The consultant plays a key role in recommending strategies for collecting and summarizing such information and in framing discussions in the context of the classroom ecology, not the child's deficits. One promising method is the Ecological Congruence Assessment (ECA) process (Wolery et al., 2002), which identifies intervention goals by using information about how the participation of a child with disabilities during classroom activities, routines, and transitions compares with that of his or her peers. The ECA should not be used to replace developmental assessments of the child but, rather, to supplement those measures. Following the ECA process, a teacher could document whether the child needs more help than his or her peers during specific times such as arrival and departure, snacks and meals, toileting and hand washing, playground transitions, outdoor play, free play or center time, and so forth. The teacher notes his or her ideas about the nature of the help needed. This information provides both the teacher and the consultant with much information they can use to identify goals and strategies that accommodate the child's strengths in the classroom (Wolery et al., 2002).

In addition to taking turns observing the child in the classroom and debriefing after their observations, the consultant and consultee should invite the family's input about the child at home and their ideas about supporting the child in the classroom. Other members of the child's team who occasionally work with the child and the program (e.g., a doctor, a social worker) also may have valuable input and data to share—for example, about medication side effects—that could be influencing the child's behavior.

The assessment process also may examine factors that facilitate and inhibit success for the child and teacher working together, such as environmental components that can be modified to increase the child's desired behavior or to decrease interference with the child's skill acquisition (Parsons, 1996; see the case illustration at the end of this chapter). This examination may reveal the need for changes on the part of the teacher—for example, the need for a deeper understanding of the situation or for different skills—thus expanding the consultation focus from the child to the consultee. The assessment process may identify factors that facilitate or inhibit the family's full participation and feeling of acceptance in the program, implying that the focus of consultation might shift to include program-level issues such as the strategies used to promote family communication and involvement. An effective consultant anticipates when there will be a need to shift the focus of consultation and may introduce this idea to the consultee as the two of them interpret the assessment findings. Table 3 presents examples of differences in consultation focus, from child to consultee to program.

When the focus of consultation expands to include consultee- and program-related concerns, the consultant may find it helpful to use his or her knowledge of the consultee's longevity with the program, the consultee's previous efforts to create change in the classroom, and the daily demands of the consultee's job as a backdrop for understanding the assessment results. As the consultant considers how assessment results compare to the consultee's own perceptions of the presenting problem, the consultant should evaluate his or her own areas of knowl-

Table 3.   Examples of differences in consultation focus across levels

Child	Consultee	Program
Needs appropriate care and early learning experiences →	Lacks knowledge about disabilities →	Needs a comprehensive staff development plan
Needs to accomplish individualized family service plan (IFSP) or individualized education program (IEP) goals →	Lacks skills to individualize instruction →	Lacks information about community and state resources
Needs to increase interactions with peers →	Lacks confidence about his or her ability to facilitate meaningful and appropriate interactions between children with and without disabilities →	Wants to develop and disseminate a mission statement addressing the program's commitment to inclusion

The arrows indicate that needs at different levels can be related and that the consultant should consider each area of focus.

edge, skill, and experience related to the identified areas of need and then identify any additional necessary resources.

The consultant should consider whether needs are indicated in an area where resistance to change may be expected. For instance, the program just invested in new playground equipment and design, but there is no equipment that the child with disabilities can use. Or perhaps the assessment indicates a need in an area previously described to the consultant as a program strength—for example, the program director is proud of the program's full inclusion of children with disabilities, but the classroom observations reveal that a child with cognitive challenges is left out of most activities. The consultant may refer to the Contact Summary form (see Form 2 in Chapter 3 for a sample; see the appendix for a full-size, blank version of this form) and the Classroom Strengths, Needs, and Resources form (see Form 3 for a sample; see the appendix for a full-size, blank version of this form) completed at the beginning of the assessment stage to refresh his or her memory of the areas identified by the program as strengths.

The *consultee* may be wondering

- Whether he or she will have the knowledge and skills to participate in the assessment process

- How his or her participation in the assessment process will be possible, given his or her duties in the classroom

- Whether the assessment process will make him or her look like a bad teacher

- Whether his or her ideas about assessment methods will be considered

- Whether each participant's observations and data will be considered equally

- Whether the assessment results will support the consultee's own perceptions of the classroom and program

- Whether the assessment results will be shared outside the classroom

- Whether the assessment results will have an impact on his or her performance review with a supervisor or with the trust placed in him or her by a family

- Whether he or she and the consultant will agree on the assessment results

- When he or she and the consultant will begin to actually address the consultee's concerns about the client

- Whether he or she will have the knowledge and skills needed to address an area of need indicated by the assessment process

COMMUNICATION STRATEGIES AND INTERPERSONAL APPROACH

Achieving a smooth entry into the program by taking time to establish a trusting relationship lays the groundwork for a successful assessment stage. At this point in the consultation process, the consultant has developed a sense of the general aspects of teaching practice with which the consultee is most pleased and perhaps those that he or she would like to change. Ideally, the consultant and the consultee approach Stage Three with an energetic desire to learn more about a specific concern.

The consultant should stress that a collaborative assessment process will reveal the most accurate and helpful information. He or she may want to remind the consultee about the importance of the consultee's perspectives and observations. At the same time, the consultant needs to rely on his or her expertise to ensure that the appropriate assessment methods are used. Most important, although the consultant is aware of his or her own hypotheses about the classroom (and, indeed, may have considered these hypotheses in recommending assessment strategies), he or she must be careful to wait on the findings of the assessment process before jumping to any conclusions.

An effective consultant recognizes the tension that may be created for the consultee during a process involving joint scrutiny of the classroom. This tension is affected, of course, by the consultee's attitudes and perceptions of his or her own work, and it may vary according to whether the child, the consultee, or the program is the primary focus of concern. The consultee's reason for accepting consultation may have been to affirm that as a teacher, he or she is doing the right thing. For the consultee, the assessment stage may represent a threatening situation. Some teachers may feel that they already should know how to work with every child and that they should be able to do their job without any help (Erchul & Martens, 2002). In situations in which such sentiments are detected, the consultant may want to move slowly through the assessment process, taking care to review the rationale for each strategy and to reaffirm the consultee's agreement about how to proceed.

Whereas the consultant relied on many open-ended questions during Stages One and Two to gather information about the consultee and the program, he or she now also may use several closed questions in an effort to gather specific information about the presenting need. For example, during the second visit, the consultant asked the consultee to describe a typical day in the classroom in general terms, but now the consultant may want to know exactly which materials are used during certain activities and how many children constitute small groups at interest centers. Typically, both open-ended and closed questions are needed to achieve a thorough understanding of the presenting concerns (see the case illustration at the end of this chapter). The consultant should be careful not to rush any interview with the consultee but, rather, to invite the consultee to tell his or her story unhurriedly. The consultant must introduce relevant questions in a patient and timely way, paraphrasing and summarizing the content (both implied and explicit) of the consultee's statements in an accurate way that enhances not only the flow of conversation but also the consultant and the consultee's shared understanding of the issues (Hughes, 1997). For example, a consultant may ask, "What led you to conclude that your room arrangement isn't working?" and then follow the consultee's response with, "You've described a general concern that children's noisy, animated play may be disturbing other children who are enjoying quiet activities. In what specific area of the room is this most problematic?" During the assessment process, the consultant and consultee will begin to interpret the meaning of their findings and analyze which steps are indicated next.

During the assessment stage, the *consultant*

- Recognizes that the consultee could feel vulnerable or exposed during the assessment stage and offers many opportunities for his or her active participation (Wallace & Hall, 1996)

- Continues to determine the consultee's willingness and availability to participate in the consultation process, taking note of the extent to which he or she is involved in assessment

- Recognizes the importance of having the consultee's agreement about assessment methods and results, as these results form the basis for goal setting, and invites the consultee to participate fully in the assessment process

- Avoids asking the consultee a lot of "why" questions at this point and focuses on creating an accurate description of the current situation

- Is aware of how questioning may negatively affect the consultation process and uses questions to enhance the collaborative relationship (Hughes, Erchul, Yoon, Jackson, & Henington, 1997)

- Avoids quick solutions and problem solving at this point

- Avoids assuming that he or she has understood what has been observed and practices the habit of clarifying his or her own observations with the consultee

- Avoids minimizing or maximizing a strength or need

- Maintains neutrality during the meeting, avoiding judgmental or critical statements (Scott, 2000)

- Recognizes that assessment results should reward and not punish the consultee and models framing the discussion of findings positively, perhaps in terms of good news or opportunities (Scott, 2000; see case illustration at the end of this chapter)

- Points out which program strengths and resources can help address which needs

- Watches for any signs of resistance on the part of the consultee during this phase and considers possible sources of the resistance—these may include factors related to the consultant's approach (e.g., rushing, being insensitive to the consultee's previous attempts to solve the problem) and factors concerning the consultee's perceptions of his or her own ability to participate in the assessment process (e.g., believing that he or she lacks the skill or time required); the consultant also may want to reflect on the consultee's participation up to this point in the consultation process as the consultant decides whether simply to slow the process or address the resistance by discussing his or her perceptions of it with the consultee

It is also important for the consultant to watch for the consultee's dependence on the consultant's expertise and to resist the consultee's invitation to "Just tell me what you think is going on—you're the expert!" An effective consultant carefully selects his or her communication strategies to reflect a symmetrical or nonhierarchical consulting relationship. He or she uses opportunities such as a consultee's invitation to be the expert to reinforce the valuable contributions of the consultee—for example, "I was thinking myself about how much I still have to learn about your classroom and how I need your input and ideas during this next phase."

WHAT IF?

While planning the approach to assessment, what if the consultee attributes a classroom problem to the child (e.g., she reports that the child will not stay seated during circle time and wanders about, creating distractions for the other children)? The consultee asks that the consultant focus observation during the assessment stage on the child and resists including an examination of curricular and instructional aspects in the assessment process. The consultant has observed, however, that there is a problem in the schedule or teaching approach (e.g., circle time is 30 minutes long, teacher directed, and does not require active participation from the children) and would like the assessment process to include a broader look at classroom practices. What does the consultant do?

The consultant and the consultee already may have discussed the concept that many factors often contribute to a problem that initially seems to have one source; if so, the consultant may be able to resolve the situation by emphasizing this point again. Also, by noticing and showing an eagerness to learn about many aspects of the classroom during Stages One and Two, the consultant has signaled an interest in a broad view and, it is hoped, has established a positive regard for the complexity of the consultee's work.

To broaden the focus during the assessment process beyond a specific child, the consultant can engage the consultee in a conversation about the consultee's goals for all children in the classroom. The consultant and consultee may want to list broad outcomes for all of the children (e.g., "We want all children to feel safe and secure, to become independent, to be engaged with the materials and each other, to learn how to get along with others, to gain skills to help them learn to read"). The consultant and consultee then should identify how these goals are supported in the classroom for all children. For example, the teacher can promote children's feelings of safety and security by going on home visits to get to know children before they start the program. Program staff can conduct safety checks of playground equipment every week. As a way to help children become independent, the consultee may make cleanup easy for the children by labeling shelves with pictures of the items stored within. She can ensure that cubbies are accessible to children who want to store and retrieve personal possessions. One way to promote children's engagement in classroom activities, including circle time, is to ensure that the activities are developmentally appropriate, that they involve the children's active participation, and that they are stimulating and brief enough to hold their interests. This discussion may identify issues that the consultee wants to address through the assessment process. Furthermore, using the example of the child who will not stay seated during circle time, it may provide a way for the consultant to guide the consultee's attention to the length and content of circle time, thus setting the stage for the possibility that many factors may affect children's behavior.

The previously described process could take the form of a brainstorming activity with the consultee and other program staff during Stage Two. Led by the consultant, this process provides an opportunity to learn more about the program's philosophy and practices prior to making decisions about the assessment methods used.

CONCLUSION

During Stage Three, the consultant and consultee purposefully and systematically explore the concern or problem area they have discussed during the early stages of consultation. Through questioning and other methods of data collection, the consultant guides the assessment process and, with the consultee, summarizes their findings. One of the biggest challenges in consultation is not rushing into the process of setting goals. As discussed previously, sometimes several meetings are needed to fully discuss and understand assessment results. Once the consultant and consultee have defined the problem or focus of concern clearly and concisely, they are ready to move into the process of determining goals.

Gathering Information Through Assessment: Stage Three Case Illustration

Consultant: Karen   Parents: Juan and Patricia

Consultees: Lakesha, Molly   Child: Benita

During the next several meetings, Karen spent time working directly with Benita on her IEP goals in the classroom and talking with Lakesha. The conversations between Karen and Lakesha shifted to focus on gathering additional information about Benita's adjustment to the classroom. Karen had observed the classroom several times, and as she and Lakesha entered Stage Three of the consultation process, Karen wanted Lakesha to get more involved in the process of assessing Benita's needs and her own needs. Karen was curious about whether Lakesha had any particular concerns about how Benita was doing.

Karen: How do you think things are going with Benita?

Lakesha: We are really enjoying Benita. She is such a wonderful little girl, but I am a little concerned about whether I can spend enough time with her and still manage the rest of the class. I see how you label things for her in the classroom and encourage her to walk with the walker, and I don't know when I could do that. There are other things that I'm not sure about, too.

Karen: I can see that there are many demands on your attention and time. It must be hard to imagine fitting in anything else. I'd like to explore this a bit more with you. When do you feel that you should be spending more time with Benita?

Lakesha: Pretty much all of the time. I mean, she just sits and watches the other children or stands in her walker unless Molly or I go over and talk to her.

Karen: How do you and Molly typically handle this?

Lakesha: Usually, one of us will sit and talk with Benita, although we're not sure how much she understands. Sometimes we pick her up and carry her to another part of the room where the other children are playing. It would probably help if we could spend a lot more time with her, but we can't because we have to attend to all of the other children.

Karen: How many times a day would you say that you and Molly are working with Benita to try to get her more involved in classroom activities?

Lakesha: A lot. I couldn't give you an exact number.

Karen: What would you like to see happening with Benita?

Lakesha: Well, that's difficult to answer, because I'm still getting to know her and I'm not really certain what she's capable of doing. But I'd really like to see Benita be a part of the class more—to communicate and participate in any way she can, to play with the other children, and to be a part of everything we do.

Karen: That helps me understand what you hope will happen. I'd like to learn more about how things are going now. What happens when one of you approaches Benita?

Lakesha: She lights up. She really does. Her favorite thing is to listen to a story with one of the teachers in the quiet corner, but 17 other children need our attention. I just can't spend all of my time with Benita.

Karen: No, of course you can't. I can see how this concerns you. What about the other children? Do they ever approach Benita and try to talk to her or play with her?

Lakesha: Oh, sure.

Karen: Which children?

Lakesha: I really don't know, but I know that the other children like Benita and they were really interested in her, especially when she first arrived. Some of the girls really showed an interest in helping Benita during breakfast and on the playground.

Karen: We may want to gather more information to find out which other children are continuing to show an interest in Benita and if there are any particular activities or times of the day when this occurs more often.

Lakesha: How will we do that?

Karen: Well, one way would be for you to make an anecdotal record to document how and when the other children and adults interact with Benita and how she responds to them. I have an observational record form that is divided into different parts of the daily schedule; you and Molly can use the form to help you record these occurrences.

Lakesha: That sounds simple enough.

Karen: You also mentioned that Benita sometimes stands in her walker. Does she ever use her walker to get around the classroom? If so, when?

Lakesha: Sometimes, like in the morning when she first arrives, but she also enjoys standing and watching. I'm not sure if I should encourage her to use her walker more often or just let her do it when she feels ready. And sometimes I feel like she won't walk unless I stay right beside her telling her to.

Karen: Let's both observe Benita over the next several weeks to see how she uses her walker in the classroom and on the playground. Then, we can discuss this more during our next meeting. Would that be helpful?

Lakesha: Yes, because I think that it is important for her to become more independent and move around the classroom on her own.

Karen: It sounds like your main concern right now is finding ways to help Benita participate more fully in classroom routines and activities and helping her become more independent. We have talked about Benita's ability to communicate and interact with others and about her mobility in the classroom. I think you and Molly also would like some more guidance about the best way of working with Benita in those particular areas. Do you have anything to add to this summary?

******

For the next several weeks, Karen and Lakesha spent part of each consultation visit discussing the strategies they were using to better understand Benita's activity in the classroom; they also reviewed Benita's IEP goals and objectives. Between Karen's visits, Lakesha and Molly continued to gather information about Benita. Lakesha and Molly's observational record revealed that adults were providing direction and children were initiating social interactions with Benita throughout the day, but Benita's responses were limited primarily to smiling at them. This showed that she was interested in others but had a limited repertoire of communication and social behaviors to sustain these interactions. It also raised more questions about Benita's ability to understand and use language—both English and Spanish.

After further observation, Karen agreed with Lakesha's assessment about Benita's limited use of her walker. She also had a hunch that the room arrangement and cluttered environment might be contributing to this problem. She decided to follow up on this in her next meeting with Lakesha by suggesting that they each administer the Early Childhood Environment Rating Scale–Revised Edition (ECERS-R; Harms, Clifford, & Cryer, 1998). Karen also hoped to introduce sections of the Quality of Inclusive Experiences Measure (QuIEM; Wolery, Pauca, Brashers, & Grant, 2000) to gather more details about child–child interactions and Benita's participation and engagement in activities; however, she will wait to do this until she and Lakesha have completed the ECERS-R. Karen thought that the information from these instruments could be used not only to improve the room arrangement to support Benita in the classroom but also to address Lakesha's priorities for improving the global quality of the learning environment for all children. The scales also would aid in preparing for the NAEYC accreditation process. Karen gave Lakesha and Molly each a copy of the ECERS-R and provided training on how to complete the instrument. Karen, Lakesha, and Molly then targeted 2 weeks during which they would each administer the assessment tools.

******

As she prepared for the meeting to discuss the assessment results, Karen recalled that Lakesha mentioned being pleased with the recent rearrangement of the block center; yet, one observation that Karen hopes to discuss during the meeting is the problematic location of the block center. It is in a high-traffic area of the room, and obstacles limit Benita's access to that area. Because Karen perceives that Lakesha and Molly consider the room arrangement a strength, she is eager to learn how they completed ECERS-R sections on Space and Furnishings and Activities. Karen hopes to share her concerns in an objective way, based on the ECERS-R results, and to frame them positively. To set the stage for this conversation, Karen decides to tell the story about her previous challenges in administering the scale in her own classroom.

Karen: I was a teacher when I first learned to use the ECERS-R, and I administered it in my own classroom from time to time. I remember one of the hardest things was to realize sometimes that what I had taken for granted as a plus in my classroom wasn't necessarily scoring high on the scale. I remember trying really hard to make sure that I always rotated the children's artwork on the walls so that the room would seem fresh and cheerful. Then, I realized when I did my scale that a lot of that artwork wasn't at eye level for the children! It was a simple thing to change, but what a surprise. Based on the way I rated child-related display in your room, I'd have to say you and Molly seemed to have thought of everything! I'm wondering, though, if you had any surprises on other items along the way.

Lakesha: Well, I think we have done a lot with the kids' art. Yeah, I gave us a 6 on child-related display. But let me think. There may have been a couple of surprises on other items. . . . I think we may have more work to do on the room, but nothing specific jumps out at me. Let me look at the scale's items about interest centers.

Karen: Good idea; we haven't talked about those observations yet.

When Karen and Lakesha review Item 22 (blocks) on the ECERS-R, they realize that Karen has rated it a 5 (*Good*) whereas Lakesha has given it a 7

(*Excellent*). Karen agrees that all of the indicators of quality under 7 are present and congratulates Lakesha on creating such a well-stocked area and on including some block play outdoors. For Item 22 to receive a score of 7, all of the quality indicators under the 5 rating also would have to be present. One of those indicators states that the block area is set out of traffic. Karen does not agree that the block area is out of the way of traffic and wants to raise this issue with Lakesha. She wants to point out the positive aspects of the block center also.

Karen: You know, as I spent time in your classroom completing the scale, I wondered about whether the location of the block center affected Benita's access to it. I remember you shared with me that you thought the new location of the center was really working, and I have seen how the children gravitate to it! My concern, though, is that the children create their constructions in the center's entrance, which makes it difficult for others to enter. Because children have to pass by the block center to get to many other interest areas, I did not give credit for the block center being out of traffic under the 5, or *Good*, rating on the scale.

Lakesha: Oh. Well, blocks are the main attraction at center time, and it looks like a tornado has hit the room when the children finish in there. I never thought about how you have to go by blocks to get to the other centers.

Karen: I appreciate the fact that you are willing to think about this, especially after the energy you and Molly recently put into rearranging that center. How about if we make a note about this idea so we are sure to revisit it when we develop our goals? Let's keep going through the items under Activities to see if anything else strikes us about the centers in terms of access or materials, and let's keep Benita's needs in mind in particular. Would that be okay?

Lakesha: Sure. I'll write "blocks/traffic" in our notes here so we won't forget.

Classroom Strengths, Needs, and Resources

Consultee Lakesha

Classroom Threes

Date 10/1/04

> Wee Care Child Care
>
> Program

Strengths (e.g., all staff participate in professional development activities, written philosophy of inclusion, accredited by the National Association for the Education of Young Children NAEYC, spacious classrooms)

1. Teachers are caring and sensitive.

2. Staff have positive relationships with parents.

3. Interest centers are well stocked.

4. Center is working on NAEYC accreditation.

5. Children get along pretty well.

Needs (e.g., lack age-appropriate playground equipment, director position vacant)

1. Ways are needed to store additional classroom materials and toys.

2. Teachers lack experience with children with special needs.

3.

4.

5.

Resources (e.g., dependable substitute teachers, program "adopted" by church club, volunteer parent carpenter)

1. Parent volunteers are available on a regular basis.

2. Substitutes are available to relieve staff for professional development opportunities.

3.

4.

5.

From Wesley, P.W. (2000). *Improving the quality of early childhood programs: The PFI model of consultation.* Chapel Hill: The University of North Carolina, FPG Child Development Institute; adapted by permission.

Form 3.   Completed Classroom Strengths, Needs, and Resources form. (From Wesley, P.W. [2000]. *Improving the quality of early childhood programs: The PFI model of consultation.* Chapel Hill: The University of North Carolina, FPG Child Development Institute; adapted by permission.)

Chapter 6

Setting Goals

STAGE FOUR

During Stage Four, the consultant and consultee identify the specific goals for change on which they agree to concentrate. Goals should be related directly to the problems or concerns identified during the assessment stage, and as much as possible, they should be framed in concrete terms that are easily understood by the consultant and consultee (Hughes, 1997; Parsons, 1996). As noted in the discussion of Stage Three, this process often naturally falls during or immediately following the discussion of the assessment results, but goal development may be postponed to a separate meeting, depending on factors such as time and the energy of the participants. The meeting may include other adults, such as the child's family members or therapists, who may have been involved in the assessment process and who have an interest in supporting the goals identified.

KEY TASKS

The consultant and consultee participate in a meeting to develop goals reflecting the priorities for change during the consultation process. In Stage Three, during the meeting to discuss results of the assessment process, the consultant and consultee began to note themes, strengths, and areas that may need attention as related to the child, the consultee, or the program. They should use this information along with notes from the Classroom Strengths, Needs, and Resources form as they select a few specific goals on which to focus their efforts (see Form 3 in

Chapter 5; also see the appendix for a full-size, blank version of this form). These goals are recorded on the Intervention Plan form, which the consultant and consultee will continue to develop and refer to throughout the remaining stages of consultation (see Form 4 for a sample; also see the appendix for a full-size, blank version of this form). It is important to write each goal in terms of outcomes that can be observed or measured with a clear understanding of the criteria that will determine whether the goal is accomplished. Goals also should be framed positively. For example, if it is found during assessment that a child does not consistently follow instructions, the goal would address an increase in follow-through, not a decrease in noncompliance.

The consultant and consultee may specify goals concerning the child, the teacher and classroom, the early childhood center's policies and procedures, or any combination of these areas. They should consider both short-term and long-term goals. Research suggests that for consultation to have a long-lasting effect, the consultant must target not only the child but also extrapersonal variables in the child's environment (Kurpius, 1985). Such variables could include the role of the consultee and other adults in the classroom, their beliefs and attitudes, the schedule of daily activities, and the physical environment. As pointed out in Chapter 5, various levels of need (child, consultee, and program) may be targeted during the assessment stage or may surface in general discussions during the early phases of the consultation process. On the basis of the assessment results, the consultant and consultee may set goals specifically related to what the child will do—for example, the child will increase interactions with peers throughout the day. For any goals selected for the child, the consultant and consultee should work together to determine the levels of outcome they can expect from the child (see Chapter 11 for information on using a goal-attainment scaling process to assess children's progress on goals selected during consultation). They also may choose to develop goals for the consultee—for example, that he or she will acquire knowledge and skills related to a type of disability.

Sometimes the consultant and consultee identify program-level changes that are needed to address child-specific concerns. Examples of program-level goals include the acquisition of additional sturdy and secure tables for diaper changing or the scheduling of bookmobile visits. In cases when the consultant's purpose from the outset is to promote global quality, consultation likely will concentrate on needs of the consultee and program and not on specific children. In turn, goals may address areas such as staff–child ratio, health and safety, classroom schedules, curriculum and materials, teaching strategies, interactions in the classroom, and professional development. It is advantageous to include the program director in the entire consultation process when the focus of concern is program quality; at the very least, the administration's input during goal and strategy selection may ensure that the Intervention Plan is realistic and supported at the highest level of management within the program.

Stage Four (Setting Goals) and Stage Five (Selecting Strategies) provide opportunities to clarify the areas of focus by specifying goals, strategies, people re-

---

Intervention Plan

Consultant _____

Consultee _____

Classroom _____

```
┌────────────────────────┐
│                        │
│                        │
│               Program  │
└────────────────────────┘
```

Consultation start date _____   Consultation end date _____

Month/Date/Year   Month/Date/Year

Goals/objectives	Strategies	Evaluation activities	Responsible person(s)	Start date	Target date	Completed date

From Wesley, P.W. (2000). *Improving the quality of early childhood programs: The PFI model of consultation* (p. 36). Chapel Hill: The University of North Carolina, FPG Child Development Institute; adapted by permission.

Form 4.   (From Wesley, P.W. [2000]. *Improving the quality of early childhood programs: The PFI model of consultation* [p. 36]. Chapel Hill: The University of North Carolina, FPG Child Development Institute; adapted by permission.)

sponsible, resources, and time lines for future work. By summarizing the goals after they initially are developed and allowing time for the consultant and the consultee to modify them, the consultant ensures that there is agreement about the goals before moving on to the selection of strategies.

During Stage Four, the *consultant and consultee*

- Discuss possible causes of some of the assessment results (introduce "why" questions) and may extend the assessment phase if it is determined that more information is needed

- Determine which goals are a priority and why—for instance, goals to address a current and pressing need (e.g., a health or safety issue)

- Identify goals that will likely result in immediate, visible results (e.g., teaching sign language to all children in the class, rearranging classroom furnishings)

- Determine the knowledge and skills needed by both the consultant and the consultee to support goal work

- Determine additional resources needed to support the accomplishment of each goal (e.g., outside expertise, centerwide training, money)

- Consider whether the commitment of someone other than the consultant and the consultee is needed to agree on or accomplish the goals—that is, consider with whom or what must the goals align (e.g., director's goals for the program, upcoming licensing process, family's priorities for the child, current budget)

- Discuss the relationship among goals, and break broad goals down into subgoals (e.g., a goal for a child to increase engagement during class time may require a goal to improve access to and appropriateness of centers and materials)

- Review who, in addition to the consultee, would be interested in the goals (e.g., the child's family, the program's board, a teacher with a similar classroom) and make a plan for involving these people or groups and keeping them abreast of progress

- Decide how the consultant and the consultee will know if the goal is accomplished (i.e., introduce evaluation process)

- Begin to envision how working on each goal will affect the classroom structure (e.g., adult roles, classroom rules, procedures, policies, routines), the organizational and cultural norms (e.g., values, staff recognition, program rituals), and the human resources (e.g., the consultee's need for support beyond that of the consultant; Bolman & Deal, 1997)

- Anticipate how accomplishing each goal will affect the child, other children, families, staff, and the overall program

CRITICAL CONSIDERATIONS

During Stage Four, the consultant encourages the consultee to lead the process of identifying goals. This is especially important if the consultee has led the meeting to discuss assessment results, and it becomes the second opportunity for the consultee to increase his or her leadership in managing the consultation process. Continuing to promote the active participation and increasing responsibility of the consultee facilitates his or her sense of empowerment and ownership of the change process. If the consultee has not had experience with developing goals that are clearly specified and measurable, the consultant may provide direction while making sure to seek ideas and feedback from the consultee. For example, the consultee may refer to information gathered during the assessment phase that supports a general goal that he or she has in mind for the child, whereas the consultant may suggest a specific way to word that goal. Regardless of whether the consultee leads the discussion, the consultant can help to set goals by relying on a combination of facilitation, analysis, and interpretation skills to make sense of the assessment results (Parsons, 1996; see the case illustration at the end of this chapter). He or she should strive to keep things "doable," ensuring that not too many goals are identified and that the selected goals are feasible given the resources.

During goal setting the *consultant*

- Encourages the consultee to consider his or her motivation for addressing each goal (i.e., consider where the energy lies)—for example, the assessment results indicate general program needs in the area of appropriate outdoor opportunities for children of diverse abilities, as well as the need to increase the independence of a child with a disability during transitions and mealtimes; the consultee prefers to address goals related to the child first and to revisit the outdoor needs in the spring as staff plan their annual retreat

- Considers the goals that he or she deems as urgent, critical, or otherwise important to include in the Intervention Plan form and why, and determines which goals are of less importance; he or she develops a plan for presenting these goals for discussion if the consultee does not raise them

- Encourages the consultee to determine whether any themes noted during the meeting to reach consensus about the assessment results relate to each other (e.g., the assessment showed several times that children with disabilities are often unengaged—perhaps resulting from interest centers being inaccessible or inadequately stocked, which was also noted as a theme)

- Is mindful of the number of goals being set and the possibility that the consultee may equate a high number of goals with personal incompetence or failure

- Considers how feasible the goals are given the particular child, teacher, and classroom and begins to think ahead about reasonable and appropriate strategies

The *consultee* may be wondering

- Whether he or she has the experience and expertise needed to identify goals

- Whether he or she gets to choose the goals that he or she wants to work on and the time line for attaining them

- Whether each participant's ideas will be considered equally

- Whether the consultee and the consultant have selected the "right" goals

- Whether he or she will have time in the future to tackle the goals

- Whether additional resources will be available to support goal work

- What is in it for the consultee—that is, how his or her efforts and success in attaining the goals will be recognized

- How much the consultant is going to help him or her work on the goals

- How to go about working on the goals and when to get started

- Whether having many goals means that the consultee has not been doing a good job

COMMUNICATION STRATEGIES AND INTERPERSONAL APPROACH

During Stage Four, the consultant and consultee bring new definition to the consultation process by pinpointing the targets for change. The consultant needs to maintain a high awareness of the consultee's and his or her own priorities and to weigh many factors as the two of them come to an agreement. The consultant must continue to reflect on conversations with the consultee and on his or her observations of the program during initial visits, then compare the assessment findings with those impressions. Although the consultant and the consultee discuss specific goals, the consultant may want to frame this discussion in terms of the big picture—that is, in view of the program. For example, although several staff training needs emerged during Stage Three, which the consultant realizes initially may seem overwhelming, he or she can boost consultee confidence by pointing out how quickly the teacher and his or her assistant implemented a family's mealtime suggestions for a child with significant motor challenges. He or she also can help to identify easily available training resources. At the same time, the consultant should be cautious not to minimize important areas that need attention.

In the field of early childhood, the population of children served is changing both in terms of abilities and cultural diversity. This increases the probability that consultees who are caregivers will have needs related to their understanding of the children and families they serve and to their skills in the classroom. The same can be said of a consultant who works in these ever-changing classrooms. It is critical for the consultant to anticipate this possibility and to work hard to identify areas in which he or she and the consultee can be resources for each other as they both develop professionally. An effective consultant relies on his or her observational and interview skills in determining consultee needs for knowledge and skills (Parsons, 1996). Consultee needs in the areas of understanding typical child development, cultural diversity, and recommended professional practices for the field may influence the way that he or she and the consultant identify problems and concerns, envision goals and strategies, and approach implementation.

During goal setting the *consultant*

- Is aware of the consultee's energy level throughout the goal-setting process and adjusts expectations and approach accordingly

- Talks with the consultee about how approaching change may create anxiety and how feeling some degree of resistance is typical when it is time to set goals; for many people in a consultation process, goal identification signals that implementation is just around the corner and that changes cannot be far away

- Strives to maintain shared decision making and collaboration when goals are needed related to consultee skills, and encourages the consultee to set clear and attainable objectives and activities

- Demonstrates a nonevaluative stance toward problem solving, neither avoiding areas of disagreement nor approaching them as negative occurrences (Hughes, Hasbrouck, Serdahl, Heidgerken, & McHaney, 2001)

Consultants and consultees should expect some disagreement as a natural part of the consultation process. Although disagreement can occur at any stage, it is especially important for consultants to resolve disagreement effectively at the critical point of setting goals and strategies. Hughes (1997) offered several strategies for skillful management of disagreements between the consultant and consultee. These include clarifying areas of agreement and disagreement, highlighting strengths within the relationship, identifying plans to achieve a better understanding of the different views or misgivings, and facilitating a brainstorming session about compromises.

WHAT IF?

What if the consultant's documented observations during the assessment stage cause concern about safety practices but the consultee does not identify this area as a priority for change? How should the consultant present his or her item for discussion? After the consultant raises the issue, what if the consultee agrees that it is a concern—for example, that it would be nice to have diaper changing tables with raised edges to prevent children from rolling off—but maintains that such a target for change would be futile because the director would not support additional expenditures in the classroom?

This is a two-part dilemma. The first question is how to raise an issue that the consultee has not identified as a need. The hallmark of a mutual exchange during discussion of assessment findings is that all parties contribute their ideas to the conversation. Throughout the consultation process, the consultant needs to create the tone that two heads are better than one. If the consultant has made observations not noted by the consultee, the consultant should simply state that he or she would like to share an additional observation. He or she should then describe it and provide the reason it is a priority in his or her view. It is likely that during the early assessment stage, the consultant and consultee have had a conversation about the importance of addressing any concerns identified in important areas such as health and safety. With this as a backdrop, the consultant easily can recommend that he or she and the consultee should consider addressing the safety concern as they develop goals.

The second question presented in this dilemma concerns the consultee's perception that the safety concern cannot be addressed at the present. Many factors should be considered in determining the best way to handle this situation. In the preceding safety concern example, the consultee believes that the program lacks the resources to purchase a new changing table. Further discussion may reveal that the consultee has in mind other priorities that will require the director to make purchases for his or her classroom and that he or she believes purchasing a new changing table will jeopardize the acquisition of these other items. The consultant may want to confirm with the consultee that the table is a concern (thus ensuring that the problem is not a lack of understanding or knowledge) and then facilitate a brainstorming session about solutions. It may be that the consultee has not considered other resources such as a parent who has carpentry skills or a community donation.

CONCLUSION

Stage Four is a critical point in the consultation process upon which the rest of the consultant's and consultee's activities depend. Specifying goals that are related directly to the assessment findings and that are endorsed, if not identified, by the consultee are key tasks. As goals are selected, the discussion naturally will progress toward promising methods and necessary resources for achieving the goals.

Setting Goals: Stage Four
Case Illustration

Consultant: Karen   Parents: Juan and Patricia
Consultees: Lakesha, Molly   Child: Benita

During her next meeting with Lakesha, Karen focused on summarizing and drawing conclusions from their earlier discussions as well as from their classroom observations. She continued to facilitate the exchange of ideas with Lakesha and sought validation from Lakesha periodically to ensure that they shared the same goals for Benita. Karen also suggested that they consider a broader goal of making programmatic changes to improve the room arrangement and center activities. The meeting ended with a discussion of resources that might be useful to address these goals. A portion of this meeting's conversation follows.

Karen: We've covered a lot of ground, Lakesha. Let's see where we are. Benita has adjusted well to her new classroom and is liked and accepted by the other children. At the same time, you have some concerns about Benita's lack of participation and independence, and you're worried that she is taking too much time away from the other children. Is that right?

Lakesha: Right. But I also want to make sure that we are doing everything that we can to help her learn.

Karen: Yes. When we looked at the assessment data we gathered, we decided that you and Molly were spending a considerable amount of individual time with Benita, but much of that time was spent making comments to Benita about what to do or carrying her from one place to another. We also learned that Benita has a limited number of ways in which she responds to you and the other children. She uses some gestures and wonderful facial expressions to communicate but rarely uses words or verbalizations. She mainly just smiles a lot when others approach her.

Lakesha: Right. You know, she's really like a much younger child in her lack of language and the fact that she doesn't move around very much. But she clearly likes what's going on around her, and she seems to understand and enjoy it. I think there's more we can do throughout the day to help her communicate.

Karen: You've given a good description of Benita. It makes me wonder what the other children think of her. I think we are right on target with our first goal to help Benita start to use her communication board at school while we explore other ways to help Benita respond to requests and comments from others. I think it will be easy to monitor Benita's success by whether she points to the pictures to express herself. Do you still think this sounds like a reasonable goal?

Lakesha: That makes sense to me, and I know that her parents would be pleased to see her communicate more with us. I try to touch base with them when they drop her off in the morning.

Karen: I'm glad you brought that up. We'll need to make sure that we continue to share our ideas with them and get their input before proceeding. I think it's great that you are staying in touch with Benita's parents about Benita's progress and our work together. Why don't you let me know when you think it might be helpful for me to contact them? And I will make a note to discuss the communication board with Benita's parents the next time we meet. You also mentioned that you would like some suggestions for working with Benita to promote her mobility. Is this still a priority?

Lakesha: Yes, I don't think she's going to do it on her own, and I'm getting tired of carrying her.

Karen: To accomplish this, you may find it helpful to learn about cerebral palsy in general. I've got some nice handouts about cerebral palsy that I will give to you. We can go over them together on my next visit and talk about how each point applies to Benita. I also know of a workshop next month that's about working with children who have physical challenges. We could make this another goal on the Intervention Plan form and develop some strategies specifically related to how you work with Benita.

Lakesha: Okay, and I know Molly would like to go to the workshop, too, so I'll put in a request for a substitute teacher and a volunteer on that day. Let me know the date as soon as you can.

Karen: I'll make a telephone call to find out before I leave today. So, we've got a goal for Benita to increase her communication with others and one for you to learn about cerebral palsy and strategies for promoting Benita's mobility. How does that sound?

Lakesha: That sounds good. I'd also like to include Molly in the plan because she and I work equally with all of the children in our classroom.

Karen: Of course. We need to include Molly in any plan we develop together and make sure that the ideas we come up with make sense to her. It sounds like we need to set up some meeting times when Molly can join us. In conjunction with this, I will share some information with both of you to ensure that you have the knowledge and skills you need to carry out the activities we decide on. For example, we'll talk about the fact that the strategies we develop will need to be implemented throughout the day rather than just during a specific time. Also, we'll talk about the notion of beginning with a less intensive approach at first and moving to a more intensive strategy if Benita doesn't respond as hoped. I want to make sure that you have the tools and resources you need to carry out the plan we develop together. Do you have any questions or concerns about that?

Lakesha: It makes sense to me, but I think we also need to keep in mind that whatever we come up with cannot take too much time away from the other children.

Karen: You're right. When we start thinking about various strategies, please be sure to ask questions and share anything that's on your mind, including reminding me about your other day-to-day responsibilities. Now, let's both think back to our last discussion about the assessment results and look one more time at our notes from the last meeting. What other goals do we want to consider?

Lakesha: Well, I sort of hate to bring this up, but we did say we wanted to think some more about access to the block center and whether we need to do anything with the room arrangement.

Karen: Sounds like you aren't sure you have the energy to go there!

Lakesha: No, it's not really that. It's just a hard room to arrange. There are so many doors and so little storage, but I do think we need to consider Benita and how easy or hard it is for her to use all the areas.

Karen: I know what you mean. Sometimes the room layout can make it hard to envision many alternatives. I've been thinking a lot about Benita. During my visits to your classroom, I've noticed that there are aspects of the physical environment and room arrangement that might be contributing to Benita's reluctance to use her walker and move independently from center to center. For one thing, the room is long but not necessarily wide, which makes it hard to arrange the furniture in a way that provides adequate pathways for Benita's walker. I've also noticed that although your resourcefulness and Molly's diligence have paid off in terms of stocking the block center and housekeeping with a variety of appropriate and stimulating materials, those centers now have almost too many toys while others have limited materials or materials that are rarely changed.

Lakesha: Yeah, and you and I talked about a problem with the blocks being strewn all over the middle of the floor all of the time. I just don't know what to do about room arrangement. I guess we ought to make that a top priority because so much of what we work on with Benita will have to depend on her being able to get around the room.

Karen: I can tell this is feeling like a big job. I don't want us to rush into it, but I think that we could come up with some ideas to improve the room arrangement and reorganize the centers that would help us address Benita's goals and also would improve the learning environment for all of the children, which will help with getting accredited. How does that sound?

Lakesha: I guess we ought to go for it. Maybe we could find a way to make the book corner more inviting for all of the children. But is it going to take a long time?

Karen: You and I will sketch out a time line that is comfortable for you. I like the idea of building on Benita's interests. I'm going to add a goal about making the block center and the book area more accessible and inviting. I want to hear more about your ideas for improving the book corner, so be thinking about it in preparation for our discussion next week about strategies. Okay, where are we?

Lakesha: Well, according to our notes, we've got three goals. One goal is to help Benita learn to use a communication board at school. Another goal is for Molly and me to learn some strategies for working with Benita to increase her independent mobility. And how did you word that third one?

Karen: The third goal is to make changes to the classroom environment to enhance center activities for all of the children and to improve access for Benita. What do you think about that?

Lakesha: Okay. That's good. And that's it, right?

Karen: Yes, I'd say that sums it up! We will review these again when we sit down next time to develop our strategies.

Lakesha: Wow, we've got a lot to do!

Karen: Yes we do. That's why it's a good thing we are working together! Let's take a minute to think about our goals. Are they doable? Can you think of anything you want to add or change?

Lakesha: No, for now it seems like we've covered everything. And, like you say, if you, Molly, and I are working together, I think we can accomplish this.

Karen: Okay. Before we end our discussion today, let's jot down these goals on the Intervention Plan form and then spend a few minutes talking about some resources that we might need to address the goals that we've identified. We'll want to reconsider our resources as we think in more detail next time about strategies.

Intervention Plan

Consultant _Karen_

Consultee _Lakesha, Molly_

Classroom _Threes_   _Wee Care Child Care_
                                                                          Program

Consultation start date ___10/6/04___   Consultation end date ___5/31/05___
                         Month/Date/Year   Month/Date/Year

Goals/objectives	Strategies	Evaluation activities	Responsible person(s)	Start date	Target date	Completed date
Benita will use her communication board, pointing to at least 25 familiar pictures upon request.	Include pictures of Benita's family and her favorite foods and books; ask Benita's parents for other ideas; and start with only a few pictures at a time.	Goal Attainment Scaling	Lakesha, Patricia	10/21/04	5/1/05	4/1/05
Teachers will gain knowledge about cerebral palsy through a workshop on this topic and will apply this knowledge in the classroom.	Use teacher-identified strategies to promote Benita's mobility in the classroom, drawing on ideas learned from the workshop.	Summary conference	Lakesha, Molly	11/1/04	11/2/04	11/2/04
The room arrangement will be improved by increasing access to and organization of centers.	Define center boundaries clearly, and move blocks out of traffic; rotate materials in the housekeeping and block centers; and build on Benita's interest in books by integrating relevant books in various centers.	ECERS–R, classroom observation	Lakesha, Molly, Karen	11/10/04	11/30/04	11/30/04

From Wesley, P.W. (2000). *Improving the quality of early childhood programs: The PFI model of consultation* (p. 36). Chapel Hill: The University of North Carolina, FPG Child Development Institute; adapted by permission.

Form 4.   Completed Intervention Plan form. (From Wesley, P.W. [2000]. *Improving the quality of early childhood programs: The PFI model of consultation* [p. 36]. Chapel Hill: The University of North Carolina, FPG Child Development Institute; adapted by permission.)

Chapter 7

Selecting Strategies

STAGE FIVE

Just as the process of setting goals may begin during the meeting to discuss assessment results, so can the process of strategy selection run parallel with the process of setting goals. Strategies are selected based on the likelihood that they will be effective in achieving the agreed-on goals, their appropriateness given the characteristics of the child or program, their feasibility in terms of the demands of the context (e.g., their fit with the classroom schedule and materials) and available resources, and their match with the philosophies and beliefs of the consultee (Hughes, 1997). The consultant and consultee have to specify what the tasks are, who is responsible for each task, when and where the tasks will occur, which resources are needed, and when start and completion are anticipated. Along with the goals set by the consultant and consultee, these details about strategies comprise the Intervention Plan form that drives the remainder of the consultation process.

KEY TASKS

The consultant uses knowledge of available resources, including the consultee's experience and skills, to guide strategy selection. He or she asks the consultee which strategies have previously been tried and found to be effective that may apply to the goal in question (see the case illustration at the end of this chapter). After jointly brainstorming about possible strategies and selecting the ones that they want to employ, the consultant encourages specificity in terms of who will do what when and where. The consultant or the consultee records this information on the Intervention Plan form, on which they already documented the goals in Stage Four (see Form 4 in Chapter 6; also see the appendix for a full-size, blank version of this form). The consultant and the consultee then plan how the strategies will be communicated among stakeholders in the classroom and the family. They also begin to discuss the methods that they will use to determine the effectiveness of the strategies, a conversation that will be revisited during the implementation and evaluation stages. For example, they may design a data collection form that the consultee will complete during the first week a strategy is introduced to track changes in the child's behavior.

As strategies are developed and people are assigned responsibilities for carrying them out, the consultant likely will have to take on new roles. An effective consultant is flexible and helpful in forecasting and clarifying these roles. For example, if he or she and the consultee center their focus on the child's acquisition of new skills as directed by the IEP, strategies may involve the consultant's direct work with the child, his or her observations of the child in the classroom, the consultee's work with the child, and the consultant's feedback to the consultee. If a consultation goal focuses on the consultee's need for a deeper understanding of the child's needs, strategies may call for the consultant to serve as a resource for information and education. If a goal is developed for the consultee to acquire new skills, strategies may include the consultant's demonstrating various intervention techniques, coaching the consultee as he or she tries them, and creating numerous opportunities for guided practice and feedback.

CRITICAL CONSIDERATIONS

Although it is a good idea for the consultee to take an active part in setting goals, the consultant's expertise and experience play an important role in selecting effective and practical strategies. He or she may introduce alternate views or model strategies to help the consultee determine feasibility and fit in the classroom. The consultee ultimately must determine what is practical for him or her given his or her philosophy and beliefs, the classroom and its daily demands, and his or her skills and confidence. It is especially critical that the consultant draw on his or her own expertise and resources to provide accurate answers to the consultee's questions. These questions may address areas such as typical or atypical child development, specific disabilities, classroom interventions, curriculum, and community or state resources. The active participation by the consultee in setting goals and selecting strategies boosts the probability of successful implementation (Brown et al., 1998).

As strategies are being identified, the consultant and consultee may realize that it is not possible to focus intervention on every need at the same time. The consultant may want to facilitate a discussion about how to set priorities. Five guidelines offered by Parsons (1996) may be helpful. First, consider strategies that provide the broadest impact for the effort. An example would be rearranging interest centers in the classroom to make them more inviting and to define more clearly their purpose for the children. This rearrangement also would increase access and interrupt open traffic zones that encourage running. Next, consider strategies that cause the least strain or costs for the consultee in terms of program resources. This means building on the consultee's existing skills and resources and providing ample support as interventions get underway. The third and fourth considerations are that consultees are most likely to embrace strategies that directly address what Parsons refers to as "their immediate pain" (p. 162) and that address the issues that the consultees state they are most motivated to address. Finally, it is important to begin with a problem or an issue that is manageable and with a strategy that appears to have a high likelihood of success. For example, the consultee's first strategy to facilitate the children's ability to clean up independently at the end of an activity is to label accessible shelves and plastic storage bins with photos and pictures that correspond to the toys and materials to be replaced. Next, the consultee and the assistant learn and implement a simple modeling procedure for providing children who do not follow through with directions to clean up. Using this strategy, the teacher says what needs to happen and shows the children how to do it. Then, he or she asks the children to do it and follows through by participating with them, physically guiding them if necessary.

As the intervention plan comes together, the consultant is aware of the internal, personal transition process that has begun for the consultee. In selecting strategies, the *consultant* asks the following:

- What does the consultee say he or she wants to do? What are his or her areas of emphasis or importance (Parsons, 1996)?

- What resources are available to support the strategies considered?

- Are any old practices ending or being replaced? How can the consultant and the consultee take time to honor past achievements (Bridges, 1991, as cited in Scott, 2000)?

- Are new vocabulary terms, pieces of equipment, methods, or procedures being introduced? Is it possible to use the old way and the new way for a while—that is, to create a transition period (Bridges, 1991, as cited in Scott, 2000)?

- Will the strategy require additional knowledge and skills for implementation?

- How does the strategy align with the consultee's philosophy and beliefs about child development and teaching?

- How can support be enhanced for the first-time use of a new strategy? Can the consultant be present when a strategy is first tried? Can two people work together to implement the strategy initially? Is it possible to try the new strategy only once per day for a while (Scott, 2000)?

- How can the strategy be monitored, and how will the consultee communicate deviations and innovations to the consultant?

- Which strategies offer the best potential for immediate success? The consultee may have experienced the problematic situation for some time prior to consultation. Encountering some degree of success in achieving first goals builds hope for the situation and for the consultation process itself (Parsons, 1996).

The *consultee* may be wondering

- How quickly the strategies will work

- How he or she will be viewed by the consultant if the strategy does not work as planned

- Whether the strategies will work in similar situations or with other children

- Whether he or she will require new skills, training, or knowledge

- Whether research has demonstrated that the strategies are effective in the classroom context

- Whether the time lines and strategies can be adjusted along the way, and if so, when and by whom

- Whether he or she will have to take time away from other children or duties to implement the strategies

COMMUNICATION STRATEGIES AND INTERPERSONAL APPROACH

By Stage Five, the consultant and consultee most likely have settled into an effective style of communication and approach to problem solving. Ideally, they both are comfortable brainstorming with each other and sharing their honest reactions to ideas. They may find it helpful to clarify the nature of the contributions they each can make to the strategy selection process. For example, the consultee knows the classroom inside and out, likely has developed a positive relationship with the child and family, and has a realistic perspective about what is feasible in his or her program. The consultant has the benefit of working in several different programs and previously may have implemented strategies to achieve similar outcomes (Wesley & Buysse, 2004). Both may appreciate having time to research and think about strategies before beginning implementation. For this reason, they may want to hold several meetings to discuss strategies over a period of a couple of weeks. It is up to the consultant, however, to ensure that this process does not delay implementation too long.

As is also true during goal setting, the consultant requires skills that promote agreement on the selection of strategies. Skillful communication includes asking a general question related to agreement, pausing to allow the consultee to reflect and respond, and then adding a follow-up question concerning any needed corrections or clarifications (Hughes, 1997). For example, the consultant should summarize the strategy that has been agreed on and ask, "How do you think that sounds?" If the consultee replies that the strategy sounds fine, the consultant should then ask at least one additional question: "Can you think of anything we need to add or change?" By establishing the habit of these simple but methodic steps of seeking agreement, the consultant models a predictable process that may result in the consultee's increased initiative and participation. After considering several strategies in this way, the consultee may offer clarifications or amendments to the strategies spontaneously or may assume more leadership for the agreement-seeking process in the future.

During strategy selection the *consultant*

- Assesses the consultee's energy level and continued availability during the consultation process

- Conveys an attitude of flexibility, openness, and innovation

- Does his or her homework and brings relevant information and resources to the strategy selection process

- Helps the consultee to anticipate obstacles to implementing the strategies planned

- Reflects the content and feelings expressed by the consultee (e.g., "You haven't worked with knee braces before and worry you won't have the time to deal with them after nap")

- Prepares the consultee for the probability that the consultant's role will change as implementation gets underway and the consultee assumes increasing responsibility

WHAT IF?

What if the jointly identified goal requires the consultee to learn new skills but the consultee seems to avoid strategies involving his or her own professional development? For example, say that a consultant and a consultee agree to concentrate on an IEP sign language goal during snack and meal times. The consultant loans the teacher a sign language book and suggests as a first strategy that the consultee learn at least 10 signs, including the 5 signs that the child already knows and the new ones indicated on the child's IEP. The consultee worries aloud that he or she won't have time to learn the signs and probably won't be able to remember them throughout the day. He or she suggests an alternative strategy of laminating drawings of the signs and what they represent and then taping them to the table where the child sits. That way, the child will be reminded to use the signs and the consultee will not have to worry about trying to become an expert in an area about which he or she knows nothing.

As strategies are identified and added to the intervention plan, some consultees may feel a bit overwhelmed. They may begin to wonder about the feasibility of parts of the intervention plan or even about their choice to participate in consultation. An effective consultant is sensitive to these stresses during Stage Five, discusses them with the consultee, and allows sufficient time to think about and finalize strategies. For teachers who have never worked previously with a child who has disabilities, the prospect of having to learn new skills may represent a considerable professional challenge. It may require new resources, extra time, and a departure from their comfort zone. These changes may seem less scary when the consultee sees the consultant actively seek new knowledge and skills for him- or herself as a part of the consultation process. The consultant may use the consultee as a resource but at the very least shares his or her own strategies for acquiring the new information as a way of modeling continued professional development. The consultant also may allow the consultee to see him or her practice and refine these skills.

In cases like the preceding example, it is important for the consultant to understand the consultee's notion that he or she has to be an expert to teach a child who is learning sign language. The consultant could validate the consultee's feelings about facing this new challenge (e.g., "Learning a new language can seem overwhelming at first") and then clarify that fluency in American Sign Language will not be necessary (e.g., "It will be important for the child to use just a few signs at first, adding only those signs that she may need in her daily routines"). These steps provide a way for the consultant to clarify any of the consultee's misunderstandings about the strategy. The consultant also may want to consider his or her own actions in setting the stage for implementation. Handing the consultee a book of signs rather than drawings of only the relevant signs may have contributed to the consultee's fearful reaction.

There may be times, however, when the consultant has to challenge a consultee to consider his or her own contribution to a situation, both in terms of understanding factors influencing the problem and, as in the preceding example, implementing strategies toward a solution. In the sign language example, the consultant should let the consultee know that his or her idea to use laminated pictures of the signs is a good way to prompt and reinforce sign language for the child. At the same time, the consultant should stress the teacher's role in using the signs and the need for communication to be sent and received between at least two people. In other words, the child may not understand the effectiveness of signs as a form of communication if others are not using them too. Perhaps the consultant will want to emphasize the important role that being able to communicate effectively with others plays in building social competence. The consultant may want to remind the consultee of another time when his or her extra effort resulted in a child learning needed skills and, if relevant, emphasize that although extra effort was required from the teacher at first, it paid off in the end by eliminating the child's dependence on adults in the classroom. The consultant may ask the consultee if it would help to break the strategy down into more steps, perhaps introducing only one new sign per week. The consultant may step up his or her support by offering to make for the teacher a notebook of new signs, to which the consultant, teacher, or parent can add as the child and consultee progress. In short, through a combination of social influence and clear explanation of the rationale for the strategy, it is hoped that the consultant can convince the consultee to use the signs him- or herself.

CONCLUSION

The closure of Stage Five marks a pivotal point in the consultation process as the consultant and consultee prepare for implementation. Gaining the consultee's input and agreement on the selected strategies may build confidence and commitment as he or she tries them in the classroom. It is wise to keep in mind that as implementation unfolds, it may be necessary to select alternative or new strategies if certain strategies do not work or if progress occurs more quickly than anticipated.

Selecting Strategies: Stage Five
Case Illustration

Consultant: Karen   Parents: Juan and Patricia

Consultees: Lakesha, Molly   Child: Benita

At their next meeting, Karen and Lakesha reviewed the goals that they listed on the Intervention Plan form and began developing strategies to address each goal. The following excerpt from that conversation addresses the first goal.

Karen: I think we're ready now to tackle the first goal: Benita's communication. We said we would help her start using a communication board at school while we explored other ways she could respond to people. As we consider strategies, it would be helpful if you could briefly review how you are working with Benita now in terms of her communication.

Lakesha: Well, when Benita first came, we weren't sure what we were supposed to do. We spent a lot of time talking to her and reading books to her, and we also carried her to different parts of the classroom because she wasn't able to move on her own. But now we've figured out that one way to get Benita to participate more during circle time is to have her sit next to one of us and to physically prompt her through the fingerplays and music activities.

Karen: How well does that seem to work?

Lakesha: She seems more involved in the activities than before, but I'm not sure what she is getting out of them. I also understand now that her fine motor skills are affected by her cerebral palsy, so there are some things, like fingerplays, that she just struggles with.

Karen: Understanding how cerebral palsy affects Benita definitely is going to help you and Molly know how to work with her. I know it is hard sometimes to know what Benita is understanding; what else can you tell me about her communication?

Lakesha: She has her good days and bad days. Some days, she really seems tuned in to what the other children are saying to her. She smiles and maintains eye contact with them. Other days, she doesn't show much interest.

Karen: Are there strategies that you've tried to help Benita communicate? Are there things you are doing that we may want to consider as we think about introducing the communication board?

Lakesha: Well, I point to things and label them for her. I'm trying to use Spanish words now for a few things in the classroom, but I also say them in English. Whenever there's a picture in one of our books of something that we have in the classroom, Molly will go and get it and show it to Benita. Just yesterday, Molly was showing Benita our toy boat that looks a lot like the one in the story Molly was reading.

Karen: That is such an effective way to teach language and to get children excited about communicating! What else have you tried?

Lakesha: I can't think of anything else really. I mean, we just try to talk with her when we can.

Karen: What do you think about using the communication board to give Benita a more precise way of communicating her wants and needs?

Lakesha: I think that would be very helpful because I don't always know what Benita wants.

Karen: I was thinking that we might make a file with a few pictures of things that are meaningful to Benita. Perhaps we should start with some of the objects you have been labeling in Spanish and English. We can add other pictures later, once Benita gets the hang of it.

Lakesha: Well, we'll also need pictures of her family, her favorite foods, and her favorite books.

Karen: Good ideas. Anything else?

Lakesha: I think we also should include pictures of Molly and me, as well as of Caitlin and Stephen* because they spend time with Benita and she really perks up when they are around.

Karen: I agree. I can bring my camera and take the photos we discussed. Then, we can mount the pictures on a tag board and laminate them. Why don't we ask Benita's mother to help us come up with other ideas for photos? Perhaps she can help get us started with photos of her family or a couple of favorite foods.

Lakesha: That's a good idea. I've been wanting to touch base with her anyway. When should we use the picture board?

Karen: We want to start out with just a few pictures on the board. I was thinking that we might introduce the board when Benita arrives and then use it during times when we want Benita to make choices or indicate her preferences. We don't want to overwhelm her.

Lakesha: How about during snack time? We could ask Benita to point to the foods she wants.

Karen: I think that's a great place to start. Food can be very motivating! Maybe then we can think about other times of the day when we

*This fictional example assumes that Caitlin's and Stephen's parents have signed a permission form to have their children's photographs taken by the teacher and used for this purpose.

can get Benita to participate more through communication. Let's also think about how we can get some ideas from Molly and Benita's parents.

Lakesha: Yes. They may have other ideas about pictures that we need to add later on. I do have one question. I'm not exactly sure about how to introduce the communication board to Benita and how to teach her to use it.

Karen: We'll work together on this. I'll show you how to get started with it. We could ask Benita's mother to plan to join us so she can see, too. We could also ask Patricia to help us with the Spanish words so that we can label each picture in both Spanish and English. Perhaps we should start writing some of these strategies onto the Intervention Plan form.

Lakesha: Okay. I can do that. I've always wanted to learn Spanish!

Karen: This will be an opportunity for both of us! Before we move on, let's summarize these strategies for the first goal on the Intervention Plan form. I want to be sure that we write down who is going to do what, and while we are at it, let's develop a time line.

Chapter 8

Implementing the Plan

STAGE SIX

During Stage Six, the consultee, with the support of the consultant, implements selected strategies to accomplish the agreed-on goals for change. Although the consultant continues to visit the program, implementation occurs largely in his or her absence. Depending on the goals, implementation may last several weeks or several months. The consultant and the consultee check in with each other frequently to share views about how things are going and to make adjustments in the strategies as necessary.

KEY TASKS

Implementation has been called the moment of truth in the consultation process. After agreeing on the goal-related strategies that define the consultation's focus from this point, the consultee, with the consultant's support, now must try the strategies and see if they are effective. After discussing the consultee's and the child's readiness for implementation, the consultant makes regular visits to the program, calling ahead to confirm appointments. While at the program, he or she observes in the classroom and meets with the consultee to gain a sense of how things are going. The consultant may want to step up support as implementation is launched by increasing his or her accessibility and encouragement to the consultee. For example, the consultant could demonstrate continued interest and presence between visits by sending e-mails or relevant articles as a follow-up to conversations.

During implementation, the consultant assumes different roles based on the needs of the consultee (e.g., classroom volunteer, trainer, coach, confidant, observer) and on the three tasks of helping to solve problems, using social influence, and offering professional support to the consultee (see Chapter 1). Transitions among roles are smoothest when the consultant prepares the consultee by discussing this flexibility as they approach the implementation stage. As they select strategies, for example, they may agree that the consultee will learn new methods to allow a child who is nonverbal to make choices in various interest centers. The consultant should suggest that he or she can share her experience regarding which methods are likely to be effective, demonstrate these methods to the consultee during class time, observe the consultee as he or she tries them, provide feedback and encouragement, and later assist the consultee as he or she modifies the methods to best suit the situation. The consultant may volunteer to share resources or locate training opportunities for the consultee and other teachers about ways to work with children who are nonverbal—from reading the cues that indicate emotions, needs, and intentions to making simple communication boards. Although the consultant probably has adjusted his or her approach to meet the needs of the consultation process prior to implementation—for example, by shifting to a training role as he or she introduced new assessment instruments to the consultee—the active nature of the implementation stage increases this likelihood.

The consultant should continue to keep a written Contact Summary about each communication with the consultee. The Contact Summary form provides an opportunity for the consultant and consultee to track the purpose, activities, and outcomes of each contact in addition to plans for next steps (see Form 2 in Chapter 3; also see the appendix for a full-size, blank version of the form). Because this form provides a helpful history of tasks, accomplishments, concerns, and challenges in the consultation process, as well as the consultant's own reflections about how things are going, it can be especially valuable as a planning tool during implementation. The consultant can refer to summaries of recent contacts during implementation as a way to prepare for the next visit.

During implementation, the consultant also may want to connect the consultee with other people and programs engaged in similar activities. Helping the consultee to build a network of professional peers can provide validation and encouragement during this most challenging stage of consultation. The consultant and consultee should acknowledge and celebrate their accomplishments during this stage as a part of an ongoing dialogue about the effectiveness of the strategies and the continued applicability of the goal.

CRITICAL CONSIDERATIONS

Gutkin and Conoley (1990) described components of consultation that contribute to the likelihood of consultees' implementing intervention plans. These include a minimal need for time and resources to implement the interventions, the interventions' minimal intrusiveness in terms of the ecological context, and the consultees' sense of controlling the implementation. Understandably, some resistance is to be expected from the consultee during implementation. Up to this point in the consultation process, the consultant and consultee have been gathering data and discussing needs, ideas, and plans. During implementation, the consultee will take specific actions to accomplish the specified goals for change. These actions may have an impact on children's behavior, parents' perceptions of the classroom, and the perceptions of the consultee and his or her co-workers about their work. It is important to keep in mind that resistance is a normal reaction to the prospect of change. The consultee's awareness of the importance to evaluate each strategy's effectiveness as it is implemented may create additional stress.

Although both the consultant and consultee discuss their readiness for implementation, the consultant also may want to consider the likelihood of successful follow-through based on the consultee's current energy and previous participation during the consultation process. Throughout Stage Six, the consultant must determine the degree of the consultee's involvement and commitment and identify who else is supporting implementation. In some situations, it is also important to discuss the readiness of the child and family for implementation, especially if several new child-related strategies are planned. At the same time, it is important for the consultant to confront his or her own fears about the success of implementation.

The *consultant* can boost confidence and success during this critical stage of the consultation process when he or she

- Provides sufficient information to support the consultee's belief in the effectiveness of the interventions (Witt, 1986)

- Encourages the consultee's steady focus and maintains an awareness of how much time, energy, and attention the consultee has

- Asks the consultee about what else is competing for his or her time and attention and shows understanding and support

- Offers leadership, particularly by facilitating problem solving and sharing resources

- Models the spirit and technique of reflecting on his or her own actions (e.g., shares his or her notes about recent observations of the child in the classroom with the consultee and thinks aloud with the consultee about what can be concluded from that observation)

- Reminds the consultee that results may not be immediate

  During implementation the *consultee* may be wondering

- To what extent the consultant will participate in actual implementation and who is ultimately responsible for the outcomes

- What barriers and supports to anticipate

- What new skills he or she will need to be successful during implementation

- Whether his or her alternate ideas will be accepted during implementation

- What process to use to troubleshoot and whether the consultant will be available when needed

- How immediate results will be

COMMUNICATION STRATEGIES AND INTERPERSONAL APPROACH

Although the implementation stage is characterized by action, continued and careful communication and planning are nonetheless critical. The consultant should ask the consultee to share his or her fears and concerns about implementation, and together they can anticipate any obstacles. The consultant needs to summarize the intervention plan in a way that helps the consultee understand its details, and he or she should provide sufficient opportunity for the consultee to ask questions or make changes to the plan.

The consultant must affirm continued flexibility, openness, and commitment to the consultation process and the program and build in many opportunities to model this flexibility and resiliency. The consultant should discuss with the consultee plans for checking in during implementation, call ahead to confirm each scheduled appointment, and invite suggestions for actions that would be most helpful to the consultee during visits (Wesley & Buysse, 2004). As strategies are being implemented, both the consultant and consultee need to discuss the effectiveness of the strategies. The consultant can be a sounding board for the consultee and accurately reflects the consultee's feelings (see the case illustration at the end of this chapter). The consultant then should offer authentic support and understanding and, when necessary, demonstrate his or her willingness to adjust the time line and revisit the goals and strategies to ensure their relevance. Most important, the consultant must demonstrate patience during implementation. He or she understands that a teacher's job is full of many pressures and responsibilities and never blames or finds fault when follow-through does not meet an expected time line.

WHAT IF?

What if implementation hits a snag because the consultee does not attempt intervention strategies for one goal? For example, although the classroom teacher agreed during the assessment and goal-setting stages that a girl with severe visual impairments would benefit from accomplishing the IEP goal of increased independent mobility in the hallway, the teacher does not follow through with any of the mobility training strategies that have been demonstrated to her. What steps can the consultant take to solve this dilemma?

For many reasons, there are times when carefully and skillfully developed intervention plans are not implemented fully, even though the consultee initially seemed in agreement with the goals and strategies. Perhaps the consultee did not understand how to carry out a particular step or lacked the skills, time, money, or support to implement it in the classroom. Perhaps the consultee tried to implement the strategies reflected in the intervention plan but believed that some were not producing the desired outcome or were exacerbating the problem. It may also be that there is a mismatch between the goal and strategies and the consultee's philosophy, beliefs, or values. In the preceding example, the consultee may believe in theory that children with visual impairments should become as independent as possible, but he or she also may believe that this particular child is too young for such independence at school. The consultee may not see it as his or her role to promote independent mobility, or perhaps he or she derives great pleasure from personally guiding the child.

To identify the obstacles, the consultant must share his or her observation that parts of the intervention plan are not being implemented. The consultant should do so in a manner that acknowledges that he or she is not present all of the time while being clear about his or her observations when present in the classroom. The consultant can assure the consultee that snags are not unusual during implementation and may choose to relay an example of a previous experience in which obstacles were identified and overcome. The consultant must balance the need to be clear and honest with the need to avoid blaming the consultee. The consultant's communication should be straightforward yet supportive. He or she should not ask the consultee, for example, how he or she thinks the strategies are working if the consultant knows that they are not being implemented. The consultant simply should state his or her concern that the child is not attaining the goal of independent mobility in the hallway and suggest that they revisit the strategies, considering their feasibility and appropriateness as well as the consultee's feelings about implementing them. In this way, the consultant and the consultee work together to identify and, it is hoped, to overcome the barriers to implementation.

The consultant must remember that the goal is to clarify and understand the situation, not to embarrass the consultee or exhibit power or one-upmanship (Parsons, 1996). Communication should be descriptive, not judgmental or evaluative. It may be helpful for the consultant to consider how the confrontation will be perceived by the consultee and to practice his or her communication prior to the meeting.

CONCLUSION

Implementation is an exciting and active time during the consultation process. The consultee's role primarily is to carry out the strategies identified on the Intervention Plan form while the consultant provides a variety of supports such as encouragement, coaching, observation, and feedback. Both consultant and consultee may engage in evaluating and documenting the effectiveness of the strategies being implemented. They also monitor and discuss the way they continue to work together and ideally make adjustments as needed in areas such as communication and follow-through. Through their continued dialogue and data collection, they develop a sense of the success of intervention and prepare for the next stage in which the intervention plan and the consultation process as a whole will be evaluated.

Implementing the Plan: Stage Six
Case Illustration

Consultant: Karen

Consultees: Lakesha, Molly

Parents: Juan and Patricia

Child: Benita

Over the course of several weeks, Karen played several key roles as Lakesha and Molly implemented the agreed-on plans. She facilitated the discussion about how the children reacted to changes in the block center and showed Molly how to keep a daily log to document Benita's increasing mobility. She participated in brainstorming sessions with Lakesha and Molly about ideas for encouraging other children to use Benita's communication board. Karen offered technical advice ("It might work better if we stabilize the board using Velcro") and served as an instructor ("Be sure to give Benita plenty of time to point to the picture before giving her the object") and a coach ("That worked well today—tomorrow, let's try asking Benita to walk a little bit farther"). Karen provided additional resources, including an annotated bibliography of children's books to guide decision making about additions to the book center.

During their meetings, Lakesha and Karen worked together to adjust their plan and fine-tune their strategies. Throughout the implementation process, Karen was available to listen and offer support or to observe how things were going firsthand and provide another perspective. She also tried to gauge Lakesha's willingness to try new approaches and her reaction to implementing them in the classroom. As shown in the following excerpt, Karen and Lakesha discussed their progress with changes to the furniture arrangement and classroom materials and the impact of these modifications on the children. Based on Lakesha's suggestions, new strategies were added to the Intervention Plan form.

Karen: How are the children adjusting to the new classroom arrangement?

Lakesha: Well, for one thing, they aren't all congregating in two centers anymore. I think moving the block center and widening its entrance has really helped the room feel less cluttered, and yesterday I saw Benita enter the center twice! Can you believe that?

Karen: This is encouraging news. You sound pretty excited.

Lakesha: There's a lot going on! The other thing we've noticed is that rotating books in the book center means there's something new to attract the children nearly every week. The children spread themselves out much more across the different interest centers. I don't think we've had as many disputes over toys and materials. Also, Molly and I can address individual needs more easily.

Karen: It sounds like the room changes have been beneficial. Children seem to be using the centers more, and you and Molly may be feeling a bit more relaxed.

Lakesha: You know, I think we are.

Karen: What else have you noticed about Benita?

Lakesha: Benita really hasn't started using her walker that much more; I think she still prefers to have one of us carry her. Although not every day is like this, sometimes it seems like she's glued to the floor. We're encouraging her to walk to different parts of the room, but I thought she would catch on faster than this. And I'm not sure Molly and I are both using the same procedure to help her pull up from sitting to standing at her walker.

Karen: I know it can be frustrating and tiring to care for a child who isn't walking.

Lakesha: Yes, it is. Even though I understand more about cerebral palsy now, what I don't get is how Benita's energy can vary so much each day.

Karen: Tell me more about that.

Lakesha: Well, every time I think we're getting somewhere, it seems like Benita stops trying. I don't think she's being stubborn, but it sure is aggravating.

Karen: It sounds like you've had to work hard to be patient with her. What's your best guess at what might be going on? Can you think of any reason for her to walk on some days but not on others?

Lakesha: Molly and I were talking about that. I'm not sure, but we wondered if it had to do with her motivation.

Karen: You may be onto something there. Perhaps we should gather some more information on when and where Benita is using her walker on her own. You mentioned she had entered the block area twice recently.

Lakesha: Yes, that's right. And books. She goes into the book area on her own.

Karen: Could you and Molly start writing down these times when she does walk and also the times when she just seems stuck? Pay special attention to this idea about motivation by being sure to write down where Benita is going when she does walk!

Lakesha: Sure.

Karen: Before I leave today, let's look at a couple of different ways to do that. Perhaps we can sit down with Molly, too, during naptime. Tell me more about the book area. Does Benita still prefer to be in the book corner with one of the teachers?

Lakesha: Of course. But we're helping her develop other interests. We've moved some of her favorite books into the other areas. For example, today in the housekeeping center, the children pretended that Benita's book was a cookbook, and Caitlin used it to prepare a birthday cake. Benita actually joined in by pretending to eat a piece.

Karen: Wow! What a clear indication that Benita is enjoying play with other children. It's always so interesting to hear how creative you and Molly are! I wonder if we could figure out a way to get Benita interested in the art center?

Lakesha: I bet we could if we figure out a way to use one of her favorite books. Maybe we could display the pumpkin book near the table easel while offering Benita paint the same colors as in the book. This might inspire her! What do you think?

Chapter 9

Evaluating the Plan

STAGE SEVEN

Evaluation answers more than a yes/no question about whether a strategy worked. The purpose of evaluation is to determine whether the agreed-on goals were attained and whether the collaborative processes were effective. Also of interest is the extent to which the consultee acquired sufficient knowledge, skills, and experience to prevent or manage similar problems in the future. Discussion about evaluation is ongoing throughout the consultation process, but as noted in Chapters 7 and 8, an evaluation component also is built into the Intervention Plan form. Evaluation becomes more formal at the end of consultation, when plans are made for terminating the focus on a particular goal or, possibly in the case of consultation to promote program quality, the consultant's involvement with the program. Chapter 11 provides more detail about evaluation methods and measures as well as a process for assessing and making sense of consultation outcomes across a large number of individual cases.

KEY TASKS

During evaluation, the consultant and consultee determine whether the strategies were effective in attaining the targeted goals, and they document measurable outcomes related to the child, classroom, and consultee. The evaluation process also examines the degree to which the collaborative relationship was maintained. Just as the consultant shared new ideas, practices, and resources with the consultee during strategy selection and implementation, he or she shares information about evaluation methods during Stage Seven. The consultant must ensure that the people involved in planning and implementing the consultation process are also involved in its evaluation, and he or she should seek the consultee's input while developing the evaluation plan. Evaluation plans should be integrated onto the Intervention Plan form. Depending on the complexity of evaluation questions and methods, some consultants and consultees also may write a separate summary of the evaluation plan.

Brown et al. (1998) described key considerations in planning an evaluation of consultation. These include determining the purpose of the evaluation, agreeing on appropriate measures to evaluate both outcomes and process, agreeing on data collection methods, setting up data collection schedules and roles, and determining with whom findings will be shared and how they will be used. The obvious reason for evaluation is to determine the match between desired and achieved outcomes: Were the goals on the Intervention Plan form accomplished? It is also important to assess aspects of the consultation process—that is, the consultant's skills and approach and the consultant's and consultee's overall satisfaction with their relationship. In some cases, there may be a need to determine how much time was spent by the consultee in the consultation process or how many on-site visits were made by the consultant. Other such needs that are idiosyncratic to the particular parties engaged in consultation may arise. Determining what content and process data will be needed is a decision that should be made early in the consultation process so that data collection methods can address both formative needs (i.e., addressing aspects of planning and implementation during the consultation process) and summative needs (i.e., evaluating the end result, impact, or product of consultation). Consideration also should be given to who besides the consultant and consultee will have access to the evaluation results. For example, will it be shared with families, a program director, or the board?

In selecting data collection methods, schedules, and roles, the goals are to ensure that the evaluation strategies and tools are appropriate for the purpose of evaluation, that they will be easy to use in the context of the classroom or consultation setting, and that the results can be interpreted in a way that makes sense to the consultant and consultee. It is helpful for both to have a clear understanding of their roles related to what is involved, from collecting information from others to filling out forms themselves or participating in interviews (Brown et al., 1998).

Although evaluation naturally follows implementation, an effective consultant establishes formal and informal opportunities for evaluation and feedback throughout the consultation process, clearly communicating these to the consultee. He or she seeks agreement at various points along the way and takes the time needed to make adjustments before moving to the next consultation stage. The effective consultant also models giving and soliciting feedback at each stage of consultation and, depending on the skills and comfort level of the consultee, may take the lead on analyzing the evaluation results. The Consultation Stages Checklist is a helpful tool for the consultant to monitor consultation tasks throughout each stage (see Form 5 for a sample; also see the appendix for a full-size, blank version of this form).

Consultants and consultees may want to hold a special meeting to present and react to evaluation data. This meeting differs from the final summary conference in that it creates an initial opportunity to consider evaluation results. It is not a time when concrete plans are finalized for next steps in the consultation process, although participants may float ideas about the future focus or termination of consultation. It is helpful at the beginning of this meeting to restate the reason for the consultant's involvement in the program, to summarize briefly the problems and the intervention goals, and to present the evaluation results descriptively, not interpretively (Parsons, 1996). Ample time must be provided at this meeting for all participants to interpret and react to the evaluation findings, to explore issues of confidentiality, and to consider the possible negative effects of evaluation findings at many levels, including the child, the consultee, the classroom, the program, and the consultant.

As the consultant and consultee begin to understand their evaluation results, they may identify new areas of need and schedule time to discuss options for addressing those areas in the future (see the case illustration at the end of this chapter). This may be as simple as, for instance, recognizing that a child who accomplishes his IEP goal of using his communication board at snack and lunch time may be ready to have new pictures added to expand the board's use throughout the day. However, identifying future directions may present more complex challenges. For example, evaluation data indicate positive outcomes in children's engagement resulting from simple environmental changes in room arrangement, furnishings, and materials, but children with disabilities continue to be excluded from the play of their classmates. This need may become the focus of concern for future consultation. One outcome of any meeting to discuss evaluation results is that the consultant and consultee begin to have a clearer understanding of the agenda for the final summary conference.

CRITICAL CONSIDERATIONS

The discussion of which evaluation methods to use actually begins during strategy selection. During Stage Seven, the consultant continues to consider the consultee's familiarity with various data collection procedures and his or her willingness to engage in self-reflection. In addition to frequent and open general communication, evaluation methods may include observation, data collection, a log of daily reflections, self-assessment, and interviews with the consultee, the child's family, and other professionals involved with the child. During Stage Seven, it is helpful for the consultant to remember that the evaluation data to be collected should be as objective as possible and directly linked to the evaluation question and consultation goals. Evaluation results can be used to answer at least three questions: 1) whether the goals have been accomplished and the interven-

Consultation Stages Checklist

Consultee _____

Classroom _____

Date of Initial Contact _____ Month/Date/Year

Date of Final Contact _____ Month/Date/Year

[ ] Program

____ Check completed tasks.

Stage One: Gaining Entry

____ Make initial contact.

____ Arrange the first visit.

____ Discuss the process of consultation.

____ Assess the match between the consultee's needs and priorities and consultant's skills and knowledge.

Stage Two: Building the Relationship

____ Build rapport and establish trust.

____ Visit/observe the program or classroom.

____ Learn more about the program and the consultee.

____ Learn more about the focus of concern.

____ Discuss the consultation process.

Stage Three: Gathering Information Through Assessment

____ Specify the consultee's concerns and needs.

____ Decide on methods for gathering additional information.

____ Specify the roles and responsibilities of the consultant and consultee in gathering information.

____ Formulate a definition of the problem.

Stage Four: Setting Goals

____ Discuss assessment results and the possible causes of the findings.

____ Summarize consultee's concerns and priorities related to the assessment results.

____ Identify one or a few specific goals on which to focus consultation.

____ Determine what knowledge, skills, and other resources are needed to address goals.

____ Determine how both parties will know when the goal has been accomplished.

Stage Five: Selecting Strategies

____ Determine which strategies the consultee tried in the past and how well these worked.

____ Discuss other strategies that could be employed.

____ Select strategies that are acceptable to the consultee and the consultant.

____ Determine what knowledge, skills, and resources are needed to implement the strategies.

____ Identify roles and responsibilities for implementing the strategies selected.

Stage Six: Implementing the Plan

____ Encourage and support the consultee as needed.

____ Determine if adjustments to the plan are needed.

____ Evaluate the effectiveness of the plan.

Stage Seven: Evaluating the Plan

____ Assess the match between desired and actual outcomes.

____ Review the evaluation plan.

Stage Eight: Holding a Summary Conference

____ Summarize the consultation's focus, goals, and accomplishments.

____ Shift attention to other concerns and goals for change.

____ Ask the consultee to complete the Consultation Evaluation form.

From Wesley, P.W. (2000). *Improving the quality of early childhood programs: The PFI model of consultation.* (pp. 71–72). Chapel Hill: The University of North Carolina, FPG Child Development Institute; adapted by permission.

From Wesley, P.W. (2000). *Improving the quality of early childhood programs: The PFI model of consultation.* (pp. 71–72). Chapel Hill: The University of North Carolina, FPG Child Development Institute; adapted by permission.

Form 5. (From Wesley, P.W. [2000]. *Improving the quality of early childhood programs: The PFI model of consultation* [pp. 71–72]. Chapel Hill: The University of North Carolina, FPG Child Development Institute; adapted by permission.)

tion should be terminated, 2) whether progress has been made toward achieving the goals and the intervention should be continued, and 3) whether the intervention should be restructured because of lack of progress (Hughes, 1997). The consultant and consultee may decide to use the same instruments during this stage as they used to gather information during the assessment process. For example, they likely used an environment rating scale in Stage Three if the focus of concern was enhancing global program quality. Completing the scale again in Stage Seven provides excellent pre- and postassessment comparisons.

During evaluation, the *consultant* will be forming ideas about

- The consultee's perspective concerning the energy, commitment, support, and attention required during the evaluation process

- The consultee's capacity to use assessment and goal-setting processes in the future absence of the consultant

- Other possible areas of change that were not identified during the consultation process but that may emerge as a result of the evaluation

- The best way to share evaluation results with the family and others (e.g., through a written report, at meetings)

- The consultee's readiness to terminate consultation or shift to another focus in the consultation process

The *consultant and consultee* consider layers of evaluation that examine

- How the consultee, child, and family have reacted generally to change

- What has been learned during the consultation process

- Whether the consultee has generalized behaviors and strategies to similar situations

- The unanticipated outcomes and impact of the consultation process

- The accomplishments about which the consultant and consultee are most proud

COMMUNICATION STRATEGIES AND INTERPERSONAL APPROACH

By the time the consultant and consultee arrive at Stage Seven, both have some awareness of the success of implementation and are beginning to form opinions about the effectiveness of consultation to address the needs identified by the program. During Stage Five, when strategies were selected, they discussed methods for determining whether the targeted outcomes were achieved. Indeed, an effective consultant ensures there is continuous evaluative feedback to maintain, revise, or terminate consultation activities and processes (Idol, 1990). For these reasons, the general results of evaluation should not be a surprise to either the consultant or consultee.

Sometimes consultation that was characterized by collaboration between consultant and consultee fails to achieve successful outcomes in terms of the targeted goals. Although the tendency may be for the consultant and consultee to reduce tensions and vulnerability by not focusing on the lack of success, it is critical for both of them to review efforts and processes to learn from the experience (Parsons, 1996). It is possible that consultation fails because of a critical error at some stage of the process. For example, perhaps data gathered during assessment were not adequate to formulate a comprehensive or accurate description of the problem, or perhaps the consultant rushed the entry stage and missed important information about the values and resources of the program. In addition to considering such points with the consultee, it is also helpful for the consultant to share his or her experiences and perspectives about consultation cases with a colleague to benefit from another consultant's insights.

It may be challenging to plan a more structured examination of the consulting process and relationship, an aspect of evaluation that extends into Stage Eight. In effective consultation, the consultant and consultee become comfortable with the way they communicate and address issues related to their relationship throughout the consultation process. For example, the consultant presents an open interest in feedback about his or her own skills and approach, and models active reflection about all aspects of the consultation experience—from his or her own effectiveness to the consultee's creative use of resources. Although the consultant may defer a formal assessment of the consultee's overall satisfaction with the consultation process until Stage Eight, using an approach that will allow the consultant and consultee to recognize the positive impact of the relationship, even if the terminal goals were not achieved, is important during Stage Seven (Parsons, 1996). Through experience, the consultant is able to increase his or her understanding and strategies related to this aspect of evaluation. Building on their mutual interest in their work and their partnership, the consultant and consultee may want to discuss how

- Tasks were assigned

- Resources were identified

- Conflicts were resolved

- Resistance was managed

- Agreement was gained

- Collaboration was maintained

Finally, considering that not every strategy selected is always effective and that unintended outcomes are possible, it is easy to see how the evaluation process can lead to the revision or addition of goals or strategies. In other words, the consultant and consultee may "reboot" the consultation process by returning to Stage Four or Five or even to Stage Three to initiate additional assessments. An effective consultant is mindful of how this affects the consultee and demonstrates his or her continued commitment to the problem-solving process. The consultant emphasizes positive outcomes and intentions, acknowledges and accepts the consultee's efforts without being judgmental, highlights the value of the knowledge and skill that the consultee has both contributed and developed as a result of consultation (Parsons, 1996), invites the consultee to share his or her views about the outcomes, and validates the consultee's feelings.

WHAT IF?

What if the program director, who has not been an active participant in the consultation process, follows the consultant to his or her car one day while questioning the consultant about the evaluation results? Perhaps the director wants to know specifically whether the teacher has been cooperative in his or her role as consultee or seeks the consultant's opinion about whether the classroom is up to par. How should the consultant handle this situation without betraying the confidence and trust of the consultee?

In this situation, the consultant must be mindful of at least two things. First, the consultant should be concerned about how walking to the car with the director may look to others, especially the classroom teacher with whom he or she has been working. Second, the consultant needs to respect and respond to the director's interest in the consultation process without violating the consultee's trust. The best way to avoid a situation such as this is to have frequent conversations with the director and classroom teacher about the roles of the program staff during consultation. These conversations would begin during entry and continue as the process progresses from stage to stage. The consultant should work to encourage and support the consultee to assume responsibility throughout consultation, making suggestions along the way about specific tasks such as facilitating meetings, managing implementation, and interpreting evaluation results. As Stage Seven approaches, it is helpful to share the plan for gathering and making meaning of evaluation data with the program director. Empowered consultees often take the lead on sharing evaluation results with the program director and others outside the classroom.

If the director accompanies the consultant on the way to his or her car, the consultant may want to stop in the lobby of the building or on the sidewalk to continue and conclude the conversation. Sharing general positive outcomes related to the classroom is appropriate, as is the consultant's remarking on his or her own positive feelings about working with the program. The consultant should inform the director, if necessary, about the consultant and consultee's location in the evaluation process and remind the director of the plan to share results. Certainly, if the director has been an active part of the process—for example, if he or she participated during assessment and implementation—then he or she should have participated in planning and conducting the evaluation and already would have a sense of the findings. If the director has not been an active participant in the consultation process, then the consultant should encourage the director to talk directly with the classroom teacher or offer to set up a time during the next visit when the three of them can sit down together to discuss how things are going.

CONCLUSION

Beginning during implementation, as data about effectiveness of strategies are collected, the consultant and consultee should consider the effectiveness of their intervention plan. Results of additional evaluations conducted during Stage Seven typically provide a clear picture of accomplishments related to the identified goals and the consultant's and consultee's overall satisfaction with the consultation process. Analyzing these findings and identifying next steps are the purposes of the summary conference.

Evaluating the Plan: Stage Seven
Case Illustration

Consultant: Karen   Parents: Juan and Patricia
Consultees: Lakesha, Molly   Child: Benita

After implementation was well underway, Karen and Lakesha shifted their focus to evaluating the Intervention Plan form. Karen started by reviewing each of their goals and then invited Lakesha to help assess the match between the desired and actual outcomes identified in the plan. They also completed the Goal Attainment Scaling form* together to assess Benita's progress. Although they had been discussing the consultation intervention plan all along, both found it helpful to set aside a special meeting to step back from the process and identify which aspects of the plan worked well and which did not.

Karen: I thought we should review the goals that we identified when we started this process. One of our goals was to increase Benita's communication by introducing the communication board in the classroom.

Lakesha: That's right. Do you remember when all she did was smile at us? That seems like so long ago.

Karen: It sounds like you're continuing to see some progress in this area.

Lakesha: Oh, yes. We've seen a big change in her. She now points to pictures on her picture board to communicate with us. That's made a big difference. She also points to things she wants, and she uses her communication board with other children. This may be rushing things, but it would be nice if she'd start using some words along with her gestures and pointing to pictures. Oh, and one more thing. The other children are learning Spanish. They can all say the names of all of Benita's pictures in Spanish! Their parents are so impressed!

Karen: Lakesha, that's terrific. Do you believe that Benita has accomplished her goal? She is participating more with the other children and using gestures and pictures to communicate, but are you saying that you'd like to see her start to use some words?

Lakesha: Right. But I'm not sure if learning Spanish and English at the same time is a good thing. I'm worried that Benita might get confused and that it will interfere with learning English.

Karen: Actually, experts in this area tell us that learning two languages at the same time does not cause confusion or delays in young children but actually facilitates English language learning.

*See Chapter 11 for more details.

Lakesha: That's really interesting. I didn't know that.

Karen: But we should monitor this to make sure that this recommendation applies to Benita. I, too, would like to see her use spoken language at school. She is speaking a few Spanish words at home and we know her hearing tests within the normal range, but we have to keep in mind that Benita is learning two languages, which can take some time, and that she has cerebral palsy. All of these factors could affect the rate at which she uses spoken language at school. We want to keep open the option to pursue a more comprehensive evaluation for Benita in this area.

Lakesha: Yeah, I see what you mean. Maybe Molly and I are expecting too much too fast.

Karen: I think the wonderful progress we have seen Benita make in adjusting to your classroom and playing with her peers makes us hopeful that other areas of development will advance rapidly. Expecting progress is always a good thing! But we have to be patient. Everybody has a piece of the puzzle here. That's why your notes and insights are so important.

Lakesha: So we should keep labeling things for her throughout the day and just keep our ears open for those first words, right?

Karen: Yes, and to get additional insight about Benita, I'll talk with some colleagues who know more about young children with disabilities who are English language learners. What about our second goal, which focused on you and Molly increasing your knowledge of cerebral palsy and your skills to promote Benita's mobility?

Lakesha: Well, as you know, Molly and I both were able to go to that workshop. What really helped, though, was sharing those handouts that you had—the ones we went over and you showed me how they applied to Benita. I gave those to the other teachers here at Wee Care. I also showed them to Benita's dad one day when he dropped her off. I told him you would talk to him about them, too.

Karen: I'm glad that helped.

Lakesha: Yes, and it's been great being able to count on you to share resources like that with us.

Karen: Thanks, Lakesha. I agree that one of the strengths of our consulting relationship is the way we have shared information and resources. You know, I have learned a lot from you about how child care licensing standards affect inclusion. I'm still telling my colleagues about the fact that the regulations do not include a provision for a diaper changing area in the 3- and 4-year-old room.

Lakesha: Yes, I'm glad we were able to work that out with our consultant. I can't imagine trying to coax Benita to the bathroom every time we need to change her.

Karen: Well, what is your feeling about the way you have been able to work with Benita to promote her walking? I agree with her physical therapist that consistency is needed across home and school, but what is a typical day like in terms of Benita's independent use of her walker? Let's look at our data sheets and see what they tell us.

Lakesha: I read the therapist's report, and he is coming to visit here next week. I don't know. Molly and I are both pretty comfortable helping Benita move from a sitting position to standing at her walker. Patricia worked with us to really get that procedure down. What worries me, though, is that I don't feel like we have a good way to tell what Benita's stamina should be. Here's our log. See—on these days, she did really well moving from center to center on her own in the mornings. She even got all the way to the lunchroom without stopping. But look at this: On this week and on a few other days, Molly or I had to coax her to move even a step. The strategy to let her and another child go down to the cafeteria early to help set up snack time seemed to work for a while. It really motivated her. But now I feel like the novelty has worn off. Molly and I have found out that it is better for one of us to stay with Benita to prompt her right away rather than to try to get her going again after she stops. According to our log, it doesn't look like there is a "typical day."

Karen: Yes, I see. I'm glad you felt comfortable changing your approach when you saw things weren't working the way we'd hoped. It sounds like you have accomplished the goal to learn about cerebral palsy and develop skills to support Benita's specific needs with mobility. But as we monitor Benita's progress, you will have to continue to make adjustments in the way you and Molly work with her. Why don't we all plan to meet with the physical therapist next week? I'll talk to him about this possibility, and I'll also try to find out if Benita's parents can come. Can you get time away from the class for a while? If so, this would be a good time to think about what we want to do next in this area.

Chapter 10

Holding a
Summary Conference

STAGE EIGHT

S tage Eight represents the culmination of the consultation process related to a specific intervention plan. The purpose of the summary conference is to review the Final Report form summarizing consultation highlights and outcomes and to plan next steps related to the consultation process. These steps include how to restart the process with a focus on new and/or different concerns, extend the process to consider new aspects of the original concern, or perhaps postpone or terminate consultation altogether.

KEY TASKS

As evaluation results were organized and discussed in Stage Seven, the consultant and consultee developed written notes or files of data. Information from these documents—the Contact Summary forms, the Intervention Plan form, and any other instruments such as the Goal Attainment Scaling form—is summarized in the Final Report form. At a minimum, the Final Report form provides a succinct description of the consultation focus, goals, and accomplishments. Ideally, the form serves as a guide for a more narrative and detailed summary of the consultation process. If relevant, the consultant may want to summarize continued needs and recommendations (see Form 6 for a sample of the Final Report form;

Final Report

Consultant _____	Program
Consultee _____	
Classroom _____	
Date _____	

Brief history of consultation process

Who initiated _____

Participants _____

Dates consultation began and ended _____

Number of visits _____

Program/classroom description

Ages of children _____

Number of children and adults _____

Hours of operation _____

Licensure/accreditation _____

Program/classroom strengths _____

_____

Consultation goals _____

_____

Accomplishments/changes made _____

_____

_____

_____

_____

Recommendations for next steps _____

_____

Consultant's reflections _____

_____

Form distribution (who received this report?) _____

Form 6. (From Wesley, P.W. [2000]. *Improving the quality of early childhood programs: The PFI model of consultation.* Chapel Hill: The University of North Carolina, FPG Child Development Institute; adapted by permission.)

also see the appendix for a full-size, blank version of this form). Typically, the consultant takes the lead in completing the Final Report form, inviting the consultee's input and feedback. Consultees may want to consider sharing this report with program administrators, board members, or families who are interested in the consultation process even though they did not participate directly in it. In the section of the form for reflections, the consultant may want to comment on the consultee's hard work and productivity. The consultant also may want to add his or her own perspective about positive aspects of the consultation relationship.

In addition to reviewing the consultation outcomes related to the intervention plan and considering next steps, during the summary conference, the consultant and consultee also discuss their reactions to and satisfaction with the overall consultation experience, the skills of the consultant, and the participation of the consultee. In many ways, this conversation extends the discussion begun during the evaluation process about the presence or lack of collaborative processes (see the case illustration at the end of this chapter). Consultants and consultees may want to consider the following topics during the final stage of consultation:

- What went well during consultation and what they would want to do again, especially in terms of their roles and communication

- Problems that could have been prevented and how

- What they would do differently next time

- Personal issues that got in the way of achieving the desired outcomes

- The consultant's organization, knowledge, skills, and approach

- The consultee's participation and demonstrated commitment

The consultant may ask the consultee to complete a Consultation Evaluation form to assess his or her satisfaction with the consultant and the consultation process and a Consultee Benefits form to identify specific consultation outcomes related to the consultee (see Forms 7 and 8 for a sample of each; also see the appendix for full-size, blank versions of these forms). To provide sufficient time and to increase the consultee's comfort in providing candid responses to questions about the consultant's knowledge and skills, the consultant can provide a self-addressed stamped envelope in which the consultant can return the forms through the mail at a later date.

CRITICAL CONSIDERATIONS

In defining the point at which consultation will change course or possibly terminate, the consultant and consultee consider the remedial and preventive impact of

Consultation Evaluation

Consultee _____

Consultant _____

Classroom _____

Program _____

Date _____

Please check the appropriate box to rate the extent to which you agree or disagree with each statement as it applies to your current experience with consultation.

	1 Strongly disagree	2 Disagree	3 Agree	4 Strongly agree
Effectiveness of consultation				
1. The goal of consultation was clearly defined.				
2. Methods for gathering information to assess my needs were helpful.				
3. The intervention plan makes sense for my situation.				
4. The intervention plan has been easy enough to implement.				
5. The intervention plan has been effective to this point.				
6. The consultation process met my expectations.				
7. The overall quality of the consultation was high.				
Consultant knowledge and skills				
8. The consultant is versed not only in early childhood content but also in the process of helping others.				
9. The consultant presents information clearly in oral and written form.				
10. The consultant recommends appropriate materials and resources.				
11. The consultant elicits information from others and is a good listener.				
12. The consultant demonstrates effective organizational skills (e.g., uses time efficiently, is prepared for each consultation).				
13. The consultant provides prompt feedback.				
14. The consultant has worked collaboratively to clarify our roles and responsibilities throughout the consultation process.				

(continued)

From Parsons, R.D., & Meyers, J. (1984). *Developing consultation skills.* San Francisco: Jossey-Bass. Copyright © 1984 by Jossey-Bass. This material is used by permission of John Wiley & Sons, Inc. Further reproduction prohibited without permission from the publisher.

	1 Strongly disagree	2 Disagree	3 Agree	4 Strongly agree
Consultant interpersonal style				
15. The consultant is comfortable to talk with.				
16. The consultant demonstrates flexibility and openness.				
17. The consultant is generally pleasant.				
18. The consultant expresses his or her ideas without being overpowering.				
19. The consultant has supported my active participation in the consulting process.				
20. The consultant is respectful and caring.				
21. The consultant is creative in examining problems and options.				
Overall				
22. What aspects of consultation were particularly strong and/or useful?				
23. What aspects of consultation were weak or not useful?				
24. In what way did consultation advance your professional knowledge or contribute to the quality of your services or program?				

From Parsons, R.D., & Meyers, J. (1984). *Developing consultation skills.* San Francisco: Jossey-Bass. Copyright © 1984 by Jossey-Bass. This material is used by permission of John Wiley & Sons, Inc. Further reproduction prohibited without permission from the publisher.

Form 7. (From Parsons, R.D., & Meyers, J. [1984]. *Developing consultation skills.* San Francisco: Jossey-Bass. Copyright © 1984 by Jossey-Bass, Inc. Further reproduction prohibited without permission from the publisher.)

Consultee Benefits

Consultee _____

Classroom _____

Date _____

Program

Please check the appropriate box to rate the extent to which you agree or disagree with each statement reflecting changes in your knowledge or skill as a result of consultation.

	1 Strongly disagree	2 Disagree	3 Agree	4 Strongly agree
Objectivity				
1. I am able to recognize the knowledge and experience that I bring to the collaborative change process.				
2. I am able to view situations and problems from different perspectives.				
3. I solicit and accept constructive feedback and suggestions.				
Problem solving				
4. I am better able to set goals for change.				
5. I now use a more systematic approach to solving problems.				
6. I am able to work with other adults to make positive changes in the classroom.				
Role competency				
7. I can better assess my own effectiveness in the classroom.				
8. I am a better teacher (or parent, administrator, etc.).				
9. I am more confident in my role.				
Facilitating human development				
10. I am better able to design high quality learning environments.				
11. I have developed new approaches to working with individual children that will address their diverse learning needs.				
12. I feel confident that I can develop interventions for children in the future.				

Adapted by permission from Brown, Wyne, Blackburn, and Powell, *Consultation Strategies for Improving Education*. Published by Allyn and Bacon, 75 Arlington Street, Boston, MA 02116. Copyright © 1979 by Pearson Education. Further reproduction prohibited without written permission from the publisher.

Form 8.   (Adapted by permission from Brown, Wyne, Blackburn, and Powell, *Consultation Strategies for Improving Education*. Published by Allyn and Bacon, 75 Arlington Street, Boston, MA 02116. Copyright © 1979 by Pearson Education. Further reproduction prohibited without written permission from the publisher.)

consultation (Parsons, 1996). That is, during Stages Seven and Eight, they conclude whether the intervention plan has been effective in resolving the problems that were the focus of consultation (remedial) and whether the consultee has developed knowledge and skills to deal with similar problems in the future (preventive). It is reasonable to anticipate that by the time of the summary conference, the consultant and consultee have a sense of closure if the intervention plan has been successful and are ready to refocus or terminate consultation. As pointed out in Chapter 9, termination is rarely a next step for the early intervention consultant focusing on a child with a disability, but it is a likely option for a consultant focusing on enhancing program quality. It is prudent, however, for all consultants to consider the impact that decreasing or otherwise substantially changing the consultation service may have on the consultee and program. Some consultees report that the experience of working with a consultant to solve problems in their own classroom boosts morale and instills confidence (Palsha & Wesley, 1998). For others, it represents the first time they have worked with someone outside the program who was not in a monitoring role (Wesley et al., 2001). For these reasons, it is possible that some consultees will resist terminating the consultation process, even if the intervention plan was successful (Wesley & Buysse, 2004). Stage Eight is a time when the consultant must try to discern whether any new needs that are identified are within his or her area of expertise as well as whether the consultee and the program could address them independent of consultation.

COMMUNICATION STRATEGIES AND INTERPERSONAL APPROACH

Parsons (1996) described specific tasks that the consultant can perform to maximize positive communication and rekindle energy and commitment when consultation goals are not met. The following tasks typically begin during Stage Seven, when it first becomes apparent that the interventions did not work, and continue through the summary conference to plan next steps. The *consultant*

- Conveys a sense of hopefulness that the information the consultant and consultee have gained about what has not worked will help them identify effective strategies in the future

- Shares a personal view about positive aspects of the working relationship and his or her levels of satisfaction with the outcomes

- Invites the consultee to disclose his or her view of the working relationship and his or her degree of satisfaction with the outcomes

- Resists the temptation to patch the intervention plan or to simply restart it—it is important to consider the situation in light of the new information and to generate new interventions

- Invites the consultee to begin a new consultation process that offers the opportunity to consider the new data in an effort to redefine the problem and generate related goals and strategies (Parsons, 1996)

    Just as the consultant invited continued input and feedback from the consultee in writing the final report, he or she ensures that decisions are made jointly during the summary conference and that there is clear and mutual understanding about next steps.

In some situations, the consultee may decide to discontinue consultation; the consultant may or may not agree with this decision. The consultant should reflect on his or her formal and informal relationships both within the system in which the consultee works and with the consultee and examine how the nature of these relationships has facilitated and limited consultation. The consultant should consider how his or her presence and structured interventions have affected the program, including a possible impact on those not directly involved in consultation. He or she must try to understand the pressures that such an impact may have had on the consultee. Such impacts may include possible changes in the relationships between other classroom teachers who are not involved in consultation and the consultee, who has received recognition for her efforts by the program director, or pressure on the consultee to limit his or her use of program resources in addressing consultation goals (Wesley & Buysse, 2004). The consultant needs to consider the distribution of power in the consulting relationship and to compare the outcomes with what the consultee said he or she wanted at the outset. The purpose of such reflection is not to blame the consultant for the purpose of inducing guilt but to develop insight about the complexities of consultation. The right of the consultee to voluntarily participate in consultation includes his or her right to terminate it (Hughes et al., 2001). Exercising this right does not necessarily indicate a negative reaction to the consultation process or the consultant.

WHAT IF?

What if the consultant and consultee disagree about next steps? For example, the IFSP team decides that once-weekly services in the early childhood classroom are sufficient for a young toddler with a disability; however, the consultee requests that the consultant continue visiting the classroom twice per week to help him or her feel more confident while working with the child. The consultant's perspective is that the consultee possesses the skills necessary to provide appropriate and nurturing care to the toddler and that the IFSP can be implemented with one visit per week. Or perhaps a program director has requested that the consultant continue visiting a particular classroom because he or she believes it is necessary to maintain the quality improvements that consultation has produced.

Both of these examples reflect dependency by consultees on the consultant and a lack of their confidence in solving problems independently. An effective consultant anticipates when these situations may arise well before Stage Eight. He or she has reflected on the consultee's degree of participation during the processes of assessing the situation, defining the focus of concern, and identifying goals and strategies. The effective consultant and the consultee have discussed the consultee's ability to use the same instruments and methods to assess and address similar situations in the future. This consultant routinely has invited the consultee to disclose his or her comfort level during Stage Six, when strategies are implemented largely in the absence of the consultant. He or she has increased her support and perhaps tried new strategies along the way to increase consultee confidence and skill. When a consultee continues to express a need for continued support from the consultant about issues that have, in the consultant's view, been resolved through consultation, it may be an indication that internal supports are lacking at the early childhood program.

The consultant may want to explore this possibility with the consultee by asking him or her to describe resources within the program that can be called on for continued support. Such resources may include regular meetings with other teachers serving children with disabilities, conferences with the family of the child who has a disability, participation in an e-mail discussion group with other teachers in the community who are engaged in quality enhancement initiatives, and periodic meetings with his or her supervisor or mentor teacher. The consultant may suggest some of these ideas him- or herself or may consider setting up a temporary period of time during which the teacher can check in via e-mail or telephone.

As discussed in Chapter 2, throughout the process of consultation, the consultant must be aware of the professional boundaries of the consulting relationship and take care not to step into the arena of counseling. This means focusing on work-related challenges and referring the consultee elsewhere if he or she expresses personal or psychological needs.

CONCLUSION

As detailed in Chapter 9, the evaluation process should include summative and formative methods for determining changes made as a result of the interventions and consultee satisfaction with the consultation process and the consultant. The summary conference provides an opportunity to examine these findings in detail as well as to identify any unexpected outcomes—for example, a modification in an activity center to promote access for a child with a disability increased all of the children's interest in that center. The consultant and consultee also should discuss the consultee's readiness to continue efforts to improve his or her practice in the absence of the consultant, including the consultee's comfort with designing an evaluation of future efforts. Chapter 11 presents information about various tools that can be used to evaluate consultation processes and outcomes.

Holding a Summary Conference: Stage Eight
Case Illustration

Consultant: Karen   Parents: Juan and Patricia

Consultees: Lakesha, Molly   Child: Benita

After Karen and Lakesha had fully evaluated their Intervention Plan, they scheduled a summary conference. Karen invited Benita's parents, but they could not attend, so Karen arranged to visit their home at a later time. Karen planned to continue working with Lakesha to address other IEP goals and objectives for Benita and to help Lakesha consider ways of improving her program, but Karen knew that the summary conference would be useful for several reasons. First, she had begun to signal that her direct involvement to address some of their goals was no longer needed, and this meeting would help underscore this idea. Karen was ready to shift her attention to other concerns and goals that she and Lakesha had discussed concerning Benita, and she needed to convey this to Lakesha to get a sense of her readiness.

Karen also wanted to summarize the satisfaction that she and Lakesha felt regarding their overall experience with the consultation process. She felt very comfortable with Lakesha and it appeared that Lakesha was pleased with their consulting relationship. She wanted to discuss this and to identify areas for improvement, however, so she asked Lakesha to complete the Consultation Evaluation form to assess key aspects of the consultation process, such as Karen's content expertise, her organizational skills, and her responsiveness, as well as the effectiveness of the consultation in addressing mutual goals. Karen was also interested in Lakesha's perception about other possible benefits of consultation and invited her also to fill out the Consultee Benefits form. Lakesha agreed to complete and return the forms to Karen prior to the conference so that they could discuss the outcomes together when they meet. Part of the ensuing conversation follows.

Karen: Thanks so much, Lakesha, for your willingness to complete this evaluation form. I know we have talked all along about how we thought things were going, but this really helps me get a sense of your overall reaction to the consultation process.

Lakesha: No problem. I was glad to fill it out.

Karen: I would like to suggest that we talk a little about items 22 and 23 on the form: aspects of the consultation that were particularly strong and/or useful versus those that were weak and not useful. Would that be okay with you?

Lakesha: Sure. You can see I thought everything was really helpful, and if you look at the previous items on the form, you can see that I thought you were really organized and great at helping define our goals and at identifying resources that helped Molly and me.

Karen: Thanks, Lakesha. I recall that you and I talked a lot about resources throughout the process, especially when we were working through implementation. Is there anything that you can think of that would have improved the consultation process?

Lakesha: I thought a lot about that when I answered item 23 about aspects that were weak. I guess I wouldn't say that anything was really not useful. The only weakness I can think of was that I remember always feeling surprised at how long it took us to do some things.

Karen: Oh, I want to hear more about that. Do you remember when you first felt that way?

Lakesha: Like when we started to talk about rearranging the room. I remember thinking, "Why doesn't Karen just tell me what to do?" And then I started the ECERS-R and I remember thinking we would never get through that.

Karen: The rating scale process is pretty thorough. What do you think would have helped with the way you were feeling? Can you think of anything we should have done differently?

Lakesha: Yes and no. I mean the scale is the scale, and it's really great that I now understand it so well. It's going to make life a lot easier when we go through the state assessment process. And I get the part about why you didn't just tell me everything that I needed to do. Frankly, I think if you had done that, I wouldn't know nearly what I do now about quality, and especially about helping a child like Benita. But part of what was hard was that we were the only classroom in the program using the scale at that time. Other teachers who knew we were going to make some changes in our room would stop by and ask us why we hadn't done anything yet. I think they thought we were just slow or something, but here we were getting your services, which I guess they took to mean we should have been moving right along. Then, when the state lady came and talked about the rated license and how the scales were being used, everybody wanted to know why we already knew about the scale and they didn't!

Karen: So you were feeling some pressure from others to show some results, and at the same time, it sounds like some of your colleagues may have felt out of the loop.

Lakesha: Yeah, I guess that's it. And we just had to go through that learning process and realize things weren't going to happen overnight.

Karen: I wonder if it would have helped if we had opened up the training on the rating scale to the entire staff at Wee Care? That way, everybody would have had a sense of what you and Molly were working on, and everybody would have had the same leg up when the state consultant came.

Lakesha: That's a really good idea because I think one of the weaknesses, if you can call it that, of the consultation is that it sort of separates Molly and me from the others. We missed a couple of staff gatherings one time because we wanted to sit down with you, and we just had to make a choice about our priorities on those days. But, yeah, anything you could do to bring in the others sometimes would really help.

Karen: These insights are so helpful to me, Lakesha. These are things that I would never have thought of without your help. Am I reading your reaction correctly, though, that overall you were satisfied with the consultation experience?

Lakesha: Oh, absolutely! We can't wait to start on the new goals, and I probably wouldn't have brought these other issues up, except you asked me to be honest on this form.

Karen: I knew I could count on you for a thoughtful assessment. I'm going to give a lot of thought to how we could engage the director and other teachers, especially those in the other classroom for 3- and 4-year-olds, in our activities next time.

Final Report

Consultant __Karen__

Consultee __Lakesha__

Classroom __Threes__

Date __5/31/05__

Wee Care Child Care	
	Program

Brief history of consultation process

Who initiated __Consultation was provided to support the implementation of Benita's IEP.__

Participants __Lakesha (teacher) and Molly (teaching assistant), Karen (consultant)__

Dates consultation began and ended __9/30/04–5/30/05__

Number of visits __36__

Program/classroom description

Ages of children __The class in which Benita's enrolled serves 3- to 4-year-olds.__

Number of children and adults __There are 18 children with 2 adults.__

Hours of operation __Wee Care is open 7:30 a.m.–5:30 p.m. Monday–Friday.__

Licensure/accreditation __Wee Care has received 3 out of 5 stars in the state's rated license program. The center is in__
__the process of applying for NAEYC accreditation.__

Program/classroom strengths __Lakesha and Molly show warmth and sensitivity in their interactions with the__
children. Overall, staff seem to have positive relationships with the families and to value their involvement. Wee Care is
inclusive, and some resources are available for professional development.

Consultation goals __Although Benita's IEP addresses her specific learning needs, Lakesha and Molly wanted to__
increase Benita's communication and mobility in the classroom. As a foundation, Lakesha hoped to increase her
knowledge and skills related to working with children with cerebral palsy and physical challenges in general. A third goal
was to improve room arrangement to increase accessibility and children's interest in the centers.

Accomplishments/changes made __Lakesha and Molly attended a workshop on how to work with children with physical__
limitations and shared the session materials at the center. They continued to learn strategies for both challenging
Benita and creating opportunities for her to demonstrate competence in the classroom. They worked closely with Mrs.
Alvarez to add new words to the communication board, and they showed Benita's classmates how to use it. In addition
to rearranging the room and rotating materials that interested Benita through the centers, Lakesha encouraged
Benita to increase her mobility. Evaluations this spring indicated that in the classroom Benita was using at least 25
words on her communication board functionally and that she used her walker to walk independently between activities at
least four times each day.

From Wesley, P.W. (2000). *Improving the quality of early childhood programs: The PFI model of consultation.* Chapel Hill: The University of North Carolina, FPG Child Development Institute; adapted by permission.

Recommendations for next steps __Lakesha and I discussed the need to define a new area of focus for Benita as we__
approach the summer months. We will work with the physical therapist to determine the special mobility needs Benita
and her family may anticipate. We will assess Benita's social interactions—how often she initiates and responds to
overtures from peers.

Consultant's reflections __We hope to build on the knowledge and skills that Lakesha has gained in working with Benita.__
Lakesha is interested in readministering the environment rating scale in the consultation process. Working with Lakesha and Molly has been a rewarding experience.
Their commitment to creating enjoyable and stimulating experiences for ALL children is evident in their hard work and
enthusiasm.

Form distribution (who received this report?) __Lakesha and Molly, Mr. and Mrs. Alvarez__

From Wesley, P.W. (2000). *Improving the quality of early childhood programs: The PFI model of consultation.* Chapel Hill: The University of North Carolina, FPG Child Development Institute; adapted by permission.

Form 6. Completed Final Report form. (From Wesley, P.W. [2000]. *Improving the quality of early childhood programs: The PFI model of consultation.* Chapel Hill: The University of North Carolina, FPG Child Development Institute; adapted by permission.)

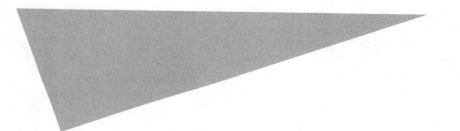

Section III

Outcomes, Applications, and Recommendations

Chapter 11

Additional Considerations for Evaluating Consultation Processes and Outcomes

Because evaluation of consultation is built into the implementation plan and reflected in Stage Seven of the consultation process, the reader may wonder why additional evaluation is addressed in a separate chapter. We believe that it is essential to think about evaluation in two distinct ways: 1) as part of the process of working with an individual program, consultee, and child to guide decision making in a particular situation and 2) as a standardized set of evaluation methods that can be used to assess consultation outcomes across a large number of individual cases as a way to understand these findings in the aggregate. The purpose of this chapter is to address this broader view of one's consultation practice as well as to provide additional information about specific tools that can be used to evaluate consultation processes and outcomes. First, however, it may be helpful to consider some of the issues and challenges related to conducting a valid evaluation of consultation practice.

In this era of public accountability in human services, the need for scientific evidence to demonstrate that consultation is both acceptable and effective should come as no surprise. Funding agencies and policymakers routinely require such evidence to justify their continued investments in an array of human service programs. Yet professionals who work with very young children and their families and engage in the practice of consultation may be motivated by other factors as well. Many express a genuine desire to understand how their work affects children, families, and professionals and programs that serve them. Given that a framework for consultation practice is still evolving and lacks an empirical foundation in the early childhood field, it is particularly important to use an evaluation of consultation processes and outcomes to guide decisions about ways to improve consultation practices. Most would agree that evaluation is a worthwhile investment of time and resources when information gained through systematic data collection leads to more effective consultation services, and, ultimately, to enhanced child and family outcomes.

Even if widespread agreement about the importance of evaluating consultation could be assumed, the fact remains that practitioners of consultation (both consultants and consultees) face a number of challenges in finding a feasible and valid approach for conducting an evaluation. For one thing, demonstrating the benefits of consultation to a third party (e.g., a young child with disabilities) through an intervention that focuses on improving the knowledge and skills of a second party (e.g., a classroom teacher) presents certain methodological challenges to researchers and practitioners alike (Erchul & Martens, 2002). Based on a review of school-based consultation outcome research, Sheridan and colleagues (1996) concluded that the majority of studies using poorly articulated models of consultation without sound theoretical bases yielded neutral or negative findings, whereas studies using models with clear conceptual frameworks (e.g., mental health, behavioral consultation) yielded positive outcomes. These findings suggest that efforts to evaluate the outcomes of consultation practice in early childhood will be strengthened when the field reaches consensus on a consultation framework and develops methods such as guidebooks and interview forms to assess standardized implementation of agreed-on consultation practices.

Another challenge in evaluating consultation is accounting for all of the possible mediating factors in the desired chain of effects (e.g., the introduction of a new curriculum, a change in the child's home situation). It is no less challenging to find appropriate methods of measuring consultation outcomes for a wide range of positive changes that are likely to occur within the child, the consultee, and the program. For example, objective measures that assess an increase in the consultee's knowledge or skills and his or her ability to solve or prevent future problems simply do not exist or are addressed mainly through self-assessment methods administered at the end of the consultation process.

Despite these challenges, researchers have developed widely accepted methods of documenting the effectiveness of consultation practice in schools. This chapter looks to this larger body of knowledge and applies these methods of evaluating consultation processes and outcomes to early childhood contexts and settings. Although much of the information presented here might be considered useful to researchers, this chapter focuses on helping practitioners of consultation find practical, effective methods of evaluating consultation, primarily for the purpose of improving their individual practices. It is hoped that in the future, there will be ways to incorporate findings from individual evaluations into the larger body of knowledge to build the evidence base for the field as a whole (Buysse, Sparkman, & Wesley, 2003; Wesley & Buysse, 2001).

The following section presents selected evaluation methods and measures that have been developed or tested through empirical research; however, they also are designed to transcend the gap between research and practice that characterizes so many evaluation efforts in education. In other words, the evaluation methods proposed here are not restricted for use only in research studies but also are appropriate for practice settings.

PLANNING FOR EVALUATION OF CONSULTATION

It is important to consider evaluation at the beginning of the consultation process rather than waiting until Stage Seven, when evaluation becomes the focus of the consultation process. Figure 5 displays an example of how a logic model can be used to guide the planning of an evaluation of consultation practice in early education contexts and settings. Although originally designed to assist in planning broad-based program evaluation efforts (Unrau, 2001), a logic model also can be used as a tool for considering the linkages among consultation services, processes, and outcomes. A logic model is based on the assumption that every human service program must have a theory of client change that provides a plausible and logical explanation of how various program components lead to desired outcomes in the children and families who receive services. Unrau noted that logic model-

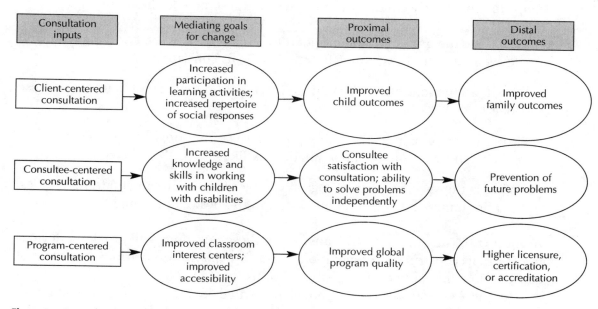

Figure 5.   Example of a logic model for evaluating consultation.

ing allows evaluators to answer questions that not only address whether a change occurred but also *how* change occurred and whether the changes were meaningful and worthwhile for clients. Moreover, whenever possible, it is recommended that client feedback be used to refine and improve the model and identify additional outcomes.

In building a logic model for evaluating consultation for an individual case, practitioners should rely on a variety of sources of information (e.g., family members, other consultants, administrators, teachers, specialists) to determine a full range of potential desired outcomes of consultation (e.g., improved child outcomes, improved program quality, enhanced professional knowledge and skill). Certainly, it is possible for a consultant to build the logic model without getting input from other stakeholders, but the end result will be limited to ideas generated by the consultant and may not reflect every important outcome, and it will not reflect all of the pathways that lead to these desired effects. Generally, the outcomes will include proximal outcomes, which are most closely associated with the direct effects of the interventions (e.g., improving the consultee's knowledge and skills), and distal outcomes, which result from the indirect effects of the intervention (e.g., improved child and family outcomes).

Gilliam and Leiter (2003) posed a number of questions that designers of program evaluation should ask themselves to help build a logic model. The questions are designed to help evaluators envision the overarching goal of the program or service as it relates to the nature of the social problem that will be addressed, the recipients of the target intervention, the desired state of change (i.e., observed changes in the child and perceived changes in the consultee's ability to assist the child in making a positive change), and the strategies used to achieved the desired results. These questions can be adapted to building a logic model for evaluating consultation in early childhood settings. Examples include the following:

- What are the primary outcome goals for children, families, and programs, and do we really think we can achieve these goals consistently?

- What are the important elements of consultation that can help us attain these goals?

- What kinds of assumptions do we make regarding how the participants will change and what that change might look like?

- What is the specific chain of logical changes that occurs in children, families, and programs that will ultimately lead to the desired outcomes?

According to Gilliam and Leiter, answering these questions will provide information to help construct the logic model and to explain how various elements of consultation are connected to goals and outcomes.

In the example of a logic model presented in Figure 5, the consultation inputs include the consultant's focus on issues of concern related to the child, the classroom teacher, and the program as a whole. This represents the full range of possible inputs, but depending on the situation, the consultant may neither focus on all of these issues at the same time nor treat them equally. Each input or area of focus is associated with mediating goals for change, such as increasing a child's participation in learning activities, increasing the consultee's knowledge and skills, or improving accessibility within a classroom. The mediating goals, in turn, are associated with both proximal outcomes (e.g., the consultee's ability to solve problems independently) and distal outcomes (e.g., improved child and family outcomes, prevention of future problems).

EVALUATING CONSULTATION PROCESSES

In considering appropriate ways to evaluate the consultation process (also referred to as *formative evaluation*), it is helpful to revisit the previously described logic model. The logic model includes assumptions about the links among consultation services, goals, and outcomes that can be used to assist in selecting an appropriate method of keeping a record of the consultation process as it unfolds. In Figure 5, the consultation focuses on child functioning, the consultee's knowledge and skills, and concerns about the quality of the early childhood program. Consequently, an evaluation of the process should include a method of monitoring whether and how each issue was addressed at every step. An evaluation of the consultation process is directly related to the continuous improvement of consultation practice as it occurs rather than at the end of the process. It answers questions such as the following:

- How did the consultee react to the suggestions that were made today?

- Did the consultation session result in a clear definition of the consultee's concerns and needs?

- How difficult was it for the consultee to implement the intervention plan in the consultant's absence?

Gathering a consistent set of information across consultation situations is critical to aggregating the findings and drawing broad conclusions to improve future consultation practice.

According to Brown et al. (1998), process data can inform the consultation process in a number of important ways. It can inform the consultant about progress toward consultation goals and assess whether key tasks within each of the consultation stages have been addressed. For example, if a consultant's records indicate that little progress is being made at the stage of selecting an appropriate strategy to address a mutual issue of concern, it may be time to shift gears and try a different approach. Over time, monitoring the consultation process across many different cases will provide consultants with normative data about how much progress to expect at different points along the way.

Another way that monitoring consultation can inform the process is by revealing certain patterns that may be used to guide the consultant's subsequent interactions with the consultee. For example, the consultant's notes or summary contact records may reveal subtle resistance to the idea of having the consultant observe a consultee's classroom or failure to implement certain agreed-on action steps, but this is discovered only after reviewing written summaries of their consultation sessions.

Process data also can be used to validate a consultant's hypothesis or promote greater understanding of the consultation case and other relevant variables. The consultant may wonder whether the consultee has additional unvoiced concerns and later find hints of these unstated concerns in written summaries of their earlier conversations. The consultant can use these insights to change course or explore other avenues as the consultant and consultee move toward addressing their mutual goals for change.

Contact Summary Form

The consultation Contact Summary form can be used by a consultant to maintain a record of every consultation session or contact (see Form 2 in Chapter 3; also see the appendix for a full-size, blank version of this form). The form includes identifying information pertaining to the consultee and program as well as the type of contact, the purpose, the focus of concern, a summary of the discussion, any decisions reached, action steps, the date of the next consultation session, and reflections on the consultation process. The consultant should complete a Contact Summary form as soon as possible following each consultation contact. Throughout the process, Contact Summary forms can be used to monitor the progress of the consultation process and to make adjustments as needed. Chapter 3 provides additional information about how the Contact Summary form is used to evaluate the consultation process.

Consultation Stages Checklist

The Consultation Stages Checklist is a tool for assessing key tasks across consultation stages. The consultant should check off when a task has been completed and use this information to ensure that no essential activities and processes have been overlooked. Chapter 9 provides additional information about how the checklist is used as a part of the evaluation process.

EVALUATING CONSULTATION OUTCOMES

Practitioners of consultation should consider assessing outcomes (also referred to as *summative evaluation*) at three levels: the client (e.g., child, child and family), the consultee (e.g., classroom teacher, parent, specialist), and the program (e.g., program quality). The following subsections explore methods for evaluating various types of outcomes.

Child Outcomes

Single-Subject Design

Sheridan et al. (1996) and many others have recommended that practitioners of consultation consider using single-subject designs in their evaluation efforts, primarily because this method offers ongoing, direct, and systematic measures of target behaviors across baseline, intervention, and follow-up phases. The traditional ABA design assesses baseline behavior (A), then introduces a treatment or intervention (B), and finally, returns to the baseline condition (A). Many variations of this basic design can involve multiple children, behaviors, and conditions. The essence of single-subject research is assessing the effects of intervention on an individual child, which corresponds with the need to understand the unique effects of consultation for individual children, consultees, and systems. Unfortunately, there is a lack of empirical evidence of the effectiveness and acceptability of single-subject design to evaluate consultation practices in early childhood settings, along with a lack of information about the evaluation of consultation in general. Consequently, we cannot offer specific recommendations about the use of single-subject design; we refer the reader to Kratochwill (1985) and Brown et al. (1998) for additional information regarding this approach. Brown et al. (1998) wisely noted that single-subject designs are consistent with the behavioral consultation model but may not correspond with other consultation models and will not be considered acceptable to all consumers of consultation. The Goal Attainment Scaling method may be more relevant and appropriate, depending on the consultation framework employed and the consumers who participate in this model.

Goal Attainment Scaling

Goal Attainment Scaling (GAS; Kiresuk, Smith, & Cardillo, 1994) has been recommended frequently to assess children's progress on a goal selected as part of the consultation process by the consultant and consultee. There are several reasons for this. First, the GAS method is consistent with the consultation process that involves setting a goal, then implementing an intervention, and finally collecting information about goal attainment. Second, the GAS method provides a consistent method for collecting outcome data across different consultation cases and clients who have a range of goals for change. Imagine how difficult it would be to select specific outcome measures to address individual goals for every child on the consultant's caseload.

For the vast majority of children receiving early education and intervention services, the consultation goal will reflect one or more goals on their IEPs or

IFSPs. The GAS consists of a 5-point scale with goal indicators representing possible outcomes along a continuum from *much less than expected* (−2) and *somewhat less than expected* (−1) on the one end, to the *expected level of outcome* (0) in the middle, and to *somewhat more than expected* (+1) and *much more than expected* (+2) on the other end (Kiresuk et al., 1994). We suggest that the consultant and consultee work together to select the goals and specify the expected level of outcomes at each level on the scale. The ratings then will represent a consensus between the consultant and consultee regarding the child's progress following intervention (see Form 9 for a sample; also see the appendix for a full-size, blank version of this form).

The following steps have been recommended for consultants and consultees to follow in completing the GAS for an individual child (Kiresuk et al., 1994):

1. Identify the issue that will be the focus of the intervention (e.g., participation in classroom activities).

2. Translate the selected issues or concern into one to three goals and label each goal (e.g., uses a communication system).

3. Select an indicator for each goal (e.g., points to pictures upon request).

4. Specify the expected level of outcome for the goal to represent the most precise indication possible of what the child is most likely to achieve as a result of the intervention (e.g., points to at least three familiar pictures upon request).

5. Specify the somewhat more and somewhat less than expected levels of outcome for the goal.

6. Specify the *much more than expected* and *much less than expected* levels of outcome.

7. Repeat these steps for each additional goal.

See the end of this chapter for an example of a completed Goal Attainment Scaling form addressing three possible goals for Benita. The GAS represents a measure of Benita's postintervention functions based on predetermined scaled goals. The consultant (Karen) and consultee (Lakesha) can use the goal attainment scale to assess the extent to which Benita met or did not meet each of her goals, reaching consensus about Benita's level of goal attainment and indicating this level by circling the appropriate box for each goal. Whenever possible, it is advisable to ask an independent, outside observer to score each goal to obtain another source of information. According to Kiresuk and colleagues (1994), the key to effective GAS is the goal-setting process itself. It is essential to set the expected level of outcome at a level that is realistic for each child—neither too easy nor too difficult.

Goal Attainment Scaling

Child _____

Program

Teacher _____

Date goals set and expected levels of outcome specified

Consultant _____

(prior to intervention) _____
                                        Month/Date/Year

Date consensus reached on goal attainment*

(following intervention) _____
                                        Month/Date/Year

*Indicate consensus ratings by circling or marking the appropriate box.

Level of attainment	Scale 1	Scale 2	Scale 3
	_____ _____ _____	_____ _____ _____	_____ _____ _____
−2 Much less than expected			
−1 Somewhat less than expected			
0 Expected level of outcome			
+1 Somewhat more than expected			
+2 Much more than expected			
Comments			

From Kiresuk, T.J., Smith, A., & Cardillo, J.E. (1994). *Goal attainment scaling: Applications, theory, and measurement* (p. 18). Mahwah, NJ: Lawrence Erlbaum Associates; adapted by permission. Further reproduction prohibited without permission from the publisher.

Form 9.   (From Kiresuk, T.J., Smith, A., & Cardillo, J.E. [1994]. *Goal attainment scaling: Applications, theory, and measurement* [p. 18]. Mahwah, NJ: Lawrence Erlbaum Associates; adapted by permission. Further reproduction prohibited without permission from the publisher.)

Consultee Outcomes

Consultation Evaluation Form

The Consultation Evaluation form can be used to assess the consultee's satisfaction with the consultation process and content as well as the consultant's interpersonal style (see Form 7 in Chapter 10; also see the appendix for a full-size, blank version of this form). The scale consists of 16 items rated on a scale from 1 (*strongly disagree*) to 4 (*strongly agree*), along with space for comments and recommendations for improving future consultations. This is one of many consultation satisfaction forms available, but it is relatively easy to complete and is organized in a way that summarizes satisfaction across key consulting domains (e.g., efficacy of consultation, consultant's expertise, consultant's interpersonal style). The consultee should complete this form at the end of the consultation process, as part of the evaluation and summary steps described in Chapter 10.

Consultee Benefits Form

The Consultee Benefits form (see Form 8 in Chapter 10; also see the appendix for a full-size, blank version of this form) consists of 12 items rated on a scale from 1 (*strongly disagree*) to 4 (*strongly agree*). This scale can be used to determine if consultees perceive that they are more prepared to address a range of issues that include understanding the complexities of the problem situation, clarifying the problem situation, identifying alternative strategies, trying out some of their own ideas, making decisions to manage the problem, and feeling equipped to address similar problems in the future. Once again, the consultee should complete this form at the end of the consultation process described in Chapter 10.

Program Quality Enhancement

Environment Rating Scales

The ECERS-R (Harms et al., 1998) and its sister scales, the ITERS-R (Harms et al., 2003), the Family Day Care Rating Scale (FDCRS; Harms & Clifford, 1989), and the School-Age Care Environment Rating Scale (SACERS; Harms, Jacobs, & White, 1995) have been used widely to assess quality for both practical and research purposes. All scales are recognized internationally and draw on research evidence, professional values, and practical knowledge to define quality and early childhood environments. These scales rate quality across 32–49 items on a 7-point scale with descriptors for 1 (*inadequate*), 3 (*minimal*), 5 (*good*), and 7 (*excellent*). Items are grouped into five to seven global categories. Studies examining the psychometric properties of the scales reported high reliability and validity (Harms et al., 1998; Peisner-Feinberg & Burchinal, 1997; Whitebook, Howes, & Phillips, 1990).

Building on the concept that improving global quality in early childhood programs is a critical first step to promoting successful inclusive placements of young children with disabilities (Bailey, McWilliam, Buysse, & Wesley, 1998; Odom & McEvoy, 1990), at least two studies have examined the use of environment rating scales as a foundation for consultation practice. Wesley (1994) and Palsha and Wesley (1998) described using the rating scales as a springboard for collaboration between consultants and consultees as they identify goals and strategies for change, including resources, methods, time lines, and work scopes. Both studies document statistically significant changes in many subscale dimensions of quality from pre- to posttest at the conclusion of consultation. The consultant and consultee should separately administer the same rating scale (choosing one that is based on the children's ages and setting) and meet to discuss their observations and scores. The purpose of this meeting is to reach consensus about the program's strengths and to identify areas in which improvements can be made. Consultants and consultees may want to develop goals corresponding to specific items on the scale and to reflect broad needs related to subscales. They also may use the scales to consider the needs of children with disabilities that are related to dimensions such as furnishings, personal care, use of language, activities, and interactions. By administering the scale again after the implementation stage, the consultant and consultee are able to measure their accomplishments by comparing pre- and post-consultation scores.

Quality of Inclusive Experiences Measure

The Quality of Inclusive Experiences Measure (QuIEM; Wolery et al., 2000) was developed specifically to assess program variables thought to influence outcomes for young children with disabilities who are enrolled in inclusive early childhood settings. The instrument is available in either an abbreviated or unabridged version. It can be used to assist in improving services for a child with disabilities who is enrolled in an inclusive setting and to collect information for evaluating a program or conducting a research study that assesses the quality of inclusive programs. The QuIEM was not designed to measure staff performance, to determine whether a given program would be a suitable placement for a particular child, or to assess the extent to which programs work collaboratively with families.

The QuIEM authors note that no other existing measures of global program quality were designed with this expressed purpose in mind, although the QuIEM was designed to be used in conjunction with the ECERS-R and other similar quality measures. One of the primary rationales for using the QuIEM stems from the fact that children with disabilities may be enrolled in high-quality early childhood programs that do not address their individual goals and needs. The QuIEM was based on five assumptions: 1) children's learning and development occur from their ongoing interactions with the environment, 2) practices of inclusive child care programs influence children's learning and development, 3) high-quality programs for typically developing children are not necessarily high-quality programs for young children with disabilities, 4) providing high-quality inclusive experiences for children with disabilities is a complex task, and 5) the QuIEM is needed because of the growing number of early childhood programs throughout the United States that enroll young children with disabilities.

The QuIEM is organized around the following seven dimensions:

1. Program goals and purposes

2. Staff supports and perceptions

3. Accessibility of the physical environment

4. Individualization

5. Children's participation and engagement

6. Adult–child contacts and relationships

7. Child–child contacts and interactions

Information for the QuIEM is collected through a variety of methods, including document reviews (e.g., the program's philosophy statement, children's IEPs or IFSPs), observations of classroom practices and children's interactions with other children and adults, staff interviews, and written questionnaires. Most items across the seven dimensions of quality are scored from 1 (*very poor*) to 5 (*excellent*). Subscale total scores are helpful for use in program evaluation and research. The QuIEM authors estimate that the comprehensive version of the instrument requires 3–4 hours on each of the 2–3 days it takes to administer, with less time required when only certain subscales are administered. The abbreviated version requires 3 hours per day for 2 days.

Because there is no research examining the use of the QuIEM to support consultation practice and to assess program level outcomes related to consultation in early childhood settings, we view the QuIEM as a promising tool to support program quality enhancement efforts. Until further research becomes available, we recommend that practitioners of consultation view the QuIEM as a method of gathering additional information about global program quality in inclusive settings in conjunction with the ECERS-R or a similar instrument. This may mean selecting one or two subscales to administer to augment information already gathered about the program's accessibility, children's participation or engagement in inclusive settings, or the availability of staff supports to address the individual needs of children with disabilities who are enrolled in the program. The QuIEM also could be used to assist programs in obtaining a higher rated license.

CONCLUSION

This chapter presented tools that can be used to plan and conduct an evaluation in early childhood settings. Although it may not be feasible to use all of these tools, it is critical that practitioners identify at least some methods that are useful to them to monitor the consultation process and determine the effectiveness of consultation for children, parents, and teachers.

Goal Attainment Scaling

Child   Benita

Teacher   Lakesha

Consultant   Karen

	Wee Care Child Care
	Program

Date goals set and expected levels of outcome specified

(prior to intervention) _____9/7/04_____
Month/Date/Year

Date consensus reached on goal attainment*

(following intervention) _____5/31/05_____
Month/Date/Year

*Indicate consensus ratings by circling or marking the appropriate box.

Level of attainment	Scale 1 Uses a communication system	Scale 2 Uses a walker	Scale 3 Responds to request from peer
−2 Much less than expected	Points to zero familiar pictures upon request	Cannot pull to stand	Does not point to, touch, or hand familiar object to peer upon request
−1 Somewhat less than expected	Points to one to two familiar pictures upon request	Pulls to stand and maintains standing for less than 10 minutes	(Points to or touches familiar object but does not hand it to peer upon request)
0 Expected level of outcome	(Points to three familiar pictures upon request)	Pulls to stand and maintains standing for 10 minutes	Hands one familiar object to peer upon request
+1 Somewhat more than expected	Points to four to five familiar pictures upon request	(Pulls to stand, maintains standing for 10 minutes and walks several steps)	Hands two to three different familiar objects to peer upon request
+2 Much more than expected	Points to six or more familiar pictures upon request	Pulls to stand, maintains standing for 10 minutes and walks at least 20 steps	Hands more than three different familiar objects to peer upon request
Comments	Include pictures from home and school.	Consider possible distractions as well as motivational factors.	Use objects from dramatic play area.

From Kiresuk, T.J., Smith, A., & Cardillo, J.E. (1994). *Goal attainment scaling: Applications, theory, and measurement* (p. 18). Mahwah, NJ: Lawrence Erlbaum Associates; adapted by permission. Further reproduction prohibited without permission from the publisher.

Form 9. Completed Goal Attainment Scaling form. (From Kiresuk, T.J., Smith, A., & Cardillo, J.E. [1994]. *Goal attainment scaling: Applications, theory, and measurement* [p. 18]. Mahwah, NJ: Lawrence Erlbaum Associates; adapted by permission. Further reproduction prohibited without permission from the publisher.)

Chapter 12

Contexts and Settings Associated with Consultation

What should practitioners know about the contexts and settings associated with consultation targeting young children and their families? Where should consultants expect to serve these children, and how do different contexts influence consultation practices? Which early education disciplines and systems of care are most likely to be associated with particular settings? What other contextual factors might influence the consultation process? This chapter explores the answers to these questions by first taking a bird's-eye view of the early childhood field and then zooming in to get a closer look at the issues within specific settings and contexts. It begins with a brief overview of early childhood services. Then, it introduces aspects of the sociopolitical context that are contributing to changes in the early education and intervention field and describes related consultation challenges.

OVERVIEW OF EARLY CHILDHOOD SERVICES

For several reasons, it has been suggested that early childhood programs in the United States resemble a loosely woven patchwork quilt. For one thing, early childhood services take many different forms: private and public prekindergarten programs, for-profit and nonprofit child care centers, regulated and unregulated family child care homes, Head Start and Early Head Start programs, and specialized programs for children with disabilities and other special health care needs, along with a variety of other programs and child care arrangements. Rather than being organized as a single system, education and care services for young children (from birth to 5 years) and their families frequently are fragmented, duplicated, disconnected, and determined by the specific eligibility requirements and priorities of various funding sources at the local, state, and federal levels. In fact, Kagan and Neuman (2000) concluded that three distinct but loosely configured early childhood fields have emerged as a result of this fragmentation: child care, early education, and early intervention. Furthermore, high teacher turnover, uneven program quality, widely varying funding mechanisms, and an increase in the cultural and linguistic diversity of preschoolers in the United States all contribute to the complexity of finding ways to integrate early childhood services into a single coherent system. Issues related to teacher compensation also have received considerable attention since the late 1990s, because it is now widely acknowledged that low compensation makes it difficult to recruit and retain qualified early childhood teachers, particularly within child care programs. Compensation packages and the education of professionals in the early education and intervention fields vary widely, with teachers in the child care sector having fewer educational opportunities and receiving lower wages than public school teachers in prekindergarten classrooms.

Despite these challenges, the demand for high-quality early care and education has surged since the early to mid-1990s, as more women with preschool children enter the work force, either voluntarily or out of economic necessity. In light of this, it is rather remarkable that the vast majority of families who seek early childhood services appear to navigate the service maze successfully, finding suitable early childhood arrangements for their children. Yet, it should be noted that many other families are forced to settle for less desirable programs because they are unaware of available options, because higher-quality programs are not accessible to them, or because they simply cannot afford certain programs. It is equally important to acknowledge that still other families choose to rear their preschool children at home, taking advantage of various community resources, neighborhood playgroups, and other informal arrangements to enrich their children's early childhood experiences. Regardless of the particular early childhood arrangements and services that parents provide for their children, mounting evidence has led to a new understanding of the importance of early life experiences as well as the changing circumstances under which families of very young children live and work in the early 21st century. These circumstances in turn affect the way in which society nurtures and cares for these children (Shonkoff & Phillips, 2000).

With this admittedly brief overview of the early childhood landscape as a framework, we now turn to a discussion of several trends that are influencing and changing the early childhood field.

CHANGES IN THE EARLY CHILDHOOD FIELD

The Sociopolitical Context

Consultants who work in early childhood settings may observe a renewed interest and enthusiasm in the early childhood field that was not as apparent even at the end of the 1990s. Prompted in part by research showing the critical importance of early brain development, many states, along with the federal government, are making major investments in developing new initiatives or improving existing early childhood services for children ages birth to 5 years and their families. Although it is undoubtedly an exciting period in the history of the early childhood field, some of the renewed interest in the early childhood period has given rise to dramatic changes in notions of what constitutes appropriate early education as well as in ideas about the best way to prepare young children to succeed when they enter kindergarten. It is important that practitioners of consultation (both consultants and consultees) be aware of these developments because they form the sociopolitical context of their work. As these trends are reflected in adopted practices through the implementation of state and federal policies, they can influence the organization and delivery of services and change the way interventions developed through consultation are perceived by parents, administrators, and policy makers.

Kagan and Neuman (2000) identified three trends in the United States that have focused national attention on early education issues and helped to influence attitudes about the importance of these services for very young children and their families. These trends include widely held beliefs regarding the importance of the quality of early childhood experiences, changes in ideas about the meaning of school readiness, and the impact of welfare reform on the availability of quality early education and intervention services. Although the specific issues that form the sociopolitical context of the early childhood field will continue to evolve, the trends identified by Kagan and Neuman represent the newest directions for the field and perhaps will result in the biggest impact on services in the future.

The Critical Importance of Quality Early Childhood Experiences

The quality of early care and education has been at the forefront of research in the early childhood field since the early 1990s. This research provides ample evidence that the quality of early childhood programs is an important consideration in determining social, cognitive, and language outcomes for young children, particularly for those who live in poverty (Bryant, Burchinal, Lau, & Sparling, 1994; Cost, Quality, & Child Outcomes Study Team, 1995; Howes, Phillips, & Whitebook, 1992; Lamb, 1997).

The definition of *quality* in the literature has been conceptualized broadly to encompass all aspects of children's surroundings, care, education, and experiences that are thought to be beneficial to development and well-being. The dimensions of quality include both process quality indicators (i.e., the curriculum, instructional practices, and teacher–child interactions) as well as structural quality indicators (i.e., characteristics of the program such as staff–child ratio, group size, and qualifications of the teaching staff). Although each dimension is important, the quality of the teaching staff (in terms of teacher education and training) may be of overriding importance in determining program quality (Cost, Quality, & Child Outcomes Study Team, 1995). Although further delineation of the quality of the teaching staff is needed, critical dimensions are likely to include teaching and caregiving behaviors such as appropriate instructional practices, responsiveness to children's socioemotional needs and individual differences, equal attention to every developmental domain, and knowledge related to creating a safe and inquiry-driven learning environment.

At least one study suggested that the definition of quality inclusive early childhood programs that enroll children with and without disabilities is still evolving (Buysse, Skinner, & Grant, 2001). Based on interviews with parents and professionals, the authors concluded that quality inclusion is a two-dimensional construct encompassing both general early childhood practices and principles (e.g., qualified personnel, a well-designed classroom, developmentally appropriate practices) and individualization (e.g., therapies and special services integrated into daily routines, adaptations of the curriculum and environment, reductions in staff–child ratios), which is considered the hallmark of special education.

The Importance of Quality Early Childhood Programs for Consultation

As of 2004, there is widespread agreement about the importance of quality in early childhood programs for young children and a growing awareness of effective strategies for enhancing the quality of existing programs. At the same time, the emphasis on quality programs and services has created some challenges and dilemmas that consultants should consider as they carry out their consultation agenda. The first challenge is that despite the research showing the importance of quality care and education for young children, the majority of early childhood programs in the United States are of mediocre to poor quality (Cost, Quality, & Child Outcomes Study Team, 1995). Perhaps more troubling is the finding that even lower quality care is evident in programs serving infants and toddlers, raising concerns about the potential for these programs to meet minimum health and safety standards for these children. There are many well-conceived ideas about how to address the problem of poor-quality programs in the United States. One recommendation is to fund early care and education programs through the public and private sectors on a per-child basis, consistent with the way funding is determined for elementary school–age children (Kagan & Neuman, 2000).

Because a solution to this problem does not appear to be just around the corner, consultants can expect the issue of quality early childhood programming to affect several aspects of their work for the foreseeable future. The issue of program quality emerges almost immediately when professionals move into consultation roles. To illustrate, consultants who work in early childhood settings frequently encounter wide variability in program quality and must decide how much effort to spend on improving a poor quality program versus addressing another goal for change identified by the consultee or prescribed by an IEP (Sadler, 2002; Wesley et al., 2001). Indeed, one study found that a primary source of discomfort with consultation among professionals in early intervention stemmed from the characteristics of the programs that served as consultation sites (e.g., high staff turnover, low levels of staff education, large classroom size, inadequate staff–child ratio) (Wesley et al., 2001). Many consultants in this study believed that factors related to the global quality of the programs were out of their control; as a result, the consultants were unable to identify strategies for improving these conditions. Even if these consultants could identify ways to improve these programs, many believed that working to improve program quality was outside their realm of responsibility.

In the case illustration presented in Chapters 3–10, the consultant (Karen) concluded that the room arrangement and cluttered environment might be contributing to 3½-year-old Benita's mobility challenges as well as to other classroomwide concerns, but she needed to balance her concerns about program quality with child-specific concerns identified by the consultee (Lakesha). Although there is no simple solution to address such dilemmas, we recommend that the consultant aim to address individual goals and particular areas of concern within broader areas for programmatic change, such as improving room arrangements and making curricular adaptations.

Some early childhood consultants may find that they lack expertise in addressing program quality issues through consultation. A consultant with a background in early intervention or early childhood special education may have little or no experience as a classroom teacher; in turn, he or she may lack knowledge and skills related to implementing a general early childhood curriculum and planning an appropriate learning environment for typically developing children. The direct experience of these consultants could be limited to working with individual children with disabilities and their families. In these cases, consultants must quickly gain new knowledge and skill in the area of developmentally appropriate practice and general early childhood education practices. One way to learn about the dimensions of global program quality is by acquiring the skills necessary to administer the ECERS-R (Harms et al., 1998) and related scales for infant-toddler programs and other child care settings (FDCRS, Harms & Clifford, 1989; ITERS-R, Harms et al., 2003; SACERS, Harms et al., 1996). Chapter 11 provides additional information about how to use the ECERS-R as part of program-level consultation in early childhood settings.

Changes in Notions of the Meaning of School Readiness

The topic of school readiness dominates national discussions regarding the need to restructure early education programs in the United States. Until recently, there has been fairly widespread agreement about the necessary foundations for helping young children to make a smooth transition into kindergarten and to experience early school success. The foundations for school readiness and school success for young children (birth to 5 years) traditionally have included child qualities related to good physical health and mental health, effective communication skills, and an enthusiastic and curious approach to learning. Qualities related to academic readiness—such as recognizing the alphabet, counting, and knowing basic concepts—have been viewed as less critical than those associated with being healthy and well adjusted (Harradine & Clifford, 1996; Morisset, 1994; Welch & White, 1999). The findings of the Goal One work group, as part of the National Education Goals Panel, essentially validated these critical dimensions of school readiness and also suggested several possible new directions for investing early in young children's transition to school—for example, providing high-quality early education for children considered at risk for school failure and enhancing parent involvement efforts (Kagan, Moore, & Bredekamp, 1995; Love, 2001; Meisels, 1999; U.S. Department of Education, 1991).

National policies that emphasize the importance of literacy and children's preparedness to read as a key goal during prekindergarten and kindergarten are changing the meaning of the term *school readiness* in the United States. In response to these policy changes as well as to less articulated concerns about the United States' future as part of a global economy, young children's readiness to succeed in school has become a critical issue (Kagan & Neuman, 2000). One example of this is the Good Start, Grow Smart early childhood initiative, which includes as its centerpiece changes to the Head Start program to focus more on children's literacy skills and academic readiness (for more information, see http://www .whitehouse.gov/infocus/earlychildhood). Such initiatives and policies appear to be influencing how states and local school districts define school readiness and have prompted the creation of new state standards to assess children's school achievement in prekindergarten and kindergarten. The new emphasis on academic learning in defining school readiness also stems from research suggesting that many children enter kindergarten ill prepared (e.g., are unable to follow directions, have difficulty working independently and as part of a group) (Rimm-Kaufman, Pianta, & Cox, 2000).

The notion of redefining school readiness to emphasize cognitive learning and early reading skills has stirred controversy and debate in the early childhood field. In reaction to changes in the school readiness agenda, numerous experts in the early childhood field have published works that reiterate the interrelatedness of development and the important contributions of social and emotional development to school readiness (e.g., see Child Mental Health Foundations and Agencies Network, 2001; Ewing Marion Kauffman Foundation, 2002; Love, 2001; Raver, 2002; Sherrod, 2002; Shonkoff & Phillips, 2000). The essence of many of these publications reflects an uneasiness with policies and programs that place too much importance on learning to read at an early age.

One study found that parents of kindergarten children, teachers, and principals also expressed similar discomfort with changes in the conceptualization of school readiness and corresponding changes in the kindergarten curriculum (Wesley & Buysse, 2003). At the same time, this study suggested some ambivalence about the meaning of *school readiness* among early childhood professionals. For example, kindergarten teachers wanted policy makers to understand that children needed time for exploration and play, but their main message to parents was to work harder to be their children's first teachers and to help their children acquire the required discipline and basic skills to succeed in kindergarten.

School Readiness and Consultation Practice

How will changes in the meaning and definition of school readiness affect practitioners of consultation in early childhood settings? Since 2001, states have been involved in developing "early learning standards" to specify clear results and expectations for prekindergarten children as a way to align child outcomes with the curriculum and to guide instruction and learning across all developmental domains and approaches to learning (Scott-Little, Kagan, & Frelow, 2003a, 2003b). These standards focus on children's development rather than on expectations for the learning environment or for the program children are attending. It is not yet clear how these standards will be applied to diverse learners such as children with disabilities or English language learners. We expect these new standards to have a significant impact on early childhood curricula and, in turn, on the child-centered and program-level goals that consultants and consultees select as part of the consultation process.

Consultants who always have sought ways to help children with disabilities gain access to the general curriculum likely will face additional challenges in assisting these children to learn academic and literacy skills that other children of this age group are now widely expected to learn. Many prekindergarten programs have shifted toward an expectation that young children will show progress developing such skills as number and letter recognition and phonemic and phonological awareness—academic outcomes formerly associated with kindergarten. Practitioners of consultation need to determine whether certain academic goals are appropriate for particular children with disabilities and to continue to rely on a range of curricular modifications and adaptations to help these children gain access to the general curriculum. Table 4 describes an approach for thinking about these modifications and examples of what they might look like in an early childhood classroom setting. In addition to these curricular modifications, consultants and consultees should consider ways of embedding learning opportunities to address goals and objectives for children with disabilities throughout daily routines and activities. To assist in planning and implementing this approach, many professionals find it helpful to create an activity matrix for a particular child, plotting learning opportunities throughout the daily schedule along the vertical axis and IEP or IFSP objectives along the horizontal axis (Horn, Lieber, Sandall, Schwartz, & Wolery, 2002).

Table 4.   Curriculum modifications

Modification	Description	Examples
Environmental support	Change the physical, social, or temporal learning environment to promote child engagement and learning.	Before children arrive, set up play scenes in a couple of interest centers to suggest possible activities in those areas. For example, arrange dolls eating at the table in the housekeeping center or create a simple garage with blocks and park a toy vehicle near it in the block center.
		Ensure that traffic areas in the classroom are wide enough to accommodate a child using a walker or wheelchair.
Material adaptations	Modify classroom toys and materials so that children can participate fully and as independently as possible.	Stabilize toys to surfaces by using Velcro or masking tape.
		Glue craft sticks as handles to the pages of board books to make it easier for a toddler to turn each page.
Special equipment	Use switches or special devices to increase a child's level of participation.	Use bolsters or pillows to support a child who has difficulty sitting without assistance.
		Integrate adaptive chairs into the interest centers to make it easy for a child with physical challenges to make smooth transitions.
Use of children's preferences	Incorporate a child's interests into activities to motivate the child to learn.	Place a favorite toy in an interest center that the child rarely explores.
		Augment classroom materials to reflect the special interests of a child. For example, add photographs of a child and his or her pet in the science area.
Simplifying the activity	Reduce an activity into smaller parts.	Help a child complete a puzzle one piece at a time.
		Provide advanced notice about classroom transitions, allowing some children to start early to make the change.
Adult support	Provide encouragement, guidance, and support or rearrange a naturally occurring event to increase a child's ability to participate in a learning activity.	Give a child directions or the words to use to participate during an activity.
		Arrange for a child to have an opportunity or turn to participate and suggest a role for that child.
Peer support	Create an environment that is conducive to positive relations with peers.	Allow ample opportunities for children to make choices and to select their own playmates and friends.
		Show all children how to use a child's unique communication system.

Sources: Odom (2002); Wesley, Dennis, and Tyndall (1998).

It is unclear how young children with developmental delays will fare in the current school readiness milieu. Parents and professionals have raised questions about the possibility of children "failing" kindergarten screenings and being sent home for another year, despite a legal entitlement to attend kindergarten at age 5 (Wesley & Buysse, 2003). Practitioners of consultation may find themselves having to advocate for young children who develop and learn at different rates from their peers so that they will not be retained or denied access to school entry. Furthermore, practitioners of consultation may need to advocate for learning goals and activities that promote development within the social and emotional domains, as well as in the cognitive and language areas. In this book's extended case illustration, the consultant and consultee agreed to focus on how Benita was relating to others in the classroom as well as on helping her learn communication and cognitive skills. In an early childhood program driven by a curriculum that primarily emphasizes literacy and numeracy skills, it may be more challenging for the consultant and consultee to find ways to incorporate social and emotional intervention goals, even though the notion that all developmental domains are inextricably linked is a fundamental tenet of early childhood education. In addition, professionals will have to consider how they will measure progress in young children who do not score well on standardized tests or end-of-grade assessments.

Finally, given the recent emphasis on academic learning for young children, it is even more important for all professionals to find ways to work in partnership with families to prepare children with diverse abilities and experiences for school success. It is hoped that parents, professionals, and administrators will engage in collective questioning and problem solving to address a host of issues related to school readiness policies and practices in the future.

Welfare Reform

Welfare reform represents yet another sociopolitical context for consultation practice in early childhood settings. The Personal Responsibility and Work Opportunity Reconciliation Act (PRWORA) of 1996 (PL 104-193) was enacted to reduce the number of young children growing up in single-parent households and to require mothers to move from welfare to work. In their commentary, Shields and Behrman (2002) concluded that families with low incomes generally have fared well under these reforms, with fewer children living in poverty and single-parent homes. In families with school-age children, welfare reform also is associated with reductions in behavior problems and improvements in academic performance. But what is known about the effects of welfare reform on young children (birth to 5 years)?

Welfare Reform and Consultation in Early Childhood Settings

One of the biggest impacts of the welfare reform movement has been the dramatic increase in state and federal spending on programs for prekindergarten children and child care (Shields & Berhman, 2002). In addition to increased enrollment within existing programs (Head Start, Early Head Start, Title I Early Education, child care initiatives), the vast majority of states now offer families of young children some other form of state-sponsored prekindergarten program, many aimed primarily at improving the likelihood that children exposed to poverty and other risk factors will succeed when they enter kindergarten. Most families in the welfare system appear to rely on relative care and other informal child care arrangements, such as neighbors or baby sitters, but there is some evidence that these families utilize more formal early childhood programs as they make the transition from the welfare system into stable jobs (Fuller, Kagan, Caspary, & Gauthier, 2002). Although research suggests that children from families that receive welfare benefit the most from early education programs, uneven access to high-quality services limits the extent to which many of these children actually participate in these programs. Finding suitable early childhood arrangements may be particularly challenging for families with low incomes that have young children with disabilities.

Practitioners of consultation must recognize that welfare reform policies have changed some of the conditions under which many intervention programs were developed (Raver, 2002). For example, new policies that require mothers of young children to work outside the home have caused early childhood programs that rely on home visiting or include parent involvement opportunities to reconsider their approach. For consultants and consultees who strive to coordinate the consultation process with families' needs and priorities, a significant challenge may stem from added stress on family functioning that results from economic demands and decreased time to participate in planning and implementing interventions developed through consultation. Finding a place and time to meet with families during the consultant's typical working hours is likely to be difficult, if not impossible. At the same time, it is essential that consultants continue to seek effective ways of serving families whose caregiving practices and beliefs may not correspond closely to their own (Fuller et al., 2002). Finding ways of building trust with families in the welfare system, many of whom have less experience and comfort with formal education programs, may be particularly important in establishing effective parent–professional partnerships.

SETTINGS AND SYSTEMS OF CARE ASSOCIATED WITH CONSULTATION IN EARLY CHILDHOOD

Table 5 presents the primary settings and systems of care associated with consultation practice in early childhood settings. The systems of care represent broad conceptual categories that reflect the various forms of early childhood services. These include general early care and education programs, early education programs targeting children from families with low incomes, early intervention and early childhood special education, mental health, and health care. As mentioned previously, these systems actually represent a loose configuration or network of programs serving similar individuals, but they are not necessarily linked organizationally. For example, both Title I and Head Start programs are included in the low-income category, but these programs are organized and administered differently and have different funding sources. The table allows the reader to identify settings, such as homes or child care centers, that consultants associated with particular service systems are most likely to encounter.

Table 5. Early childhood settings and systems of care associated with consultation

Setting	Systems				
	Early care and education	Early education for children from families with low incomes	Early intervention and early childhood special education	Mental health	Health care
Home			●		
Family child care home	●		●		
Child care center	●		●		
Private preschool program	●		●		
Head Start, Early Head Start, and Migrant Head Start		●	●		
Public school prekindergarten	●	●	●		
Public school prekindergarten for children with disabilities			●		
Specialized center for children with disabilities			●		
Other community settings (e.g., neighborhood playgroups, recreational programs)			●		
Clinics, hospitals, and public health centers					●
Mental health centers				●	
Other (e.g., foster care, relative care, homeless shelter)			●		

Although the case illustration in Chapters 3–10 focused on one primary setting—a child care center—the consultation practices and processes described could have been implemented in a home setting, a public school classroom, another community setting, or any of the other settings listed in Table 5. Similarly, the consultant in the case study represented the early intervention and early childhood special education system, but depending on the situation, a consultant also could work as part of the general early education system, the education system for children from families with low incomes, the mental health system, or the health care system.

Consultants from these various systems can be expected to differ with respect to their education, professional experience and disciplines, philosophical assumptions and beliefs, and areas of focus. For example, health care consultants who work in early childhood settings focus primarily on health and safety issues, such as injury prevention on the playground or proper diapering and hand-washing procedures. Mental health consultants with backgrounds in psychology, psychiatry, and clinical social work emphasize caregiving practices that support children's social and emotional development as well as effective strategies for addressing and preventing challenging behaviors. Early intervention consultants represent a wide range of disciplines (e.g., early childhood special education, physical therapy, speech-language pathology, psychology, occupational therapy, social work), but collectively, their work generally focuses on addressing the individual goals of children with disabilities and their families in a variety of contexts that include the home, family child care homes, center-based programs, hospitals and clinics, and neighborhood and community settings. Consultants who work in programs serving children from families with low incomes or consultants who represent the general early childhood field may focus on improving global program quality and supporting classroom practices that enhance children's academic learning and literacy skills. Although the content of the consultation will vary depending on the consultant and the system of care that he or she represents, the consultation process and strategies used in these different situations are viewed as essentially the same.

The next section explores how contexts associated with broad setting categories, such as the home or center-based programs, coincide with systems of care to influence consultation practice. It also examines specific challenges to consultation within each of these contexts.

The Home

The most commonly reported setting for early intervention services for infants and toddlers with disabilities or at-risk conditions is the home (U.S. Department of Education, 2000). Professionals from other systems of care such as early care and education or mental health are much less likely than early interventionists to work in home settings; however, many early education programs have a home visiting component, so these issues have relevance for professionals in these programs as well. Although it can be difficult for professionals in center-based programs to find effective strategies for involving parents in children's educational activities at home or school, it is not difficult to find ways of involving families in planning and implementing interventions for their children when services occur within the home. Not all professionals in early intervention envision themselves as consultants in their work with families of young children; regardless of how professionals who visit families in their homes label their roles, however, consultation practices and strategies certainly could be used to make collaboration and communication with families more systematic and more effective. In other words, professionals who call themselves home visitors can apply consultation practices to enhance their work with children and families.

Mott (1997) noted several characteristics of the home that should be considered in early intervention practice, and these suggestions are equally relevant for practitioners of consultation who work with children and families in their homes. First, it is important to recognize that the home is not just a physical place but also a personal space that reflects a family's values and beliefs and may reveal the most intimate aspects of their lives. As a result, everything the consultant says and does must communicate a fundamental respect for families who are willing to share their home with professionals for the benefit of their children. Klass reflected the need for home visitors to respect families' personal space: "As guests in parents' homes, effective home visitors take cues from parents, for example, asking the parents' permission before touching or picking up their baby. Similarly, they never enter rooms in the home unless invited to do so" (1997, p. 6). According to Klass, forming effective parent–professional partnerships in home settings hinges on the consultant's ability to address four central elements: 1) clarifying their expectations and those of the parents regarding the goals of the home visit, 2) describing what they want to do with the parents and the child, 3) specifying the roles of the parents and the professional, and 4) recognizing that work conducted in parents' personal space raises issues different form work that occurs in other settings.

Another important characteristic of the home setting is its location within the community. For example, consultants who work in homes must consider whether families have access to community resources as well as the safety of these locations. When the home is located in an unsafe environment, a consultant may want to consider meeting with a family in another location or asking another professional to accompany him or her on a visit. In addition, there may be scheduling difficulties if the home is located in a rural setting or is far from the consultant's work setting. Most consultants who work in home settings eventually confront issues related to families who are not available for scheduled home visits. Mott (1997) suggested that professionals develop and explain the policy for missed appointments to families but also examine the reasons why families might not honor these commitments (e.g., emergencies, irregular work schedules).

A third characteristic of the home setting that consultants should consider involves material resources. This category includes both basic resources, such as heat and water, and the availability of adequate meeting space, toys, and other learning materials. Nearly every home visitor or consultant eventually faces the difficult issue of whether to bring toys and learning materials into the home. This issue must be discussed openly with families and decided together, with the consultant showing a great deal of sensitivity and respect for the family's preferences. Consultants should have an array of other supports readily available to offer families if needed, such as community resources and information that will assist them in supporting their child's development and learning.

Another consideration involves the roles that family members and consultants play during a home visit. The consultant should consider how to balance times when he or she works directly with the child and times when he or she works primarily with the parents or other family members. Another question concerns which members of the child's family will be present during the home visit and how their roles will be defined.

Consultants who work in home settings may encounter some parents who assume that the consultant is the expert and that his or her role is to teach them the right way to parent (Klass, 1997). Of course, these assumptions violate a basic tenet of both consultation and home visiting—the importance of establishing a trusting relationship with the consultee—and require the consultant to make a concerted effort to help parents modify these expectations.

One of the most challenging issues for consultants in home settings is how to address difficult issues regarding abuse and neglect or inadequate parenting. It is recommended that consultants first explore the policies and supports available through their agencies in dealing with these issues. Then, they should inform families of the legal requirements for reporting these events and help them understand the procedures for assessing and intervening to address the problem (Mott, 1997). If consultants have established a trusting and open relationship with families and informed them of the legal and ethical implications of reporting abuse and neglect, many families actually come to view this process as helpful and therapeutic.

Another challenge for consultants who work in home settings is establishing appropriate professional boundaries (Klass, 1997). Some parents who have established trusting relationships with professionals may introduce intensely personal topics that extend beyond the purpose and goals of consultation. Klass recommended that consultants avoid the temptation to "rescue" these families but, rather, listen empathically and help them use a problem-solving approach to identify possible solutions.

Family Child Care Homes

Family child care homes consist of settings in which a small group of children is cared for in the home of a relative, friend, or nonrelative. Often the caregiver's own children are included in this child care arrangement. The vast majority of states regulate family child care homes, which generally amounts to ensuring only minimal health and safety standards, limiting group size, and regulating caregiver–child ratios. Yet, it is estimated that 80%–90% of family child care homes are unregulated and do not comply with state requirements to register their programs (The Annie E. Casey Foundation, 2003). Family child care homes generally fall into two groups: homes in which a small number of younger children are served (generally 6 or fewer children) and homes in which a larger number of older children are served (generally 7–12 children) (Children's Foundation, 2003). Specific group size limits for large and small child care homes may vary widely across states. Many caregivers lack formal education and training in early childhood education, and they may be unaware of resources to improve the quality of their services and advance their professional knowledge and skills. These caregivers generally work long hours for low wages and few benefits, and most are isolated from other adults who are doing similar work.

How do services in family child care homes compare to those provided in center-based programs? One study found comparable curricular materials and equipment, such as art supplies, blocks, and manipulatives in both settings; however, family child care homes were less likely to have dramatic play props, science materials, books, learning centers, individual cubbies, and materials that reflect cultural diversity (Faddis, Ahrens-Gray, & Klein, 2000). With respect to program dynamics, the study found that family child care homes were more likely than center-based programs to schedule field trips and maintain a balance between adult- and child-initiated activities, but they were less likely to promote cultural awareness, involve parents in sharing cultural experiences, display children's art work, use child-size furniture, and have providers eat with the children. The study also found no differences in children's performance on key developmental and learning indicators, suggesting that family child care homes may provide an effective child care option for families of young children.

Parents often choose family child care home arrangements over other types of programs because of flexibility, affordability, and convenience or because they prefer a home environment with small groups of children to an institutional setting. Family child care homes offer a crucial resource to families who work outside of traditional hours, when center-based child care programs generally operate. Family child care homes may offer specific benefits to families of children with disabilities, primarily because parents have more opportunities to interact with caregivers in this type of arrangement and caregivers may serve parents' social and emotional needs in addition to meeting their instrumental needs for child care (Golbeck & Harlan, 1997).

Consultants must confront several issues and challenges when consultation takes place in family child care homes. One issue involves addressing the global program quality of the child care home. This issue must be approached with a great deal of sensitivity, given that the setting is someone's home rather than a child care facility. In addition, the caregiver may have limited resources to address needs for structural changes or to purchase additional materials and equipment. However, when approached in the right way, many caregivers welcome the opportunity to learn more about easy and inexpensive ways of improving the caregiving environment. The FDCRS, a variation of the ECERS-R, is a tool that can be used to assess the environment as well as to plan and implement program-level changes and improvements in these settings.

The National Association for Family Child Care (NAFCC; http://www.nafcc.org) is another resource that consultants should consider to enhance the professionalism and work conditions of the family child care provider. NAFCC promotes high-quality family child care through accreditation, leadership training, technical assistance, and public education. The NAFCC accreditation system encourages family child care providers to set higher standards of care than those required by state regulatory agencies, which generally enforce minimum standards to protect children's health and safety. The NAFCC quality standards emphasize widely recognized dimensions of global program quality, such as caregiver responsiveness, sensitivity to cultural differences, developmentally appropriate materials and activities, and positive relationships with families. NAFCC also offers family child care providers additional opportunities for professional development that include becoming a mentor, a trainer, or an observer for NAFCC. Early childhood consultants should consider additional resources to assist family child care providers to enhance their skills and improve the quality of their services. Such resources should include educational opportunities through home visits, print materials, and the Internet to allow caregivers to take advantage of educational opportunities without leaving home. Equally important, but perhaps more challenging, is helping sometimes isolated family child care providers learn about community resources and network with other family care providers.

Golbeck and Harlan (1997) recommended that the family child care provider be considered a member of the early intervention team for a young child with a disability. When this approach is used, the provider receives support from specialists or consultants on the early intervention team to address the child's individual goals. The authors further suggested that visits with the family child care provider also include the child's parents, to the extent that this is possible, to address the parents' needs for information and support and to coordinate intervention strategies between home and child care. Although this approach represents an ideal service delivery model, a consultant may find it challenging to carry out. Finding a time to meet with both the caregiver and the child's parents on a regular basis will be very difficult, but the consultant may find other ways to communicate with the parents by telephone or writing.

Unlike teachers in center-based programs, family child care providers generally do not have access to assistants or substitutes and, as a result, do not have times when they are not supervising or caring for children. This makes it difficult for the consultant and consultee to find opportunities to have a focused conversation, an essential component of the consultation process. In these situations, consultants will have to find other ways of communicating with caregivers before the first child arrives, after the last one leaves, or during brief consultation encounters while the children are present. It is particularly important for consultants who work in these settings to adopt a participant-observer mindset, which means rolling up their sleeves and assisting with caregiving tasks as needed during visits.

Center-Based Child Care and Early Education Programs

As a broad category, center-based early care and education programs capture almost all of the remaining out-of-home group care settings for preschool children. Although each has a separate history and origin, child care programs serving 3- to 5-year-olds have become more aligned with early education programs since the mid-1990s; however, the professional image of child care professionals continues to be plagued by highly variable program quality, low compensation, and uneven teacher certification standards (Craig, 1997). Center-based programs include Head Start programs, child care centers, various public school–based programs (state-funded programs for children at risk of school failure, Title I programs for children from families with low incomes, preschool programs for children with disabilities), and private preschool programs. Since the late 1990s, blended early childhood programs have emerged as a new hybrid early education setting, particularly within the public schools. These programs mix funding sources to serve eligible children from two or more types of programs in the same classroom setting (e.g., a program that blends funds from Head Start, preschool services for children with disabilities, and Title I; a program that blends a state-funded public school program with funds from Head Start). Although more research is needed to document the effects of these unique settings on a range of child and family outcomes, one advantage of blended programs appears to be the relative ease in which inclusion of children with disabilities can be implemented within a public school environment. Increasingly, since the 1980s, children with disabilities are being served in a range of early childhood settings and other natural environments rather than in specialized programs that exclusively serve children with disabilities.

Center-based early childhood programs present a unique context for practitioners of consultation. File and Kontos (1992) described barriers to consultation practice in center-based programs that ranged from systems-level barriers to barriers at the program and classroom levels. Unfortunately, several of these barriers still exist and pertain not only to consultation practice in center-based programs but also to home settings and family child care homes. One barrier stems from the fact that most states have not articulated how indirect services in early education and intervention should be provided, nor have they defined the specific roles and competencies of professionals who provide these services. The same conclusion was reached in a study conducted by Dinnebeil and colleagues (2001). The absence of clearly defined professional roles and competencies for consultants in early childhood settings is directly related to another barrier to effective consultation practice—namely, the lack of professional development and training on consultation. Many practitioners graduate from colleges and universities without any preparation in consultation. Without a solid foundation in consultation theory and practice with supervision, consultants in early care and education programs have little to guide them and may be forced to borrow strategies from more familiar models of collaboration and help giving, such as family-centered practices. At the program and classroom levels, there is a need to clarify roles of consultants and consultees. Although the consultant bears a certain amount of the responsibility for clarifying consulting roles with individual consultees as part of the consulting process, additional clarification and support from administrators of early childhood programs would go a long way to sanction consultation as a legitimate service delivery model.

File and Kontos (1992) identified time constraints as one of the major barriers to consultation, and this is still the case in 2004. In busy early childhood classrooms, most conversations between consultants and consultees continue to occur during the rare moments when teachers do not have supervisory responsibilities (e.g., during naptime), before and after the children arrive, or as brief consultation encounters throughout daily classroom activities and routines. In some states, consultants and other disability specialists are prohibited from billing third parties such as Medicaid and private health insurance for their time unless it is spent working directly with the child and family. Obviously, this regulation serves as a disincentive to using a consultative model in which a consultant works indirectly with the child through collaboration with a classroom teacher or another adult.

Finally, barriers to consultation may stem from the consultant and consultee having a different knowledge base and worldview about child development. Professionals who function as consultants typically have attained a higher level of education and receive greater compensation than early childhood teachers, creating the possibility that staff members will either resent an external consultant or exaggerate the importance of what he or she says and does (Donahue et al., 2000). Perhaps even more important, professionals in the early childhood field may not share the same cultural models of practice related to educating children and responding to their behaviors. It is helpful to recognize that cultural models reflect professionals' own child rearing experiences as well as the beliefs and values of their profession and are expressed through variations in caregiving practices such as responsiveness and displays of affection (Finn, 2003). An effective consultant identities the cultural model that guides his or her own practices and beliefs as part of a reflective process that allows him or her to identify potential sources of conflict with the cultural model of the consultee. For example, the consultant may place a high value on promoting developmentally and individually appropriate practices but finds him- or herself in an early childhood classroom in which children are expected to learn preacademic skills primarily through large group and direct instructional approaches. Understanding how the teacher's cultural model guides his or her practices in the classroom is necessary to begin the process of negotiating these different perspectives on what and how children learn. One way that this barrier has been addressed is through the development of blended early childhood professional development programs that merge competencies for general and special education.

Other Community Settings

Because young children learn and develop in the context of everyday experiences, practitioners of consultation must be prepared to work in a wide array of community settings, as well as in formal early childhood programs and child care settings. Consultants who represent the early intervention system of care are perhaps the most likely of all early childhood consultants to work in community-based settings, largely because public law specifies that to the extent appropriate, services for young children with disabilities and their families must be delivered in least restrictive and natural environments.

Policies that support serving children in natural and inclusive environments recognize that children learn best when they can practice existing skills and master new ones in everyday settings rather than through contrived learning situations and deliberate curricula that may not reflect real life challenges. Naturally occurring opportunities include child and family routines in the home (e.g., meals, bath time, dressing and undressing tasks, grocery shopping, attending church), neighborhood playgroups (organized and informal), family and community celebrations and traditions (e.g., parades, county fairs, neighborhood potlucks), park and recreation programs (e.g., YMCA programs, summer camps), and many other daily living contexts. Each of these settings is associated with activities that present naturally occurring learning opportunities to enhance children's early experiences (Dunst et al., 2001). For example, within a neighborhood playgroup, playground equipment promotes balance and coordination skills, sandbox play facilitates learning basic concepts such as empty and full, and socialization with playmates promotes positive relations with peers.

Practitioners of consultation who work in community settings should consider the framework offered by Dunst and colleagues (2001) to develop interventions that connect natural learning environments situated in community settings and activities with children's learning and development goals. In this framework, professionals build on children's intrinsic interests that stem from everyday settings, routines, and activities. Children's interests help to engage them in learning opportunities that lead to exploration, the practice of existing skills, and mastery over new ones. Together, consultants and consultees should identify all of the possible ways that young children learn through daily routines and activities as well as ways to improve these learning opportunities. The following recommendations developed by the North Carolina Department of Health and Human Services (2002) may be helpful in this regard:

1. Identify settings in which the child and family normally spend their time or would spend their time if the child did not have developmental delays (e.g., local parks, recreation programs, sports events, public libraries, bookmobiles, stores, friends' and relatives' homes, child care programs, places of worship, restaurants, playgrounds, nature trails, museums, community events).

2. Determine service settings that are appropriate for the individual child and family and reflect the family's resources, concerns, and priorities.

3. Use familiar materials that are naturally available in the home and community.

4. Assist parents and caregivers in providing their child with opportunities to practice skills throughout the child's daily life.

5. Identify key players who could contribute ideas about the delivery of services in natural environments, such as families, early interventionists, therapists, child care providers, and community agency staff.

6. Identify which resources exist and which are needed in the community to enhance the child's learning opportunities (e.g., accommodations for physical accessibility, special equipment).

7. Work with community groups to establish new inclusive opportunities such as toddler storytime at the public library and play equipment for infants and toddlers at community parks.

8. Integrate goals and activities of programs in the community in the child's intervention plan.

Family Contexts

Families represent another context influencing consultation practice in early childhood settings. A large body of knowledge about working with families exists to inform professional practice and support parent–professional partnerships in the early childhood field (e.g., see Dunst, Trivette, & Deal, 1988; Turnbull, Turbiville, & Turnbull, 2000; Simeonsson & Bailey, 1990). Turnbull et al., for example, conceptualized partnerships with families as having evolved along a power continuum from parent counseling and training to a collective empowerment model in which parents and professionals share power to gain access to resources and achieve mutually desired outcomes. We make no attempt to replicate this impressive body of knowledge here. Rather, our intent is to comment on aspects of working with families that strengthen or pose particular challenges to practitioners of consultation.

The increasing diversity of families poses one of the biggest challenges to consultants and consultees, primarily because this diversity increases the likelihood that professionals will encounter family contexts for which they are unprepared. Compared with previous generations, families with young children in the early 21st century can be characterized as being smaller and more linguistically and culturally diverse, with more mothers working outside the home, more single heads of households, more nonrelatives residing in the home, less time for families to spend together, and a higher chance of living in poverty (Cornwell & Korteland, 1997). As a result, practitioners of consultation must stretch their definition of *families* to include traditional and nontraditional family and household arrangements.

Cornwell and Korteland (1997) suggested that it may be helpful to think about families from the perspective of family systems theory. Using this framework, a family consists of interdependent members who function as a family for either a short or long period. The family system can be further divided into specific subsystems that are separated by boundaries and governed by rules of interaction. Family structure is one such subsystem and consists of family composition, size, socioeconomic status, geographic location, ethnicity, and culture. Family interaction defines family dynamics in general and how members relate to one another. For example, communication style, adaptability to stress, and family cohesiveness can all be used to characterize a family's style of interaction. Family functions include economic, domestic, health care, recreation, socialization, affection, self-definition, and education tasks and activities. Finally, a family's life cycle can be conceptualized along a continuum of developmental milestones that include the birth of a child, the early childhood period, school entry, adolescence, and so forth.

Consultants who work directly with families or who attempt to involve them in the consultation process must consider all of these aspects of family characteristics and functions as they develop family–professional partnerships. Unfortunately, few empirically based models for working with families or involving them in consultation exist, not even within the broader consultation literature. Although some scholars view existing knowledge about effective consultation with professionals as being consistent with the way in which consultants should be expected to work with families, others have noted that Caplan's original definition of consultation involved two professionals working together to address a mutual concern (Brown et al., 1998). The triadic nature of consultation emphasizing the consultant, the consultee, and the child has dominated consultation theory and practice. Consequently, the notion of parents as consultees or partners in consultation traditionally has received very little attention by researchers and scholars.

Despite limited information about effective ways of engaging parents, teachers, and consultants in a collaborative process, we have adopted this very approach as a potentially promising practice. In this book's extended case illustration, we included Benita's family in the consultation process, but in a realistic fashion, recognizing that many working parents have a limited amount of time to attend meetings and participate in the weekly conversations that occur between the consultant and consultee.

In addition to working with individual children and families through consultation, consultants need to develop an understanding of each early childhood program's family component when becoming acquainted with the staff and the program's mission and philosophy. Donahue et al. (2000) offered several recommendations in this regard. First, consultants should consider how early childhood professionals generally relate to families and the extent to which they provide opportunities for families to become involved in the program. Consultants likely will find wide variability among early childhood programs with respect to the parent component, with some programs offering little contact with families and others providing a range of strategies that may include home visiting, parent workshops, parent advisory boards, opportunities to volunteer in the classroom, and parent newsletters and other resource materials. Having a clearer understanding of a program's family component helps consultants understand the needs of families as they work with consultees to develop interventions.

Second, consultants should make an attempt to get to know families in the early childhood programs in which they work. Donahue and colleagues (2000) suggested that it is important for consultants to be available during arrival and departure because these times offer informal opportunities for consultants to introduce themselves, describe their role, and get acquainted with families. Needless to say, consultants must be mindful of confidentiality issues and refrain from discussing problems or concerns about a particular child in the presence of other parents and staff.

Third, consultants can support a program's efforts to involve families by giving feedback about various parent involvement strategies, facilitating a parent meeting, or leading workshops on specific topics requested by families. Finally, Donahue and colleagues (2000) suggested that consultants be available to work directly with families to help them cope with short-term needs, such as a child-related concern or family crisis, noting that families may be more likely to seek help from a professional who is familiar to them and affiliated with their child's early childhood program. It should be noted that the services offered by consultants employed by a school district or early intervention agency typically are limited to working with children who have an IEP or IFSP, and consultants who work in other systems may face similar limitations. Consequently, early childhood consultants may be restricted from implementing some of these suggestions offered by Donahue and colleagues, particularly those related to parent education activities or other families who are not on their caseloads. At the same time, it is helpful to envision a variety of ways that consultants could work with families in early childhood settings if these restrictions did not exist.

Ultimately, the early childhood field must develop specific guidelines to address the role of the family in consultation, both when an individual child with specific needs is involved and as part of a larger effort to improve the family component of early childhood programs. Once these guidelines have been developed, the effectiveness of these practices must be validated through research. In the meantime, in recognition of the high value that the field places on family–professional partnerships, consultants who work in early childhood settings must look for every opportunity to involve families, seek their input, and share information at every step in the process.

Cultural Contexts

Because consultation unfolds within a multicultural context, it requires sensitivity to cultural, racial, ethnic, and philosophical differences that may exist between the consultant and the consultee. Unfortunately, the consultation field has not developed research-based strategies to assist the consultant in achieving this goal. Just as most early childhood professionals who provide direct services may be unprepared to address the diverse educational and linguistic needs of children and families from other cultural backgrounds, consultants may be unprepared to work with consultees from diverse backgrounds. The limited research on this topic suggests that early childhood professionals in general (including practitioners of consultation) may lack knowledge of the cultural beliefs and values that families from diverse backgrounds find important, and they may lack understanding of the strengths and adaptations of child-rearing systems different from their own (Fuller, Eggers-Pierola, Holloway, Liang, & Rambaud, 1994; Harry, 1992). There is growing consensus that to provide high-quality services, early childhood professionals must learn about child-rearing practices in other cultures, facilitate language development among children whose primary language is not English, and promote continuity between the child's experiences at home and within the early childhood program (Barrera, 1993; García, McLaughlin, Spodek, & Saracho, 1995; National Association for the Education of Young Children, 1996; Sánchez & Thorp, 1998).

With respect to consultation, there is some evidence to suggest that consultees from different cultural and ethnic groups may perceive consultation services in different ways. For example, African American consultees may focus on the interpersonal aspects of the consultation process, whereas European American consultees may be more interested in the activities and tasks central to accomplishing consultation goals (Gibbs, 1980, cited in Brown et al., 1998). This fundamental difference in responding to consultation is manifested in several ways. For example, an African American consultee may remain aloof during the initial stages of consultation as he or she "sizes up" the consultant and evaluates his or her personal life, opinions, and values. In contrast, a European American consultee may concentrate on the professional skills of the consultant, the specifics of the consultation process, and the potential effectiveness of consultation. Consultants need to recognize their own cultural style in communicating and relating to consultees and must determine how this style differs from that of consultees. Otherwise, the consultation literature offers very few guidelines to assist consultants who are working within a multicultural context.

One notable exception is Soo-Hoo's (1998) recommendation to apply frame of reference and reframing techniques as a means of improving multicultural consultation. Consistent with the previously described cultural models perspective, a frame of reference orientation helps a consultant understand a problem that the consultee is facing within a cultural and sociopolitical context. This approach requires that during the early stages of the consultation process, the consultant listens carefully, reads or studies information to understand the cultural context more fully, and asks culturally sensitive questions that help the consultant enter the consultee's worldview. It is important for consultants to operate from an outsider's perspective and, at the same time, develop a better understanding of the insider's perspective. According to Soo-Hoo, consultants who become skilled at utilizing a frame of reference approach come to understand a variety of cultural values systems and are more likely to be effective with consultees from diverse groups.

Once the consultant comes to understand a consultee's frame of reference, the goal is to assist the consultee in changing certain elements of that frame. Soo-Hoo (1998) noted that human problems stem from how an individual perceives the situation and that it may be possible to develop a different explanation based on the same set of facts. Changing certain elements within the frame changes the consultee's perspective from which these events are viewed. For example, if the consultee expresses a concern that the family is not interested in participating in the consultation process, the consultant might introduce the notion that the family could be experiencing difficulty understanding their role as part of the team.

The challenge for the consultant is to change only certain key elements of the frame, not the entire frame, and to do so in a way that does not conflict with the consultee's cultural values and beliefs. Soo-Hoo recommended that any changes to the consultee's perception of the situation:

1. Are consistent with the consultee's fundamental cultural values and beliefs

2. Foster a more positive image of the consultee's competence and abilities

3. Assist the consultee in achieving more power and control over the situation

4. Result in more effective solutions

In this book's extended case illustration, the consultant (Karen) used a reframing technique to help the consultee (Lakesha) view an issue from another perspective. For example, when Lakesha expressed concern that learning Spanish and English at the same time might confuse Benita and cause delays in learning English, Karen pointed out that learning two languages simultaneously is actually thought to promote English language learning. In keeping with Soo-Hoo's (1998) recommendations, Karen also suggested that it would be important to monitor the situation to ensure that Benita continued to develop language skills. By adding this suggestion, Karen recognized that Lakesha's concerns were legitimate, and she assisted Lakesha in having some control in determining whether this approach was effective in the future.

Certainly, additional research on the issue of multicultural consultation is needed. In the meantime, consultants who strive to be effective with consultees from diverse backgrounds should consider applying frame of reference and reframing techniques in their consultation practice.

CONCLUSION

Consultation can be used in an array of different settings that include children's homes, family child care homes, child care centers, early childhood classrooms, and other community settings. The consultation process and strategies in these different settings are essentially the same, even though the content of the consultation may vary depending on the consultant's professional training and the system of care that he or she represents. It is important for early childhood consultants to recognize the specific issues and challenges to consultation within each of these settings and to understand how contextual factors that are both internal and external to the program influence the practice of consultation.

Chapter 13

Future Directions for Consultation in Early Childhood Settings

C onsultation is essentially a method of working effectively with other adults to achieve desired changes in children, their caregivers, and the environment. The key elements of consultation may differ somewhat across various models of consultation, but generally these elements include a focus on resolving work-related concerns for the benefit of a third party (or parties) and preventing similar problems in the future; a joint problem-solving process; and a consulting relationship characterized as collegial, respectful, and mutually beneficial (Zins et al., 1993). Becoming an effective early childhood consultant requires a complex set of interpersonal and communication skills in addition to a solid foundation in early childhood. This chapter offers several recommendations for moving the early childhood field toward a consensus on what constitutes effective consultation practice: 1) develop a conceptual framework for consultation practice, 2) create professional standards, and 3) evaluate consultation through scientific research.

DEVELOP A CONCEPTUAL FRAMEWORK FOR CONSULTATION PRACTICE

Undoubtedly, the biggest challenge with respect to consultation in early education and intervention is the absence of a shared conceptual framework from which practitioners of consultation (both consultants and consultees) are expected to operate. As the field begins to address this pressing need, it should consider whether there should be one framework for consultation practice in early childhood settings or various models designed for specific purposes. Brown and colleagues (1998) suggested that it may be useful to consider a taxonomy of consultation models based on different theoretical approaches (e.g., behavioral, mental health, organizational), professional roles (e.g., itinerant teacher, consultant, inclusion specialist), or goals of consultation (e.g., child centered, consultee centered, program centered). They noted that such a classification scheme could assist consultants in selecting the appropriate consultation model to fit a particular philosophy or orientation and to match the consultee's needs and priorities for consultation services. We believe that an integrated approach to consultation described by Parsons (1996), with its multidimensional focus *across* key domains (e.g., the goal of consultation, the nature of the interaction between the consultant and consultee, the role of the consultant, the theoretical model) and its flexibility *within* each domain might be more useful to the early childhood field. In using this approach, the consultant might vary his or her role from that of a facilitator to that of a coach or might shift from an indirect to a direct service delivery model, depending on the consultation context and whether the consultant is addressing an immediate need or a long-term goal.

For consultation to be effective, the field must offer specific guidelines for consultation practice rather than expecting professionals to rely on approaches borrowed from more familiar help-giving relationships and collaborative models, such as teaming and in-service training. The guidance offered to consultants who work in the early childhood field must include more than a list of recommended or evidence-based practices focused on direct service to children and families. Such lists reflect the *content* of consultation but not the complex *process* of sharing one's expertise through social influence and professional support within a consulting relationship that develops over time. Yet, existing interventions available to early childhood consultants primarily consist of strategies that focus on working directly with children rather than with the teachers and adults who care for these children at home, in early childhood classrooms, and in many other community settings.

In their discussion of this issue as it relates to school psychologists, Gutkin and Conoley (1990) concluded that the goal of bringing about lasting and meaningful improvements in children's lives can only be accomplished by exerting influence on parents and teachers, the primary people who control the environments in which children grow and learn. The authors noted, "Many of the problems facing school psychologists are actually the result of trying to solve indirect service delivery problems with direct service delivery methodologies" (p. 209).

They questioned whether school psychologists should continue their almost exclusive focus on serving children directly while ignoring a need for the field to evolve toward more adult-centered interventions targeting children's teachers and caregivers.

The early childhood field faces similar challenges. Consultants who work in early childhood settings are in an excellent position to advocate for children by sharing information with others that could lead to positive changes in child behaviors, teacher competencies, and program quality. Yet, the majority of these consultants are ill equipped to transfer their expertise because they lack important knowledge and skill in persuading others to improve their knowledge and change their practices. These qualities are important largely because the consultant must rely on the consultee to carry out the interventions that they design together through the consultation process. Gutkin and Conoley (1990) identified a number of reasons why many teachers and other adults may be reluctant to implement interventions developed with the assistance of a consultant: 1) a lack of motivation to focus one's time and energy on a particular child, 2) concerns about the effectiveness or feasibility of the intervention approach, 3) the quality of the relationship with the consultant, 4) limited knowledge or skill to carry out the agreed-on plan, and 5) demands of the organization or classroom environment that make it difficult to focus on the needs of a particular child.

In short, effective consultation depends on the consultant's ability to influence the consultee. The ability to influence others within a consulting framework requires a number of related skills. Among the many necessary skills for effective consulting, consultants must learn how to tailor their consulting style and approach to address the needs of consultees from diverse educational and cultural backgrounds. They also must acquire knowledge about effective methods for modeling exemplary practices, helping adults reframe problems to support self-efficacy, and identifying organizational variables that influence various intervention approaches.

A related aspect of consultation that must be explicated through future research is the role of collaboration. In a comprehensive review of this issue, Schulte and Osborne (2003) noted the absence of shared meaning and a formal definition of collaboration, even though this construct is universally endorsed by scholars and practitioners alike. The authors questioned, for example, whether collaboration should be defined by joint decision making, joint responsibility for implementation, or both. They suggested that a conceptual and operational definition of collaboration is needed to identify the behavior, processes, and products associated with collaboration.

In reaching consensus on a conceptual framework for consultation, it is critical for the field to recognize that *consultation is an indirect service delivery profession.* This recognition should lead to specific guidelines for consultants that focus on intervening with the teachers and other adults who care for children on a daily basis as well as on knowing how to work directly with these children and families.

CREATE PROFESSIONAL STANDARDS

Several studies document a lack of professional comfort with consultation among both consultants and consultees in early childhood settings (Buysse et al., 1996; Wesley et al., 2000; Wesley, et al., 2001). This finding raises questions about the effectiveness of consultation practices and lends a sense of urgency to the need for additional professional development on this topic. Creating professional standards to guide consultation in early childhood settings should begin with an examination of current professional development coursework and field-based experience, although it is likely that most programs are doing an inadequate job of preparing professionals for consulting roles.

It is clear from the discussion in the previous section that the relationship-based nature of consultation and the complex challenges associated with implementing effective consultation practices require both content and process expertise. Knoff, McKenna, and Riser (1991) identified five dimensions contributing to consultation effectiveness that go beyond the traditional content–process dichotomy, which also should be considered as part of the content of a professional development program in consultation. These dimensions include 1) process skills (e.g., stages of consultation, roles, responsibilities), 2) expert skills (e.g., technical knowledge, skills related to intervention strategies), 3) personal characteristics (e.g., personality, sense of humor, attitude), 4) interpersonal skills (e.g., warmth, tact, authenticity), and 5) style (e.g., self-disclosure, respect, confrontation). See Chapter 2 for a comprehensive description of the characteristics of the effective consultant.

Designers of professional development programs should consider methods to foster these interpersonal and communication skills by providing multiple opportunities for guided practice sessions followed by field-based experiences under the supervision of a skilled consultant. In our experience teaching a graduate-level course on consultation, it is helpful for students to videotape a consultation role-play session, evaluate their performance using a consultation observation rating form, and have the instructor complete the same observation form to offer another perspective on a student's performance as a consultant.

In addition to identifying content areas and methods to teach them, the field must consider the form that professional development addressing early childhood consultation will take. One option is to provide professional development through in-service training activities. We have recommended that professional development efforts through continuing education offer training to consultants and consultees together to promote a shared understanding of consultation practice (Wesley et al., 2001). Providing joint training activities to early education specialists and classroom teachers would also promote a shared understanding of consultation practice and contribute to an enlarged perspective about the respective roles of the consultant and the consultee. Training on consultation through continuing education and in-service training should incorporate regular opportunities for supervision and reflection with experienced mentors to support ongoing professional development.

The field also should consider professional development opportunities as part of preservice training programs for professional in early childhood education, early intervention, and early childhood special education. Faculty in colleges and universities who design professional development programs should consider whether additional coursework and field experiences could be added to the existing curriculum to incorporate knowledge and skills on consultation or whether a separate program focusing specifically on consultation in early childhood would be needed. At the heart of this issue is whether consultation is a separate profession or specialization area or one of many hats that an itinerant early childhood teacher wears. Several colleges and universities in Iowa offer a master's-level program in special education with a focus on consultation in early childhood settings that may serve as a model for other states. Obtaining the consultant endorsement requires eight graduate semester hours and content in the following areas: curriculum design; consultation process in special or general education (i.e., application of a methodological model for consulting with teachers and other adults in education, interpersonal relations, interaction patterns, interpersonal influence, and communication skills); and skills required for conducting a needs assessment, delivering staff in-service needs, and evaluating in-service sessions (Iowa General Assembly, 2001).

EVALUATE CONSULTATION THROUGH SCIENTIFIC RESEARCH

As mentioned several times throughout this book, the field requires additional empirical evidence to examine the effectiveness of consultation in early education and intervention. Far more work is needed to understand the impact of consultation on children, families, and the programs that serve them. Chapter 11 presented concepts and tools to support practitioners in conducting a systematic evaluation of their consultation practices; however, these evaluation methods were drawn from research conducted in school-based consultation and have not been applied to the early childhood field.

The evaluation process should begin by exploring components of consultation commonly evaluated in school-based consultation, such as consultee satisfaction with the consultation process. In addition, a range of consultation outcomes should be examined, including 1) progress in reaching children's learning and behavioral goals, 2) positive changes in the consultee's ability to address similar goals for change independently in the future, and 3) improvements in program quality.

Methods are also required for monitoring the integrity with which specific consultation practices actually are followed (Sheridan et al., 1996). The process measures described in Chapter 11 may prove useful in this regard. There needs to be a better understanding of professional comfort with consultation, factors that contribute to views about consultation effectiveness and the acceptability of various consultation approaches to parents and professionals. Also needed are additional ways of involving families in planning and implementing evaluation of consultation, as well as methods to assess follow-up and generalization of positive change to understand the long-term effects of consultation services (Sheridan et al., 1996). Regardless of the dimensions of consultation emphasized in evaluation efforts, the methods of evaluation should be relevant and acceptable to practitioners to ensure that an evaluation of consultation can be implemented at the program level and through large-scale research studies. Finally, it is necessary to consider how the evaluation findings can be used to support continuous improvement of consultation practice, to identify any unintended consequences, and to contribute to the knowledge base to advance and improve these practices for the field as a whole. Until all of these contributors of consultation effectiveness have been adequately examined, the full extent to which individual teachers, parents, and children benefit from consultation cannot be determined, nor can methods for improving the practice of consultation be identified.

At present, practitioners of consultation and researchers in early intervention operate in isolation of each other in their respective worlds of practice and science. A promising approach for bringing researchers and practitioners together to advance knowledge on consultation in early education and intervention is to build communities of practice that are based on collective expertise and designed to scrutinize and improve specific areas of practice (Buysse et al., 2003; Buysse et al., 2001; Wesley & Buysse, 2001). The potential for practitioners and researchers to co-construct knowledge exists in this approach because communities of practice represent an ongoing enterprise that invites both groups to share, build on, and transform what they know about effective practices. The key to transforming existing research and practice activities into communities of practice is to give consultants and consultees a legitimate role in constructing knowledge by linking their ideas with those of researchers and the broader early childhood community (Barab & Duffy, 2000).

CONCLUSION

Our goal in writing this book was to present a promising framework for understanding the key tasks and processes associated with the practice of consultation in early childhood settings. We recognize that this framework must be elaborated and evaluated through future scientific research. Until then, the strategies and concepts presented here may assist practitioners who are already serving as consultants to move toward a more systematic process for sharing content expertise and thereby reach mutually determined goals for children and families. Consultation holds tremendous potential to influence and improve early childhood in the United States but only if it is viewed as a valid service delivery model and receives adequate institutional support. Practitioners of consultation who find themselves working in the absence of these conditions should seek frequent opportunities for professional development, supervision, and peer support to advance and improve their consultation practices. We hope that this book serves as one resource to further this goal.

References

Alpert, J.L. (1995). Some guidelines for school consultants. *Journal of Educational and Psychological Consultation, 6*(1), 31–46.

The Annie E. Casey Foundation. (2003.) *Care you can count on: Section 5. Family child care.* Retrieved December 27, 2003, from http://www.aecf.org/publications/child/fam.htm

Bailey, D.B., McWilliam, R., Buysse, V., & Wesley, P.W. (1998). Inclusion in the context of competing values in early childhood education. *Early Childhood Research Quarterly, 13,* 27–47.

Barab, S.A., & Duffy, T.M. (2000). From practice fields to communities of practice. In D.H. Jonassen & S.M. Land (Eds.), *Theoretical foundations of learning environments* (pp. 25–55). Mahwah, NJ: Lawrence Erlbaum Associates.

Barrera, I. (1993). Effective and appropriate instruction for all children: The challenge of cultural/linguistic diversity and young children with special needs. *Topics in Early Childhood Special Education, 13*(4), 461–487.

Bergan, J.R. (1977). *Behavioral consultation.* Columbus, OH: Merrill.

Bergan, J.R. (1995). Evolution of a problem-solving model of consultation. *Journal of Educational and Psychological Consultation, 6,* 11–123.

Bergan, J.R., & Kratochwill, T.R. (1990). *Behavioral consultation and therapy.* Norwell, MA: Kluwer Academic/Plenum Publishers.

Bianco-Mathis, V., & Veazey, N. (1996, July). Consultant dilemmas: Lessons from the trenches. *Training and Development Journal,* 39–42.

Bolman, L.G., & Deal, T.E. (1997). *Reframing organizations.* San Francisco: Jossey-Bass.

Brown, D. (1993). Training consultants: A call for action. *Journal of Counseling and Development, 72,* 139–143.

Brown, D., Pryzwansky, W.B., & Schulte, A.C. (1998). *Psychological consultation: Introduction to theory and practice* (4th ed.). Boston: Allyn & Bacon.

Brown, D., Wyne, M.D., Blackburn, J.E., & Powell, W.C. (1979). *Consultation strategies for improving education.* Boston: Allyn & Bacon.

Bryant, D.M., Burchinal, M.R., Lau, L., & Sparling, J.J. (1994). Family and classroom correlates of Head Start children's developmental outcomes. *Early Childhood Research Quarterly, 9,* 289–309.

Busse, R.T., Kratochwill, T.R., & Elliott, S.N. (1995). Meta-analysis for single-case outcomes: Applications to research and practice. *Journal of School Psychology, 33,* 269–285.

Buysse, V., Schulte, A.C., Pierce, P.P., & Terry, D. (1994). Models and styles of consultation: Prefer-ences of professionals in early intervention. *Journal of Early Intervention, 18*(3), 302–310.

Buysse, V., Skinner, D., & Grant, S. (2001). Toward a definition of quality inclusive child care: Perspectives of parents and practitioners. *Journal of Early Intervention, 24*(2), 146–161.

Buysse, V., Sparkman, K., & Wesley, P.W. (2003). Communities of practice: Connecting what we know with what we do. *Exceptional Children, 69*(3), 263–277.

Buysse, V., & Wesley, P.W. (2001). Models of collaboration for early intervention: Laying the groundwork. In P. Blasco (Ed.), *Early intervention services for infants, toddlers, and their families* (pp. 258–293). Boston: Allyn & Bacon.

Buysse, V., & Wesley, P.W. (2004). A framework for understanding the consultation process: Stage-by-stage. *Young Exceptional Children, 7*(2), 2–9.

Buysse, V., Wesley, P.W., & Able-Boone, H. (2001). Innovations in professional development: Creating communities of practice to support inclusion. In M.J. Guralnick (Ed.), *Early childhood inclusion: Focus on change* (pp. 179–200). Baltimore: Paul H. Brookes Publishing Co.

Buysse, V., Wesley, P.W., Keyes, L., & Bailey, D.B. (1996). Assessing the comfort zone of child care teachers in serving young children with disabilities. *Journal of Early Intervention, 20*(3), 189–203.

Caplan, G. (1970). *The theory and practice of mental health consultation.* New York: Basic Books.

Caplan, G., & Caplan, R.B. (1999). *Mental health consultation and collaboration.* Prospect Heights, IL: Waveland Press. (Original work published 1993)

Child Mental Health Foundations and Agencies Network. (2001). *A good beginning: Sending America's children to school with the social and emotional competence they need to succeed.* Chapel Hill: University of North Carolina at Chapel Hill, Frank Porter Graham Child Development Institute.

Children's Foundation. (2003). *2003 Family Child Care Licensing Study.* Retrieved December 27, 2003, from http://www.childrensfoundation.net/publications/fccls.htm

Cormier, W., & Cormier, L. (1985). *Interviewing strategies for helpers: A guide to assessment, treatment, and evaluation.* Belmont, CA: Brooks/Cole.

Cornwell, J.R., & Korteland, C. (1997). The family as a system and a context for early intervention. In S.K. Thurman, J.R. Cornwell, & S.R. Gottwald (Eds.), *Contexts of early intervention: Systems and settings* (pp. 93–109). Baltimore: Paul H. Brookes Publishing Co.

Cost, Quality, & Child Outcomes Study Team. (1995). *Cost, quality, and child outcomes in child care centers public report*. Denver: University of Colorado–Denver, Economics Department.

Craig, S.E. (1997). Child care centers. In S.K. Thurman, J.R. Cornwell, & S.R. Gottwald (Eds.), *Contexts of early intervention: Systems and settings* (pp. 191–200). Baltimore: Paul H. Brookes Publishing Co.

Dinnebeil, L.A., McInerney, W.F., Roth, J., & Ramaswamy, V. (2001). Itinerant early childhood special education services: Service delivery in one state. *Journal of Early Intervention, 24*(1), 35–44.

Donahue, P.J., Falk, B., & Provet, A.G. (2000). *Mental health consultation in early childhood*. Baltimore: Paul H. Brookes Publishing Co.

Dougherty, A.M. (1990). *Consultation: Practice and perspectives*. Belmont, CA: Wadsworth.

Dougherty, A.M. (2000). *Psychological consultation and collaboration in school and community settings*. Belmont, CA: Wadsworth.

Dunst, C.J., Bruder, M.J., Trivette, C.M., Hamby, D., Raab, M., & McLean, M. (2001). Characteristics and consequences of everyday natural learning opportunities. *Topics in Early Childhood Special Education, 21*(2), 68–92.

Dunst, C.J., Trivette, C.M., & Deal, A. (1988). *Enabling and empowering families: Principles and guidelines for practice*. Newton-Upper Falls, MA: Brookline Books.

Erchul, W.P., & Martens, B.K. (2002). *School consultation: Conceptual and empirical bases of practice* (2nd ed.). Norwell, MA: Kluwer Academic/Plenum Publishers.

Ewing Marion Kauffman Foundation. (2002). *The Kauffman Early Education Exchange: Vol. 1. Set for success: Building a strong foundation for school readiness based on social-emotional development of young children*. Kansas City, MO: Author.

Faddis, B.J., Ahrens-Gray, P., & Klein, E.L. (2000). *Evaluation of Head Start family child care demonstration*. Washington, DC: U.S. Department of Health and Human Services, Administration for Children, Youth and Families.

File, N., & Kontos, S. (1992). Indirect service delivery through consultation: Review and implications for early intervention. *Journal of Early Intervention, 16*, 221–234.

Finn, C.D. (2003). Cultural models for early caregiving. *Zero to Three, 23*(5), 40–45.

Fuller, B., Eggers-Pierola, C., Holloway, S.S., Liang, X., & Rambaud, M. (1994). *Rich culture, poor markets: Why do Latino parents choose to forego preschooling?* (Tech. Rep. No. ED 371 855). Washington, DC: American Educational Research Association.

Fuller, B., Kagan, S.L., Caspary, G., & Gauthier, C.A. (2002). Welfare reform and child care options for low-income families. *Children and Welfare Reform, 12*(1), 97–119.

García, E.E., McLaughlin, B., Spodek, B., & Saracho, O.N. (1995). *Meeting the challenge of linguistic and cultural diversity in early childhood education: Yearbook in early childhood education: Vol. 6*. New York: Teachers College Press.

Gilliam, W.S., & Leiter, V. (2003). Evaluating early childhood programs: Improving quality and informing policy. *Zero to Three, 23*(6), 6–13.

Golbeck, S.L., & Harlan, S. (1997). Family child care. In S.K. Thurman, J.R. Cornwell, & S.R. Gottwald (Eds.), *Contexts of early intervention: Systems and settings* (pp. 165–189). Baltimore: Paul H. Brookes Publishing Co.

Gutkin, T.B., & Conoley, J.C. (1990). Reconceptualizing school psychology from a service delivery perspective: Implications for practice, training, and research. *Journal of School Psychology, 28*, 203–223.

Gutkin, T.B., & Curtis, M.J. (1982). School-based consultation: Theory and techniques. In C.R. Reynolds & T.B. Gutkin (Eds.), *The handbook of school psychology* (pp. 796–828). Hoboken, NJ: John Wiley & Sons.

Hanft, B.E., Rush, D.D., & Shelden, M.L. (2004). *Coaching families and colleagues in early childhood*. Baltimore: Paul H. Brookes Publishing Co.

Hansen, J.C., Himes, B.X., & Meier, S. (1990). *Consultation: Concepts and practices*. Upper Saddle River, NJ: Prentice Hall.

Hanson, M.J., & Widerstrom, A.H. (1993). Consultation and collaboration: Essentials of integration efforts for young children. In C.A. Peck, S.L. Odom, & D.D. Bricker (Eds.), *Integrating young children with disabilities into community programs: Ecological perspectives on research and implementation* (pp. 149–168). Baltimore: Paul H. Brookes Publishing Co.

Harms, T., & Clifford, R.M. (1989). *Family Day Care Rating Scale (FDCRS)*. New York: Teachers College Press.

Harms, T., Clifford, R.M., & Cryer, D. (1998). *Early Childhood Environment Rating Scale–Revised Edition (ECERS-R)*. New York: Teachers College Press.

Harms, T., Cryer, D., & Clifford, R.M. (2003). *Infant/Toddler Environment Rating Scale–Revised Edition (ITERS-R)*. New York: Teachers College Press.

Harms, T., Jacobs, E.V., & White, D.R. (1995). *School-Age Care Environment Rating Scale (SACERS)*. New York: Teachers College Press.

Harradine, C.C., & Clifford, R.M. (1996, April 8–12). *When are children ready for kindergarten? Views of families, kindergarten teachers, and child care providers*. Paper presented at the annual meeting of the American Educational Research Association, New York. (ERIC Document Reproduction Service No. 399 044)

Harry, B. (1992). An ethnographic study of cross-cultural communication with Puerto Rican-American families in the special education system. *American Educational Research Journal, 29*, 471–494.

Henning-Stout, M. (1993). Theoretical and empirical bases of consultation. In J.E. Zins, T.R. Kratochwill, & S.N. Elliott (Eds.), *Handbook of consultation services for children: Applications in educational and clinical settings* (pp. 15–45). San Francisco: Jossey-Bass.

Horn, E., Lieber, J., Sandall, S., Schwartz, I.S., & Wolery, R.A. (2002). Classroom models of individualized instruction. In S.L. Odom (Ed.), *Widening the circle: Including children with disabilities in preschool programs* (pp 46–60). New York: Teachers College Press.

Horton, G.E., & Brown, D. (1990). The importance of interpersonal skills in consultee-centered consultation. *Journal of Counseling and Development, 68,* 423–426.

Howes, C., Phillips, D.A., & Whitebook, M. (1992). Thresholds of quality: Implications for the social development of children in center-based child care. *Child Development, 63,* 449–460.

Hughes, J.N., (1997). *The Consultant Evaluation Rating Form scoring manual.* Unpublished document (available from the author), Department of Educational Psychology, Texas A&M University, College Station.

Hughes, J.N., Erchul, W.P., Yoon, J., Jackson, T., & Henington, C. (1997). Consultant use of questions and its relationship to consultee evaluation of effectiveness. *Journal of School Psychology, 35*(3), 281–297.

Hughes, J.N., Hasbrouck, J.E., Serdahl, E., Heidgerken, A., & McHaney, L. (2001). Responsive systems consultation: A preliminary evaluation of implementation and outcomes. *Journal of Educational and Psychological Consultation, 12*(3), 179–201.

Hunsaker, P.L. (1985). Strategies for organizational change: Role of the inside change agent. In D.D. Warrick (Ed.), *Contemporary organizational development* (pp. 123–137). Glenview, IL: Scott Foresman.

Idol, L. (1989). Reaction to Walter Pryzwansky's presidential address to the American Psychological Association on school consultation. *Professional School Psychology, 4,* 15–19.

Idol, L. (1990). The scientific art of classroom consultation. *Journal of Educational and Psychological Consultation, 1*(1), 3–22.

Idol, L., Paolucci-Whitcomb, P., & Nevin, A. (1986). *Collaborative consultation.* New York: Aspen Publishers.

Idol, L., & West, J.F. (1987). Consultation in special education: Training and practice (Part II). *Journal of Special Education, 20,* 474–497.

Iowa General Assembly. (2001, September 5). *Educational examiners.* Retrieved March 4, 2004, from http://www.legis.state.ia.us/Rules/Current/iac/282iac/28215/28215pp7.pdf

Kagan, S.L., Moore, E., & Bredekamp, S. (1995). *Reconsidering children's early development and learning: Toward common views and vocabulary.* Washington, DC: National Education Goals Panel.

Kagan, S.L., & Neuman, M.J. (2000). Early care and education: Current issues and future strategies. In J.P. Shonkoff & S.J. Meisels (Eds.), *Handbook of early childhood intervention* (2nd ed., pp. 339–360). New York: Cambridge University Press.

Kiresuk, T.J., & Lund, S.H. (1978). Goal attainment scaling. In C.C. Attkisson, W.A. Hargreaves, M.J. Horowitz, & J.E. Sorensen (Eds.), *Evaluation of human service programs* (pp. 341–370). San Diego: Academic Press.

Kiresuk, T.J., Smith, A., & Cardillo, J.E. (Eds.). (1994). *Goal attainment scaling: Applications, theory, and measurement.* Mahwah, NJ: Lawrence Erlbaum Associates.

Klass, C.S. (1997). The home visitor–parent relationship: The linchpin of home visiting. *Zero To Three, 17*(4), 1–9.

Klein, S., & Kontos, S. (1993). *Best practices in integration in-service training model: Instructional modules.* Bloomington: Indiana University Press.

Knoff, H.M., McKenna, A.F., & Riser, K. (1991). Toward a consultant effectiveness scale: Investigating the characteristics of effective consultants. *School Psychology Review, 20*(1), 81–96.

Kratochwill, T.R. (1985). Case study research in school psychology. *School Psychology Review, 14,* 204–215.

Kratochwill, T.R., VanSomeren, K.R., & Sheridan, S.M. (1990). Training behavioral consultants: A competency-based model to teach interview skills. *Professional Psychology: Research and Practice, 4,* 41–58.

Kurpius, D.J. (1985). Consultation interventions: Successes, failures, and proposals. *The Counseling Psychologist, 13,* 368–389.

Lamb, M.E. (1997). Nonparental child care: Context, quality, correlates, and consequences. In W. Damon, (Series Ed.) & I.E. Sigel, & K.A. Renninger (Vol. Eds.), *Handbook of child psychology: Vol. 4. Child psychology in practice* (5th ed., pp. 75–117). Hoboken, NJ: John Wiley & Sons.

Lippett, G., & Lippett, R. (1986). *The consulting process in action* (2nd ed.). La Jolla, CA: University Associates.

Love, J.M. (2001, December). *Instrumentation for state readiness assessment: Issues in measuring children's early development and learning.* Paper presented at the State of State Assessments symposium. Atlanta, GA.

Maher, C.A. (1993). Providing consultation services in business settings. In J.E. Zins, T.R. Kratochwill, & S.N. Elliot (Eds.), *Handbook of consultation services for children* (pp. 317–328). San Francisco: Jossey-Bass.

Medway, F.J., & Updyke, J.F. (1985). Meta-analysis of consultation outcome studies. *American Journal of Community Psychology, 13,* 489–504.

Meisels, S.J. (1999). Assessing readiness. In R.C. Pianta & M.J. Cox (Eds.), *The transition to kindergarten* (pp. 39–66). Baltimore: Paul H. Brookes Publishing Co.

Morisset, C.E. (1994). *School readiness: Parents and professionals speak on social and emotional needs of young children* (Tech. Rep. No. 26). Baltimore: The Johns Hopkins University, Center on Families, Communities, Schools, and Children's Learning.

Mott, D.W. (1997). The home environment. In S.K. Thurman, J.R. Cornwell, & S.R. Gottwald (Eds.), *Contexts of early intervention: Systems and settings* (pp. 139–163). Baltimore: Paul H. Brookes Publishing Co.

Munn, M. (2003). *Quality enhancement: Staffing for a strong system.* Raleigh: North Carolina Partnership for Children.

National Association for the Education of Young Children. (1996). Responding to linguistic and cultural diversity: Recommendations for effective early childhood education. *Young Children, 51*(2), 4–12.

Newman, J.L. (1993). Ethical issues in consultation. *Journal of Counseling & Development, 72*(2), 148–156.

North Carolina Department of Health and Human Services. (2002). *Growing up naturally: Early intervention in natural environments.* Raleigh: North Carolina Department of Health & Human Services, Division of Public Health, Women's and Children's Health Section, Early Intervention Branch.

Odom, S.L., & McEvoy, M.A. (1990). Mainstreaming at the preschool level: Potential barriers and tasks for the field. *Topics in Early Childhood Special Education, 10*(2), 4–61.

Palsha, S., & Wesley, P.W. (1998). Improving the quality in early childhood environments through on-site consultation. *Topics in Early Childhood Special Education, 18*(4), 243–253.

Parsons, R.D. (1996). *The skilled consultant: A systematic approach to the theory and practice of consultation.* Boston: Allyn & Bacon.

Parsons, R.D., & Meyers, J. (1984). *Developing consultation skills.* San Francisco: Jossey-Bass.

Peisner-Feinberg, E., & Burchinal, M. (1997). Relations between preschool children's child care experience and concurrent development: The Cost, Quality and Outcomes Study. *Merrill-Palmer Quarterly, 43*(3), 451–477.

The Personal Responsibility and Work Opportunity Reconciliation Act (PRWORA) of 1996, PL 104-193, 42 U.S.C.

Pianta, R.C., & Cox, M.J. (Eds.). (1999). *The transition to kindergarten.* Baltimore: Paul H. Brookes Publishing Co.

Raver, C.C. (2002). Emotions matter: Making the case for the role of young children's emotional development for early school readiness. *Social Policy Report, 16*(3), 3–19.

Ross, M., & Fletcher, G.J. (1985). Attribution and social perception. In G. Lindzey & E. Aronson (Eds.), *The handbook of social psychology: Vol. 2* (3rd ed., pp. 73–114). New York: Random House.

Rimm-Kaufman, S.E., Pianta, R.C., & Cox, M.J. (2000). Teachers' judgments of problems in the transition to kindergarten. *Early Childhood Research Quarterly, 15,* 147–166.

Sadler, F.H. (2002). The itinerant special education teacher in the early childhood classroom. *Teaching Exceptional Children, 35*(3), 8–15.

Sánchez, S.Y., & Thorp, E.K. (1998). Policies on linguistic continuity: A family's right, a practitioner's choice, or an opportunity to create shared meaning and a more equitable relationship? *Zero to Three, 18*(6), 12–20.

Sandall, S., McLean, M., & Smith, B. (Eds.). (2000). *DEC recommended practices in early intervention/early childhood special education.* Longmont, CO: Sopris West Educational Services.

Schulte, A.C., & Osborne, S.S. (2003). When assumptive worlds collide: A review of definitions of collaboration in consultation. *Journal of Educational and Psychological Consultation, 14*(2), 109–138.

Scott, B. (2000). *Consulting on the inside: An internal consultant's guide to living and working inside organizations.* Alexandria, VA: American Society for Training & Development.

Scott-Little, C., Kagan, S.L., & Frelow, V.S. (2003a). *Standards for preschool children's learning and development: Who has standards, how were they developed, and how are they used: Executive summary.* Greensboro, NC: SERVE.

Scott-Little, C., Kagan, S.L., & Frelow, V.S. (2003b). Early learning standards for young children: A survey of the states. *Young Children, 58*(5), 58–64.

Senge, P. (1990). *The fifth discipline: The art and practice of the learning organization.* New York: Doubleday.

Sheridan, S.M., Welch, M., Orme, S.F. (1996). Is consultation effective? A review of outcome research. *Remedial and Special Education, 17*(6), 341–354.

Sherrod, L.R. (2002). From the editor. *Social policy report, 16*(3), 2.

Shields, M.K., & Behrman, R. (2002). Children and welfare reform: Analysis and recommendations. *Children and Welfare Reform, 12*(1), 5–25.

Shonkoff, J.P., & Phillips, D.A. (Eds.). (2000). *From neurons to neighborhoods: The science of early childhood development.* Washington, DC: National Academies Press.

Simeonsson, R.J., & Bailey, D.B. (1990). Family dimensions in early intervention. In S.J. Meisels & J.P. Shonkoff (Eds.), *Handbook of early childhood intervention* (pp. 428–444). New York: Cambridge University Press.

Soo-Hoo, T. (1998). Applying frame of reference and reframing techniques to improve school consultation in multicultural settings. *Journal of Education and Psychological Consultation, 9*(4), 325–345.

Turnbull, A.P., Turbiville, V., & Turnbull, H.R. (2000). Evolution of family–professional partnerships: Collective empowerment as the model for the early twenty-first century. In J.P. Shonkoff & S.J. Meisels (Eds.), *Handbook of Early Childhood Intervention* (2nd ed., pp. 630–650). New York: Cambridge University Press.

Unrau, Y.A. (2001). Using client exit interviews to illuminate outcomes in program logic models: A case example. *Evaluation and Program Planning, 24,* 353–361.

U.S. Department of Education. (1991). *America 2000: An education strategy.* Washington, DC: Author.

U.S. Department of Education (2000). *Twenty-second annual report to congress on the implementation of the Individuals with Disabilities Education Act.* Washington, DC: Author.

Varney, G.H. (1985). OD professionals: The route to becoming a professional. In D.D. Warrick (Ed.), *Contemporary organizational development* (pp. 49–56). Glenview, IL: Scott Foresman.

Villa, R.A., & Thousand, J.S. (1996). Instilling collaboration for inclusive schooling as a way of doing business in public schools. *Remedial and Special Education, 17,* 169–182.

Wallace, W.A., & Hall, D.L. (1996). *Psychological consultation: Perspectives and applications.* Belmont, CA: Brooks/Cole.

Welch, M.D., & White, B. (1999). *Teacher and parent expectations for kindergarten readiness.* Unpublished report. (ERIC Document Reproduction Services No. 437 225).

Wesley, P.W. (1994). Providing on-site consultation to promote quality in integrated child care programs. *Journal of Early Intervention, 18,* 391–402.

Wesley, P.W. (2000). *Improving the quality of early childhood programs: The PFI model of consultation.* Chapel Hill: The University of North Carolina at Chapel Hill, Frank Porter Graham Child Development Institute.

Wesley, P.W., & Buysse, V. (2001). Communities of practice: Expanding professional roles to promote reflection and shared inquiry. *Topics in Early Childhood Special Education, 21*(2), 114–123.

Wesley, P.W., & Buysse, V. (2003). Making meaning of school readiness in schools and communities. *Early Childhood Research Quarterly, 18*(3), 351–375.

Wesley, P.W., & Buysse, V. (2004). Consultation as a framework for productive collaboration in early intervention. *Journal of Educational and Psychological Consultation, 15*(2).

Wesley, P.W., Buysse, V., & Keyes, L. (2000). Comfort zone revisited: Effects of child characteristics on professional comfort in providing consultation. *Journal of Early Intervention, 23*, 106–115.

Wesley, P.W., Buysse, V., & Skinner, D. (2001). Early interventionists' perspectives on professional comfort as consultants. *Journal of Early Intervention, 24*(2), 112–128.

Wesley, P.W., Dennis, B., & Tyndall, S. (1998). *Quick-Notes: Inclusion resources for early childhood professionals*. Lewisville, NC: Kaplan Press.

West, F., & Idol, L. (1990). Collaborative consultation in the education of mildly handicapped and at-risk students. *Remedial Education and Special Education, 22*, 22–33.

Whitebook, M., Howes, C., & Phillips, D. (1990). Who cares? Child care teachers and the quality of care of America. *Final report of the National Child Care Staffing Study*. Oakland, CA: Child Care Employee Project.

Whitt, E.J., & Kuh, G.D. (1991). Qualitative research in higher education: A team approach to multiple site investigation. *Review of Higher Education, 14*, 317–337.

Witt, J.C. (1986). Teachers' resistance to the use of school-based interventions. *Journal of School Psychology, 24*, 37–44.

Wolery, M., Brashers, M.S., & Neitzel, J.C. (2002). Ecological congruence assessment for classroom activities and routines: Identifying goals and intervention practices in childcare. *Topics in Early Childhood Special Education, 22*(3), 131–142.

Wolery, M., Pauca, T., Brashers, M., & Grant, S. (2000). *Quality of inclusive experiences measure (QuIEM)*. Unpublished assessment manual. Chapel Hill: University of North Carolina at Chapel Hill, Frank Porter Graham Child Development Institute.

Zins, J.E., Kratochwill, T.R., & Elliot, S.N. (Eds.). (1993). *Handbook of consultation services for children: Applications in educational and clinical settings*. San Francisco: Jossey-Bass.

Appendix

BLANK FORMS

Knowledge and Skills Inventory for Consultants

Contact Summary

Classroom Strengths, Needs, and Resources

Intervention Plan

Consultation Stages Checklist

Final Report

Consultation Evaluation

Consultee Benefits

Goal Attainment Scaling

Knowledge and Skills Inventory for Consultants

Please check the appropriate box to rate the extent to which you agree or disagree with the statement regarding your knowledge and skill as a consultant.

	1 Strongly disagree	2 Disagree	3 Agree somewhat	4 Agree	5 Strongly agree
With regard to basic knowledge, I					
1. Understand the stages/phases of the consultation process					
2. Understand the need to match possible consultation approaches and specific consultant situations, settings, and needs					
3. Am able to discuss the purpose of consultation in the early childhood setting and the roles of the consultant and consultee					
4. Am familiar with the major areas of child development: a. cognitive b. language and literacy c. motor d. socioemotional					
5. Am familiar with disabilities and their impact on development					
6. Can identify quality indicators in the child care center or home					
7. Understand the early childhood and early intervention service system					
With regard to systems change, I					
8. Strive to understand the philosophical/theoretical perspective of the early childhood program in which I am consulting					
9. Am able to identify positive and negative effects that might result from efforts to change part of the program					
10. Can implement strategies to empower individuals and systems to change when necessary					
11. Am able to modify myths and attitudes that impede successful inclusion of children with disabilities					
12. Am able to identify and link resources between early childhood teachers and other agencies					
With regard to personal characteristics and skills, I					
13. Am respectful, open, and caring in consultation interactions					
14. Can establish and maintain a sense of rapport and mutual trust with all persons involved in the consultation process					
15. Maintain an enthusiastic attitude and positive self-concept throughout the consultation process					
16. Demonstrate a willingness to learn from others throughout the consultation process					
17. Am creative in examining problems and options					
18. Facilitate the consultation process by demonstrating flexibility					
19. Respect divergent points of view, acknowledging the right to hold different views and to act in accordance with convictions					

(continued)

From Klein, S., & Kontos, S. (1993). *Best practices in integration in-service training model: Instructional modules* (pp. 35–39). Bloomington: Indiana University; adapted by permission.

	1 Strongly disagree	2 Disagree	3 Agree somewhat	4 Agree	5 Strongly agree
With regard to communication skills, I					
20. Communicate clearly and effectively in oral and written form					
21. Use active listening and responding skills such as paraphrasing, clarifying, and summarizing to facilitate the consultation process					
22. Am perceptive in grasping and validating stated and unstated meanings and affect in communication					
23. Am able to elicit information from persons involved in the consultation process					
24. Enable others to examine their viewpoints of a situation or stated problem and to consider other possible views or explanations					
25. Manage conflict skillfully throughout the consultation process to maintain collaborative relationships					
26. Am reinforcing of others involved in the consultation process					
With regard to collaborative problem solving, I					
27. Identify and clarify problems and needs using a variety of data					
28. Pursue collaborative "brainstorming," withholding premature evaluation of ideas, to generate possible solutions to problems and means to objectives					
29. Integrate feasible goals and objectives into a plan of action that includes consultees as equal partners					
30. Elicit information to evaluate the effectiveness of the planned activities and interventions					
31. Provide information from my own area of expertise when needed by others without overwhelming or failing to acknowledge others' expertise					
32. Recognize and respond appropriately to the belief systems of others involved in the consultation process					
With regard to my own development, I					
33. Maintain a high standard of ethics related to such issues as confidentiality, personal and professional boundaries, and consultation efficacy					
34. Am able to assess my own effectiveness by using children's progress, parent and staff feedback, and self-rating					
35. Request and accept constructive feedback and suggestions for improvement					
36. Am able to make changes based on this feedback					
37. Seek professional development through conferences, workshops, meetings, individual study, and reading					

From Klein, S., & Kontos, S. (1993). *Best practices in integration in-service training model: Instructional modules* (pp. 35–39). Bloomington: Indiana University; adapted by permission.

Contact Summary

Consultant _____

Consultee _____

Classroom _____

Date _____

	Program

Type of contact

☐ On-site consultation

☐ Telephone call

☐ Observation

☐ Other (specify): _____

Duration
(in hours and in minutes)

Prep _____

Travel _____

Contact _____

Contact initiated by

☐ Consultant

☐ Consultee

Purpose of contact _____

_____

Focus of concern _____

_____

Summary of activities and discussion _____

_____

Decisions reached _____

_____

Action steps for consultant _____

_____

_____

Action steps for consultee _____

Date of next consultation _____

(continued)

From Wesley, P.W. (2000). *Improving the quality of early childhood programs: The PFI model of consultation* (p. 42). Chapel Hill: The University of North Carolina, FPG Child Development Institute; adapted by permission.

These questions are designed to help you think about the consultation strategies you have used as well as consultee reactions and perspectives related to these approaches. Depending on which stage you are in, address the targeted issues (below) in your reflections.

Stage One: What specific strategies did you use to learn about the program and the consultee? How well do you think the consultee understands the purpose and process of consultation?

Stage Two: What strategies did you use to build trust? What have you learned about the consultee, the program, and the focus of concern?

Stage Three: What ideas and activities did the consultee contribute during the information gathering/assessment stage? What is the consultee's understanding of the priorities for focus?

Stage Four: What specific strategies did you use to ensure collaboration during goal setting? How do you know if the consultee feels ownership of the goals?

Stage Five: How did you determine the potential success of each strategy? How confident does the consultee feel about implementing the strategies?

Stage Six: In what ways did you model flexibility, encouragement, and problem-solving skills with the consultee during implementation? What adjustments were needed in the Intervention Plan? How does the consultee feel about his or her ability to implement the plan in your absence?

Stage Seven: How do you and the consultee know you have accomplished the desired outcomes? Describe any unanticipated outcomes or the impact of the consultation process. How do you and the consultee feel about the outcomes and your relationship?

Stage Eight: What specific strategies did you use to encourage the consultee to disclose his or her view of the consultation relationship and his or her overall satisfaction with the outcomes? What are the consultee's overall perceptions of the consultation process? What work, if any, remains to be done, and what are the plans for the next steps? What new goals should be addressed through future consultation?

Consultant reflections, Stage number _____ :

_____

_____

_____

_____

_____

_____

_____

_____

_____

_____

_____

_____

_____

_____

_____

_____

From Wesley, P.W. (2000). *Improving the quality of early childhood programs: The PFI model of consultation* (p. 42). Chapel Hill: The University of North Carolina, FPG Child Development Institute; adapted by permission.

Classroom Strengths, Needs, and Resources

Consultee _____

Classroom _____

Date _____

┌─────────────────────────────────┐
│   │
│   │
│   │
│   Program │
└─────────────────────────────────┘

Strengths (e.g., all staff participate in professional development activities, written philosophy of inclusion, accredited by the NAEYC, spacious classrooms)

1. _____

2. _____

3. _____

4. _____

5. _____

Needs (e.g., lack age-appropriate playground equipment, director position vacant)

1. _____

2. _____

3. _____

4. _____

5. _____

Resources (e.g., dependable substitute teachers, program "adopted" by church club, volunteer parent carpenter)

1. _____

2. _____

3. _____

4. _____

5. _____

From Wesley, P.W. (2000). *Improving the quality of early childhood programs: The PFI model of consultation.* Chapel Hill: The University of North Carolina, FPG Child Development Institute; adapted by permission.

Intervention Plan

Consultant _____

Consultee _____

Classroom _____   Program

Consultation start date _____   Consultation end date _____

Month/Date/Year   Month/Date/Year

Goals/objectives	Strategies	Evaluation activities	Responsible person(s)	Start date	Target date	Completed date

From Wesley, P.W. (2000). *Improving the quality of early childhood programs: The PFI model of consultation* (p. 36). Chapel Hill: The University of North Carolina, FPG Child Development Institute; adapted by permission.

Consultation Stages Checklist

Consultee _____

Classroom _____

Date of Initial Contact _____
                        Month/Date/Year

Date of Final Contact _____
                       Month/Date/Year

┌─────────────────────────────────┐
│   │
│   │
│   Program │
└─────────────────────────────────┘

Check completed tasks.

Stage One: Gaining Entry

_____ Make initial contact.

_____ Arrange the first visit.

_____ Discuss the process of consultation.

_____ Assess the match between the consultee's needs and priorities and consultant's skills and knowledge.

Stage Two: Building the Relationship

_____ Build rapport and establish trust.

_____ Visit/observe the program or classroom.

_____ Learn more about the program and the consultee.

_____ Learn more about the focus of concern.

_____ Discuss the consultation process.

Stage Three: Gathering Information Through Assessment

_____ Specify the consultee's concerns and needs.

_____ Decide on methods for gathering additional information.

_____ Specify the roles and responsibilities of the consultant and consultee in gathering information.

_____ Formulate a definition of the problem.

Stage Four: Setting Goals

_____ Discuss assessment results and the possible causes of the findings.

_____ Summarize consultee's concerns and priorities related to the assessment results.

_____ Identify one or a few specific goals on which to focus consultation.

(continued)

From Wesley, P.W. (2000). *Improving the quality of early childhood programs: The PFI model of consultation.* (pp. 71–72). Chapel Hill: The University of North Carolina, FPG Child Development Institute; adapted by permission.

_____ Determine what knowledge, skills, and other resources are needed to address goals.

_____ Determine how both parties will know when the goal has been accomplished.

Stage Five: Selecting Strategies

_____ Determine which strategies the consultee tried in the past and how well these worked.

_____ Discuss other strategies that could be employed.

_____ Select strategies that are acceptable to the consultee and the consultant.

_____ Determine what knowledge, skills, and resources are needed to implement the strategies.

_____ Identify roles and responsibilities for implementing the strategies selected.

Stage Six: Implementing the Plan

_____ Encourage and support the consultee as needed.

_____ Determine if adjustments to the plan are needed.

_____ Evaluate the effectiveness of the plan.

Stage Seven: Evaluating the Plan

_____ Assess the match between desired and actual outcomes.

_____ Review the evaluation plan.

Stage Eight: Holding a Summary Conference

_____ Summarize the consultation's focus, goals, and accomplishments.

_____ Shift attention to other concerns and goals for change.

_____ Ask the consultee to complete the Consultation Evaluation form.

From Wesley, P.W. (2000). *Improving the quality of early childhood programs: The PFI model of consultation.* (pp. 71–72). Chapel Hill: The University of North Carolina, FPG Child Development Institute; adapted by permission.

Final Report

Consultant _____

Consultee _____

Classroom _____

Date _____

Program

Brief history of consultation process

Who initiated _____

Participants _____

Dates consultation began and ended _____

Number of visits _____

Program/classroom description

Ages of children _____

Number of children and adults _____

Hours of operation _____

Licensure/accreditation _____

_____

Program/classroom strengths _____

_____

_____

Consultation goals _____

_____

_____

_____

Accomplishments/changes made _____

_____

_____

_____

_____

_____

_____

_____

(continued)

From Wesley, P.W. (2000). *Improving the quality of early childhood programs: The PFI model of consultation.* Chapel Hill: The University of North Carolina, FPG Child Development Institute; adapted by permission.

Recommendations for next steps _____

_____

_____

_____

Consultant's reflections _____

_____

_____

_____

_____

Form distribution (who received this report?) _____

From Wesley, P.W. (2000). _Improving the quality of early childhood programs: The PFI model of consultation._ Chapel Hill: The University of North Carolina, FPG Child Development Institute; adapted by permission.

Consultation Evaluation

Consultee _____

Consultant _____

Classroom _____

Date _____

		Program

Please check the appropriate box to rate the extent to which you agree or disagree with each statement as it applies to your current experience with consultation.

	1 Strongly disagree	2 Disagree	3 Agree	4 Strongly agree
Effectiveness of consultation				
1. The goal of consultation was clearly defined.				
2. Methods for gathering information to assess my needs were helpful.				
3. The intervention plan makes sense for my situation.				
4. The intervention plan has been easy enough to implement.				
5. The intervention plan has been effective to this point.				
6. The consultation process met my expectations.				
7. The overall quality of the consultation was high.				
Consultant knowledge and skills				
8. The consultant is versed not only in early childhood content but also in the process of helping others.				
9. The consultant presents information clearly in oral and written form.				
10. The consultant recommends appropriate materials and resources.				
11. The consultant elicits information from others and is a good listener.				
12. The consultant demonstrates effective organizational skills (e.g., uses time efficiently, is prepared for each consultation).				
13. The consultant provides prompt feedback.				
14. The consultant has worked collaboratively to clarify our roles and responsibilities throughout the consultation process.				

(continued)

	1 Strongly disagree	2 Disagree	3 Agree	4 Strongly agree
Consultant interpersonal style				
15. The consultant is comfortable to talk with.				
16. The consultant demonstrates flexibility and openness.				
17. The consultant is generally pleasant.				
18. The consultant expresses his or her ideas without being overpowering.				
19. The consultant has supported my active participation in the consulting process.				
20. The consultant is respectful and caring.				
21. The consultant is creative in examining problems and options.				

Overall

22. What aspects of consultation were particularly strong and/or useful?

23. What aspects of consultation were weak or not useful?

24. In what way did consultation advance your professional knowledge or contribute to the quality of your services or program?

Consultee Benefits

Consultee _____

Classroom _____

Date _____

Program

Please check the appropriate box to rate the extent to which you agree or disagree with each statement reflecting changes in your knowledge or skill as a result of consultation.

	1 Strongly disagree	2 Disagree	3 Agree	4 Strongly agree
Objectivity				
1. I am able to recognize the knowledge and experience that I bring to the collaborative change process.				
2. I am able to view situations and problems from different perspectives.				
3. I solicit and accept constructive feedback and suggestions.				
Problem solving				
4. I am better able to set goals for change.				
5. I now use a more systematic approach to solving problems.				
6. I am able to work with other adults to make positive changes in the classroom.				
Role competency				
7. I can better assess my own effectiveness in the classroom.				
8. I am a better teacher (or parent, administrator, etc.).				
9. I am more confident in my role.				
Facilitating human development				
10. I am better able to design high quality learning environments.				
11. I have developed new approaches to working with individual children that will address their diverse learning needs.				
12. I feel confident that I can develop interventions for children in the future.				

Goal Attainment Scaling

Child _____

Teacher _____

Consultant _____

| | Program |

Date goals set and expected levels of outcome specified

(prior to intervention) _____
                        Month/Date/Year

Date consensus reached on goal attainment*

(following intervention) _____
                        Month/Date/Year

*Indicate consensus ratings by circling or marking the appropriate box.

Level of attainment	Scale 1 _____ _____ _____	Scale 2 _____ _____ _____	Scale 3 _____ _____ _____
−2 Much less than expected			
−1 Somewhat less than expected			
0 Expected level of outcome			
+1 Somewhat more than expected			
+2 Much more than expected			
Comments			

Index

Page references followed by *t* or *f* indicate tables or figures, respectively.